W9-CRH-905

Scope & Sequence

for Literacy Instruction

Scope & Sequence

for Literacy Instruction

Second Edition

Carol Murray

YORK
PRESS
Baltimore, MD

LEXIA
INSTITUTE
Los Altos, CA

Scope & Sequence for Literacy Instruction
by Carol Murray

Copyright © 1997 and 2002 by Carol Murray. All rights reserved including the right to reproduce this book or portions thereof in any form except for the inclusion of brief quotations in a review. All inquiries should be addressed to York Press, Inc., P.O. Box 504, Timonium, MD 21904.

This book was manufactured in the United States of America.

Typesetting by William Murray
Printing and Binding by Data Reproductions Corporation
Cover Design by Daniel Cook Design

Library of Congress Cataloging-in-Publication Data
Murray, Carol, 1937.
    Scope & sequence for literacy instruction / Carol Murray.--2nd ed..
        p. cm.
    Includes bibliographical references and index.
    ISBN 0-912752-69-6 (pkb.)
     1. Reading. I. Title: Scope and sequence for literacy instruction. II. Title.

LB1050.42.M87 2002
372.4--dc21
                                                    2002069028

Dedicated to

teachers

in memory of

Beth H. Slingerland

who influenced and enhanced

the lives of so many

Acknowledgments

Scope & Sequence for Literacy Instruction would not have been written without the encouragement and assistance of my closest colleagues at The Lexia Institute, John Anton and Jerry Elkind. John's gentle but persistent insistence to "sit down and write" gave me incentive to begin, while Jerry's willingness to format tedious tables, proofread, and advise, kept me on task.

This book could not have been written without the keen interest and financial support of The Educational Foundation of America and particularly that of board member Sharon Ettinger.

Close teacher friends who gave greatly appreciated advice and valuable time to proofread and formulate thoughtful suggestions, and who encouraged me to continue when I felt disinclined, are Patricia Beis, educational consultant and private tutor in Eugene, Oregon; Nancy Royal, former executive director of Prentice School for Dyslexics in Santa Ana, California; and Sharon Sousa, principal of Los Altos Christian School in Los Altos, California.

Thanks are extended to two San Francisco Bay Area educators who contributed the lesson plans for Chapter 5. They are Regen Murray, an Orton-Gillingham-Slingerland trained instructor who wrote the Orton-Gillingham plan, and Lynne Mayer, a whole language classroom teacher with a strong background in phonics, who contributed the whole language lesson. Ms. Murray also helped extensively with the overall copyediting.

My deepest indebtedness is to my husband Bill who reformatted and beautified the first copy of *Scope & Sequence* using Word for Windows and who surprised me with his copyediting expertise, precise standards, and tenacity.

Finally, thank you friend Larry Weaver for volunteering to do the final proofing and for finding so many errors—100, 1000, more—after I was sure there were none remaining.

Although many wonderful people helped to make this book possible—including teachers, parents, and students with whom I worked over the course of a rewarding career—I alone take responsibility for any shortcomings in *Scope & Sequence for Literacy Instruction*. I hope that its strengths will outweigh weaknesses and be of real benefit.

Foreword

Written language is an unnatural brain function that opens doors of opportunity. (shown in Wingdings code)

If you are able to decipher this written language code (Wingdings), you know that it says:

Written language is an unnatural brain
function that opens doors of opportunity.

In today's modern world, most opportunities for success require adequate reading and writing skills. While spoken lan guage evolves naturally, the use of written symbols to convey information remains a relatively recent development in the history of mankind. The ability to read, write, and spell has become an almost universal expectation, yet learning written language skills remains an unnatural process that is dependent upon the quality of instruction.

There is a lively debate over the best way to provide instruction in the language arts area. Many enlightened educators argue that effective instruction must include aspects found in "whole language" as well as in "phonetic" approaches. While it is true that every student would benefit from aspects of both approaches, it is essential for children with language processing disabilities to receive instruction utilizing structured, multisensory phonics. These youngsters, for example, cannot fully benefit from a literature course unless they understand the code—or language—in which it is written.

Unfortunately, many dedicated teachers who are proficient in whole language have not had the opportunity to master the phonetic code. This book is an excellent resource for teachers who are looking for more effective ways to teach children how to read, write, spell, and express themselves. Its instructional guides will be useful for both experienced Slingerland and Orton-Gillingham teachers, as well as for whole language teachers who want their students to be well-grounded in phonics.

Over the years, the Orton-Gillingham/Stillman Simultaneous Multisensory Techniques—including the classroom adaptation by Beth H. Slingerland—have proven to be very effective in teaching children with Specific Language Disability (developmental dyslexia). The principles first proposed by Dr. Samuel Orton have been implemented, as well as developed and refined, by Beth Slingerland, Sally Childs, Jane MacClellan (students of Anna Gillingham and Bessie Stillman), June Orton and other students who followed in the footsteps of these innovative pioneers. This is as it should be. Both Slingerland and Childs personally told me that as we learn more and more about how the brain processes information, we must use the new findings to make instruction more effective. It is also important to continue to test each new instructional technique against the most recent scientific discoveries about learning processes (Current neuroresearch, by the way, continues to support Dr. Orton's theories).

It was Beth Slingerland's wish that her books not be revised. Instead, she said, new books should be written. Carol Murray accepted this challenge, and has authored a well-written and well-organized book that discusses the similarities and differences between the Slingerland and Orton-Gillingham approaches. As Murray points out, there are actually more similarities than dissimilarities between them.

Her text is also an excellent source for clearly outlined instructional sequences in easy-to-read reference tables. These can be utilized in traditional lesson planning, or in conjunction with *Lesson Planner*, a computerized lesson planning software package. Various levels of instruction are included, along with helpful references.

Murray's ability to organize and her great passion for the intricacies of the English language make this book useful for both beginning and experienced teachers. It is an important contribution to the field of teaching children with language learning difficulties, and it is an exceptional reference tool for the professional's library.

Nancy L. Royal, Ed. D.
Executive Director, retired
The Prentice School
Santa Ana, California

Contents

Acknowledgments .... *v*

Foreword .... *vii*

Contents .... *ix*

Tables .... *xv*

Chapter 1: Introduction 1

    Alphabetics *1*

    Reading Fluency *2*

    Reading Comprehension *3*

    Relationship Between Teacher Education and Reading Instruction *4*

    Computer Technology and Reading Instruction *4*

  The Purpose of This Book *4*

  Phonics-Based Approaches *5*

  Overview of Scope & Sequence for Literacy Instruction *6*

  How This Book Helps Teachers *6*

  LessonPlanner™ and Scope & Sequence for Literacy Instruction *7*

  How to Best Use this Book: Categories of Users *8*

    LessonPlanner Users with Orton-Based Training *8*

    Orton-Based Teachers But Not LessonPlanner Users *9*

    Meaning-Emphasis Teachers with Phonics Training *9*

    School Administrators and Teachers Without Phonics *10*

Chapter 2: Handwriting *11*

  The Importance of Handwriting *11*

  Historical Perspective *12*

  Variations in Orton-Based Handwriting Programs *13*

  Why Use Slingerland's Handwriting Program? *14*

  Preliminary Considerations for Handwriting Instruction *15*

  Considerations for a Manuscript Scope and Sequence in Grade 1 .... *16*

    Introducing Letters that Look or Sound Alike *18*

First Trimester..*20*

Second Trimester..*21*

Grade One SLD Third Trimester or Non-SLD Second Trimester....................*23*

Reviewing Manuscript Formations...*26*

Continuum Manuscript Instruction...*27*

Considerations for a Cursive Scope and Sequence in Grade 3 and Beyond.........*29*

The Introduction of Cursive Handwriting..*30*

First Three or Four Cursive Lessons..*30*

Second and Third Weeks of Cursive Instruction...*32*

*Third or Fourth Week of Cursive Instruction
for an SLD Class or Slightly Earlier for Non-SLD*......................................*33*

*End of the First and Start of the Second Month of Cursive
for an SLD Class or Slightly Earlier for Non-SLD*......................................*34*

*Completing Lowercase Cursive by the End of the Second Month
or Earlier for Non-SLD*...*36*

Review of Cursive..*37*

What Else to Teach with Patterns...*38*

Handwriting Practice and Review (Manuscript and Cursive)............................*38*

Chapter 3: Visual Presentations..**39**

What Are Visual Presentations?...*39*

A Comparison of Orton-Gillingham and Slingerland Use of Visual Cards........*39*

An Orton-Gillingham Program..*40*

Sequencing Differences in Orton-Based Programs..*41*

Rationale for Visual Card Scope and Sequence...*43*

Rationale for Visual Card "Levels"..*44*

Visual Card Scope and Sequence for First and Second Grades..........................*45*

Graphemes for the First Trimester in a Beginning First or Second Grade.......*46*

Graphemes for the Second Trimester in a Beginning First or Second Grade.....*47*

Graphemes for a Continuum Second Grade SLD Class or Earlier for Non-SLD.....*48*

Rationale for More Vertical than Horizontal Instruction...............................*51*

Visual Card Scope and Sequence for Third Grade and Above...........................*51*

Graphemes for Third Grade and Above..*52*

Rationales for Deciding What to Teach Next 54

Graphemes for Third Grade and Above 55

Rationale for Slight Differences in the Advanced Checklists 63

Scope and Sequence for Fifth and Sixth Grades 63

   Advanced Group I Graphemes 64

   Advanced Group II Graphemes 66

   A Note About Visual Card Verbalizations 70

Rationale for Changes in Pronunciation of Graphemes 71

   Advanced Oddities 71

Rationale for Eliminating Prompts in Visual Cards 72

Rationales for Differences in the Introduction of Graphemes in Different Grades 73

Decoding 77

   Including Nonsense Words 80

   Rationale for Introducing the Vowel "a" Before "i" 81

   A Note About the Suffix "ed" 82

   Adding Soft c and Soft g Words 83

Rationale for Letter Combination and Phonogram Sequences in Decoding 85

   Choosing Which Phonograms to Introduce Next 86

   Decoding V-Consonant-E Words 88

   Decoding Word Families and Homonyms 91

But Where Do You Teach Vocabulary and Grammar? 93

Two-Syllable Decoding 97

   Decoding with Double-Duty g and k 99

*Pronunciation and Accenting Two-Syllable Words
   with Short Vowels in Both Syllables* 99

*Typical Review of Two-Syllable Word Decoding,
   Beginning with One-Syllable Words* 101

Syllabification — Rules II, III, and IV 104

Words With More Than Two Syllables 107

   Decoding Mixed Multisyllabic Words with Affixes 109

   Decoding Words with Three or More Syllables 111

   Last Gigantic Review 112

Preparation for Reading..113

Reading from the Book...117

Chapter 4: Auditory Presentations 119

What Are Auditory Presentations?...119

 Phoneme Awareness...119

Auditory Cards...120

Yellow Auditory Cards...121

Yellow Auditory Card Scope and Sequence..122

 Phonemes Spelled with Consonants, Consonant Digraphs, and Trigraphs..............123

 Phonemes Spelled with Short Vowels and Phonograms...............................125

 Phonemes Spelled with Long Vowels, Diphthongs, and Phonograms 126

 Phonemes Spelled with R-Controlled Phonograms or Syllables 129

 Yellow Card Exercises for C-le or Silent-e Syllables 130

 Yellow Card Exercises for the Past Tense Suffix "ed"..................................130

 A Yellow Card Exercise for the Suffix "ous" and the Noun Ending "us".................131

 Vowel Perception and Discrimination...131

The Auditory Card Tables...133

 A Quick Review of Auditory Card, Perception, Discrimination, and Yellow Card Techniques...133

Scope and Sequence for Encoding and Spelling 144

 Encoding Phonetic Words...145

 Differences in Encoding Techniques...146

 Discriminating Between the Phonemes /ă/ and /ĭ/..................................148

 Encoding Ambiguous and Phonetic Words...149

 Be Careful About Nonsense Words in Encoding......................................150

 Encoding and Spelling Non-Phonetic and Phonetic Words 151

 Encoding One-Syllable Phonogram and Letter Combination Words.................154

 A Note About the Inclusion of Suffixes in Encoding..................................157

 Choices for What to Introduce Next..159

 Techniques for Encoding v-e Words..160

 Continuing Mixed Encoding..163

Scope and Sequence for Spelling 163

 Introducing Suffixes with Concept 164

 Encoding/Spelling Non-Phonetic, Word Family, and Homonym Words 165

 Spelling Phonetic, Ambiguous, and Non-Phonetic Words 166

 Encoding and Spelling Closed Two-Syllable Words with Two or More Consonants in the Medial Position 170

 Encoding and Spelling Review 171

 Encoding and Spelling Closed Two-Syllable Words with a Single Medial Consonant 173

 Encoding and Spelling Two-Syllable Words with One Open Syllable and a Single Consonant in the Medial Position 174

 Encoding and Spelling Words of Two or More Syllables 176

Encoding and Spelling Words with Common Suffixes and Prefixes 177

 Encoding Mixed Multisyllabic Words with Affixes 178

 Encoding and Spelling Words with Advanced Suffixes and Endings 180

 The Ending /əs/ Spelled Ous or Us 181

 Encoding and Spelling Words with Latin and Greek Roots 182

 Encoding Words with Three or More Syllables 183

Learning and Incorporating Spelling Rules 184

 The Silent-E Rule 184

 The 1-1-1 Vowel Rule 185

 The Consonant-Y Rule 186

 The Extended 1-1-1 Vowel Rule 187

 The Letter "l" and the Extended 1-1-1 Vowel Rule 187

 An Active Way to Look at Spelling Rules 188

Phrase and Sentence Writing to Reinforce Spelling Skills 188

Dictations 189

Independent Writing 190

 Integrating Grammar into Dictations and Composition 191

Chapter 5: Conclusions **193**

Three Lesson Plans 193

 Overview of the Lesson's Content 193

 The Format of the Lesson Plans 194

The Slingerland Simultaneous Multisensory Lesson 195

    Question of the Day 195

    Learning to Write 195

    Visual Lesson 195

    Auditory Lesson 199

The Orton-Gillingham Simultaneous Multisensory Lesson 201

    I. Phonogram Review 201

    II. Presentation of a New Concept 201

    III. Words Read in Isolation 203

    IV. "What says . . . ?" 204

    V. S.O.S. and Dictated Phrases 204

    VI. Oral Reading 205

The Whole Language Lesson Augmented with Phonics 206

    I. Daily Oral Language 206

    II. Vocabulary Development 206

    III. Reading 207

    IV. Handwriting 208

    V. Phonics, Spelling and Writing 209

    VI. Seatwork 210

  Referencing the Research 211

  A Final Word 212

Appendix A: LessonPlanner Graphemes **215**

Appendix B: LessonPlanner Phoneme **219**

Appendix C: Two Exercises for You **223**

Glossary **227**

References **239**

Index **243**

Tables

Table 2–1. First Trimester: First Group of Letters *20*

Table 2–2. First Trimester: Second Group of Letters *21*

Table 2–3. Second Trimester of an SLD Grade One and First Trimester of a Non-SLD Grade One *22*

Table 2–4. Grade One SLD Third Trimester or Non-SLD Second Trimester *24*

Table 2–5. First Three or Four Cursive Lessons *30*

Table 2–6. Second Several Cursive Lessons *31*

Table 2–7. Second and Third Weeks of Cursive *33*

Table 2–8. Third or Fourth Week of Cursive Instruction for an SLD Class or Slightly Earlier for Non-SLD . *34*

Table 2–9. End of First and Start of the Second Month of Cursive for an SLD Class or Earlier for Non-SLD . *35*

Table 2–10. Completing Lowercase Cursive by the End of the Second Month or Earlier for Non-SLD *36*

Table 3–1. Orton-Gillingham Level I—Group I *40*

Table 3–2. Orton-Gillingham Level I—Group II *41*

Table 3–3. Orton-Gillingham Level II *42*

Table 3–4. Orton-Gillingham Level III *42*

Table 3–5. Orton-Gillingham Level IV *42*

Table 3–6. Advanced Gillingham Checklist *43*

Table 3–7. Level I—Group I Graphemes for the First Trimester in a Beginning First or Second Grade *46*

Table 3–8. Level I—Group II for the Next Trimester in a Beginning First or Second Grade SLD Class
or Earlier for Non-SLD *47*

Table 3–9. For a Continuum 2nd Grade SLD Class or Earlier for Non-SLD *48*

Table 3–10. For a Second Grade Accelerated SLD Class or Earlier for Accelerated Non-SLD *49*

Table 3–11. Level I Graphemes for Third·Grade and Above *52*

Table 3–12. Level II Graphemes for Third Grade and Above *55*

Table 3–13. Level III Graphemes for Third Grade and Above *57*

Table 3–14. Level IV Graphemes for Third Grade and Above *59*

Table 3–15. Advanced Group I Graphemes *64*

Table 3–16. Advanced Group II Graphemes *67*

Table 3–17. Choices for Teaching **w** *and* **qu** *69*

Table 3–18. Advanced Grapheme Oddities *72*

Table 3–19. Manuscript and Cursive Comparison–Level I *74*

Table 3–20. Manuscript and Cursive Comparison–Level II *74*

Table 3–21. Cursive Continuum–Level III and IV *75*

Table 3–22. Advanced Grapheme Checklist *76*

Table 3–23. Advanced Grapheme Oddities to Ponder and Perhaps Teach *77*

Table 3–24. Beginning Decoding with **cvc (- a -)** *One-Syllable Words* *79*

Table 3–25. Decoding with **cvc (- i -)** *One-Syllable Words* *80*

Table 3–26. Decoding with **cvc (- u -)** *One-Syllable Words* *81*

Table 3–27. Decoding with **cvc (- u -)** *Suffixes and Digraphs* *82*

Table 3–28. Decoding with **cvc (- o -)** *One-Syllable Words* *83*

Table 3–29. Decoding with cvc (- e -) One-Syllable Words 84

Table 3–30. Beginning Decoding with Letter Combinations 85

Table 3–31. Decoding with Phonogram oa 85

Table 3–32. Decoding with Phonogram ee 86

Table 3–33. Decoding with Phonograms ai and ay 87

Table 3–34. Decoding with y - /ī/ and v-e Words 88

Table 3–35. Decoding with More Phonograms 89

Table 3–36. Decoding with Yet More Phonograms 90

Table 3–37. Continuing Mixed Decoding 91

Table 3–38. Decoding Homonyms, Word Family Words, Phonograms, and Plurals 91

Table 3–39. C/C Syllabification 100

Table 3–40. Accenting hints 1 and 2 101

Table 3–41. Review One and Two-Syllable Word Decoding 102

Table 3–42. Two-Syllable C/C Decoding 103

Table 3–43. C/ Syllabification 104

Table 3–44. /C Syllabification 106

Table 3–45. V/V Syllabification 107

Table 3–46. Decoding Words With More Than Two Syllables 108

Table 3–47. Accenting hint 3 108

Table 3–48. Decoding Mixed Multisyllabic Words with Affixes 110

Table 3–49. Accenting hints 4 and 5 111

Table 4–1. First Phoneme-Graphemes 134

Table 4–2. Phoneme-Graphemes for First Trimester 137

Table 4–3. Phoneme-Graphemes for the Second Trimester or Beyond 138

Table 4–4. Phoneme-Graphemes for Third Grade and Above 140

Table 4–5. Advanced Phoneme-Graphemes for Third Grade and Beyond 140

Table 4–6. Advanced Phoneme-Graphemes for Fourth Grade and Beyond 142

Table 4–7. Phoneme-Grapheme Oddities for Advanced Students in Fifth Grade and Beyond 143

Table 4–8. Beginning Encoding with cvc (- a -) One-Syllable Words 147

Table 4–9. Encoding with cvc (- i -) One-Syllable Words 149

Table 4–10. Encoding with cvc (- u -) One-Syllable Words 150

Table 4–11. Encoding with cvc (- o -) One-Syllable Words 152

Table 4–12. Encoding with cvc (- e -) One-Syllable Words 153

Table 4–13. Beginning Encoding with Phonograms (oa) 155

Table 4–14. Beginning Encoding with Letter Combinations 156

Table 4–15. Continuing Encoding with Phonograms (ee) 158

Table 4–16. Continuing Encoding with Phonograms (ai and ay) 159

Table 4–17. Encoding with y - /ī/ and v-e Words 160

Table 4–18. Continuing Encoding with More Phonograms 162

Table 4–19. Continuing Mixed Encoding 163

Table 4–20. Spelling Homonyms, Word Family Words, Plurals, and Words with Rules 169

Table 4–21. Encoding and Spelling Closed Two-Syllable Words with Two or More Consonants in the Medial Position 171

Table 4–22. One and Two-Syllable Word Encoding and Spelling Review *172*

Table 4–23. Encoding and Spelling Closed Two-Syllable Words with a Single Consonant in the Medial Position *174*

Table 4–24. Encoding and Spelling Two-Syllable Words with a Single Consonant in the Medial Position and One Accented Open Syllable *176*

Table 4–25. Encoding Words of More than Two Syllables *178*

Table 4–26. Blending with Common Suffixes and Prefixes *179*

Table 4–27. Encoding Mixed Multisyllabic Words with Affixes and Endings *180*

Table 4–28. Encoding Words with Advanced Suffixes and Endings *181*

Table 4–29. Encoding with Latin and Greek Roots *183*

Table 4–30. Encoding Words of Three or More Syllables with Affixes *185*

1

Introduction

Throughout the United States and other English speaking countries there is an exciting, renewed focus on literacy instruction. Educators are now strongly advocating that reading instruction be based on proven scientific reading research.

In 1997, Congress asked the Director of the National Institute of Child Health and Development (NICHD) and the Secretary of Education to convene a National Reading Panel (NRP) to evaluate the status of scientific research literature on reading. The panel assessed various instructional approaches and designed a plan for disseminating information that would facilitate effective reading instruction. Their report provides the best summary of what is known from the research literature. It also confirms the validity of the type of instruction described in this book.

The NRP considered five main topics: alphabetics, reading fluency, reading comprehension, the relationship between teacher education and reading instruction, and between computer technology and reading instruction. These topics and the NRP findings are summarized below.

Alphabetics

Alphabetics concerns phomenic awareness and phonics instruction. *Phonemic awareness* refers to a student's understanding that spoken words and syllables are made up of sequences of speech elements. This understanding is a necessary pre-condition for learning to read alphabetic languages such as English, where speech sounds are represented by letters. The NRP determined that:

- Early phonemic awareness instruction generally does produce improvement in students' phonemic awareness, reading, and spelling—but has no impact on math performance.

- Phonemic awareness instruction produces improvements in children of varying abilities.

- Explicit, systematic phonemic awareness instruction with small groups of children, focusing on only one to two phoneme manipulations, is most effective.

- Phonemic awareness is one of two best predictors of how well children will learn to read in the first two years of school. The other strong predictor is letter recognition.

Phonics refers to the various reading and spelling instruction methodologies that focus to some degree on phoneme–grapheme correspondences.[1] Sometimes *phonics* is confused with *phonemic awareness*, or with *phonetics* (see the Glossary for a definition). Phonics instruction is extremely beneficial, but will make no sense to the student who lacks phonemic awareness. The panel identified three key characteristics of successful phonics instruction programs:

- *Systematic phonics*—Instruction should build gradually from basic units or elements toward those that are more subtle and complex. The sequence of presentation is key. The Panel found that systematic phonics instruction benefits students in kindergarten through sixth grade, including children who have difficulty learning to read; and specifically, students with dyslexia.

- *Synthetic phonics*—Students should be taught to convert letters (graphemes) into sounds (phonemes), and then to blend the sounds to form recognizable words. This corresponds to Orton-based decoding. Systematic *synthetic* phonics instruction improves disabled readers' reading skills and significantly improves low socioeconomic status children's alphabet knowledge and word reading better than methods focusing less on these initial reading skills.

- *Explicit phonics*—Important points and principles should be taught explicitly, and not merely implied or embedded in instruction as secondary considerations. Early readers should be taught as soon as possible how letters are linked to phonemes to form letter-sound correspondences and spelling patterns. The Panel found this explicit instruction to be essential to successful phonics instruction.

Reading Fluency

The panel found that repeated oral reading with guidance from a teacher or someone substituting the role of teacher has a positive and significant impact on reading fluency as well as word recognition and comprehension across several grade levels.

---

[1] A grapheme is one or more letters that represent a single sound or phoneme. A phoneme is the smallest unit of speech that distinguishes one utterance from another. Refer to the glossary for a more detailed explanation of these somewhat technical terms.

Reading Comprehension

Reading comprehension may be viewed as the intentional thinking that occurs during reading whereby meaning is constructed through interactions between the reader and what the reader is reading. This requires the reader to intentionally "think" and engage in problem solving. Research that the NRP reviewed indicates the following:

Vocabulary Instruction

- ♦ Vocabulary instruction leads to comprehension gains; how vocabulary is taught must be appropriate to the ability and age of the learners.

- ♦ Instruction should be taught both directly and indirectly.

- ♦ Vocabulary development should be an active process requiring intentional and thoughtful interaction.

- ♦ Both repetition and multiple exposures to vocabulary are important.

- ♦ Learning vocabulary in rich context, via incidental learning, and with the use of computers all enhance the development of vocabulary.

Text Comprehension Instruction

The Panel recommended that the following types of instruction at least be included in text comprehension:

- ♦ Monitoring, to help students be aware of their understanding of what they read;

- ♦ Cooperative learning, during which students learn reading strategies together;

- ♦ Question answering, to questions asked by a teacher who then provides immediate feedback;

- ♦ Question generation, to help students learn to ask themselves meaningful questions;

- ♦ Use of graphic and semantic organizers, where readers improve comprehension by making graphic representations, such as story maps;

- ♦ Story summarization, where students are taught to integrate ideas and generalize what they read;

- ♦ Story structure, where readers learn to use the structure of their readings to improve their recall and to answer questions better.

Relationship Between Teacher Education and Reading Instruction

Since teachers are important in helping develop literacy skills, the Panel sought to learn what type of education best helps improve their teaching. It was found that professional development in-services produce higher gains in students' achievements than other forms of teacher education.

Computer Technology and Reading Instruction

Fewer research studies on the usefulness of computers for literacy instruction were available. However, from those that were reviewed, the Panel was encouraged by successes and the potential for successes. In particular the Panel noted computer speech recognition capabilities, developments in the Internet with the potential to link schools and instruction, the use of hypertext as an instructional advantage, and the use of word processing to combine writing and reading instruction for overall improved literacy instruction and learning.

One important effect of the *NRP Report* is that it is helping put an end to the sometimes bitter polarization between proponents of code emphasis and meaning emphasis[2] literacy instruction. It is hoped that both phonics (code-emphasis) and whole language (meaning-emphasis) schools will gradually concur that the *NRP Report* must be reviewed and adaptations to instruction made accordingly. The time is here to begin to work in harmony to improve literacy instruction and opportunities for individuals of all ages.

The Purpose of This Book

The purpose of this book is to provide teachers with *what*, *when*, and *why* to introduce and review specific literacy concepts and skills that ensure students have the best opportunity to develop literacy competency. *Scope & Sequence* is not a detailed how-to book. Teachers must decide themselves *how* to teach literacy depending on their pedagogical preferences, the needs of their students, and hopefully the recommendations of the NRP.

---

[2] *Code-emphasis* is a term used by many educators to distinguish *phonics-based* (*code-emphasis*) reading programs from *meaning-emphasis*. In *meaning-emphasis* or *literacy-based* programs, including *whole language*, common words found in print are introduced with little or no regard to their letter-sound regularity. They include words that appear frequently in print. Students learning to read them are taught a variety of strategies or clues to decipher them from the content of pictures, word configurations, and the initial letters of words. In meaning-emphasis programs there is little attempt to control words so that the same letter represents the same sound in beginning readers. For instance, the words **some**, **do**, **don't**, **hot**, **spoon**, **spoil**, **ouch**, and **hope** might be presented in one reading lesson with the "**o**" in each word representing a different phoneme.

The author's own training, experience, and success as a literacy teacher—old as it may be—is founded on a most effective, alphabetic phonics-based instructional approach that many of the NRP findings validate.

Phonics-Based Approaches

The most respected alphabetic phonics approaches for teaching literacy are based on the works of Samuel T. Orton (Orton, 1937) and Anna Gillingham and Bessie Stillman (Gillingham and Stillman, 1997). We refer to these collectively as Orton-based in this book.

Samuel Orton, a neuropsychiatrist and pathologist during the 1930s and 1940s, is most noted for his pioneering study of neurological backgrounds of language disabilities. He invited Anna Gillingham, a psychologist, to develop a remedial teaching approach, based on his studies and philosophy, for gifted students who were unable to read, write, and spell at a level commensurate with their intelligence. Gillingham, in turn, asked Bessie Stillman, a remedial teacher, to work with her in devising the remedial approach for students with what later came to be known as specific language disability (SLD) or dyslexia.[3] (Orton Dyslexia Society Newsletter, 1994)

The original collaborative work of Orton, Gillingham, and Stillman provided the foundation for the development of Orton-based adaptations for literacy remediation to students with SLD. The most relevant, for the purposes of this book, is the *classroom* approach developed by one of Gillingham's protégées, Beth Slingerland. (Slingerland,1971, 1976, 1981)

Slingerland developed the classroom adaptation of the Orton-Gillingham-Stillman approach for the prevention and remediation of specific language disabilities.[4] As you will see throughout this textbook the NRP findings concur with practices of Orton-based instruction and particularly that of the Slingerland approach.

---

[3] Specific Language Disability (SLD) is synonymous with the term *dyslexia*. As defined by a Committee of Members of the International Orton Dyslexia Society in 1994, "Dyslexia is a neurologically-based, often familial, disorder which interferes with the acquisition and processing of language. Varying in degrees of severity, it is manifested by difficulties in receptive and expressive language, including phonological processing, in reading, writing, spelling, handwriting, and sometimes in arithmetic. Dyslexia is not a result of lack of motivation, sensory impairment, inadequate instructional or environmental opportunities, or other limiting conditions, but may occur together with these conditions. Although dyslexia is life-long, individuals with dyslexia frequently respond successfully to timely and appropriate intervention."

[4] Slingerland teacher-education courses have been offered since 1960. Currently, several course levels are offered throughout the country and abroad. Slingerland-trained teachers are those who have completed at least one graduate level Slingerland teacher-education course. For more information, contact the Slingerland Institute, One Bellevue Center, 411 108th Ave., N.E., Bellevue, WA 98004. Phone: (425) 453-1190; fax: (425) 635-7762; email: Slingerland@aol.com; www.SlingInst.org.

Overview of Scope & Sequence for Literacy Instruction

Chapter 1, *Introduction*, explains for whom this book is intended and emphasizes the impact of research in changing literacy instruction.

Chapter 2, *Handwriting*, is devoted to the scope and sequence for manuscript and cursive handwriting instruction for SLD and non-SLD students, based primarily on Slingerland's works.

Chapter 3, *Visual Presentations*, explains the scope and sequence for the introduction of graphemes and decoding words from a more global Orton-based perspective. It includes a discussion of morphemes, syllabification rules, accenting hints, and how Slingerland adapted the original Orton-Gillingham approach to teach reading in a way that is compatible with whole language instruction.

Chapter 4, *Auditory Presentations*, explains the scope and sequence for phonemes, encoding,[5] spelling, and writing skills. It includes many spelling generalizations and the four major spelling rules.

Chapter 5, *Conclusions*, begins with the presentation of three lesson plans—Slingerland, traditional Orton-Gillingham, and whole language—emphasizing their similarities. It continues with a recommendation for a "must" to read to be informed about educational research that impacts literacy instruction. The chapter concludes with a final word to the reader.

Three appendixes, a glossary of terms, and references follow the last chapter.

How This Book Helps Teachers

This book is intended to assist all teachers who strive to improve literacy instruction. The sequence for introducing language elements supports the recommendations for systematic explicit phonics instruction. The sequence, based on Orton-Gillingham pedagogy, is precisely what educators, heedful of the *NRP Report*, recommend. This book addresses read-

---

[5] Until recently, in the Slingerland approach, *encoding* and *blending* were used synonymously. Currently, however, *blending* is frequently used synonymously with the term *decoding* which is the opposite of Slingerland's *encoding*. Blending is thus now referred to as Encoding. It is on the auditory side of the Slingerland daily lesson plan where phonetic words are spelled. (Technically, encoding also includes spelling nonphonetic and ambiguously spelled words, as well.) Many educators today refer to *encoding* as *segmentation*, for the techniques of *encoding* require hearing a word and then breaking it apart or *segmenting* it into its phonemes (individual sounds) with their corresponding graphemes (letters) to spell. *Segmentation* is the basis for sounding out words, i.e., spelling.

ing instruction components and topics within a comprehensive and cohesive framework with rationales for the introduction, instruction, and review of literacy skills.

If you are a teacher using an Orton-based approach, this book explains some of the differences and similarities among Orton-based adaptations; provides rationales that you might have missed; describes opportunities to enhance what and how you already teach; graphically displays the sequence for the introduction of graphemes–phonemes, decoding, and spelling; and validates the instructional strategies and techniques to which you are committed.

No matter what type of instruction you use, this book provides guidance in developing and incorporating a sequential, phonics-based program into your own instruction to address the needs of students with SLD, of students who are learning English as a second language (ESL), and to enhance literacy skills of most students. By using *Scope & Sequence* you will keep abreast of the NRP's findings and recommendations for how to best teach literacy. You will be able to adapt and enhance your own programs.

LessonPlanner™ and Scope & Sequence for Literacy Instruction

Computers help people with learning disabilities in a variety of ways. For example, they help improve weak phonemic processing and language skills, and they help children and adults compensate for poor reading and writing skills. Computers also aid teachers who work with individuals with learning disabilities by complementing and reinforcing instruction.

LessonPlanner is a software tool that has proven especially helpful to teachers.[6] *LessonPlanner* provides a comprehensive set of resources to assist teachers in their development of sequential, highly structured, multisensory language arts lessons for students with specific language disabilities (dyslexia). *LessonPlanner* was originally developed for Slingerland teachers and others who use instructional Orton-based approaches.

---

[6] *LessonPlanner* is available from the Lexia Institute, a non-profit corporation that develops computer technology for people with learning disabilities and their teachers. Lexia's goal is to help people with learning disabilities function more effectively at home, school, and work. Lexia offers another software tool, *WordSpring*, that provides simple access to an extensive set of word lists that can also be used in conjunction with this book and a web site for teachers, www. LEXIAnet.org, that focuses on phonics instruction. *WordSpring* should be of special interest to teachers using meaning emphasis methods who want to include a strong phonics component in their instruction. LEXIAnet should be of interest to all users of this book. Lexia's address is 766 Raymundo, Suite A, Los Altos, CA 94024; Phone: (650) 964-3666; fax: (650) 969-1632; email: LexiaInst@aol.com; www.LexiaInst.org.

LessonPlanner users requested the addition of a scope and sequence guide to facilitate preparation of their lesson plans.

LessonPlanner has also been found useful for preparing lessons for students in regular classrooms. This is not surprising since the Slingerland approach was originally intended for general education—not special education—instruction.

For teachers who do not use *LessonPlanner*, this book provides essential direction and rationales for what to introduce, when to introduce specific elements or concepts, and how much students can be expected to learn within given timeframes. Teachers will want to use their own favorite resource books and materials[7] to create needed word lists.

Teachers who use *LessonPlanner* will find that *Scope & Sequence for Literacy Instruction* complements *LessonPlanner*. The book provides direction for what to introduce, when to introduce elements or concepts, and how much students can be expected to learn within specific timeframes. *LessonPlanner* provides word lists containing numerous digraphs, trigraphs, phonograms, affixes, Latin and Greek roots, homonyms, confusables, and other instructional components. This book furnishes a review of how to create and obtain these resources from *LessonPlanner*.

How to Best Use this Book: Categories of Users

Scope & Sequence is intended for four broad categories of educators:

- ◆ *LessonPlanner* users with Orton-based training
- ◆ Orton-based teachers but not *LessonPlanner* users
- ◆ Meaning-emphasis teachers with phonics training
- ◆ School administrators and teachers without phonics

LessonPlanner Users with Orton-Based Training

In the first broad category of educators are teachers with Orton-based training who already use *LessonPlanner*. This community includes teachers with training in a number of Orton-based adaptations.[8] Within this community are also *LessonPlanner* users with tra-

---

[7] Educators Publishing Service, Inc. (EPS), 31 Smith Place, Cambridge, Massachusetts 02138-1000, has a wide selection of resource books and materials intended for use with students with and without learning disabilities.

[8] Adaptations include the video-taped Barton Reading & Spelling System (Bright Solutions, 1999); Alphabetic Phonics (Cox, 1992); Multisensory Teaching Approach (MTA) (Smith and Hogan, 1987); the Dyslexia Training Program (Texas Scottish Rite, 1989); Project Read (Enfield and Green, 1988); the Wilson Reading System for Older Students with Dyslexia (Wilson, 1988); the Slingerland Approach (Slingerland,

ditional Orton-Gillingham-Stillman training approved by the Orton-Gillingham Academy of Practitioners and Educators.[9]

Slingerland teachers will want to read and use all five chapters of the book because they follow the Slingerland daily lesson plan format closely. Other Orton-based teachers may choose to use the sequence for the introduction of graphemes taught in their respective training programs or that are provided in Chapter 3, *Visual Presentations*. It is recommended that consideration be given to using either the manuscript or cursive Slingerland handwriting sequence presented in Chapter 2, *Handwriting*.

If you are a *LessonPlanner* user with Orton-based training, you should be able to use *Scope & Sequence* without special training or difficulty. For optimal benefit, however, be sure to study the *LessonPlanner* User's Manual. When using *LessonPlanner*, some adaptation of the daily lesson plan format will be required. Perusing this book will make adaptation easier and more personalized.

Orton-Based Teachers But Not LessonPlanner Users

In the second category of educators are teachers with Orton-based training who are not *LessonPlanner* users. If you are a teacher in this category, you should be able to use *Scope & Sequence* without difficulty or special training by merely skimming the comments that explain how information and word lists can be obtained from *LessonPlanner*. However, the more you use *Scope & Sequence*, the more likely you will be to appreciate the value of *LessonPlanner* as a useful, extensive resource and timesaving tool.

Meaning-Emphasis Teachers with Phonics Training

The third category includes meaning-emphasis or whole language teachers with phonics training and teachers currently enrolled in phonics training workshops that use *Scope & Sequence*. Even a quick skim of *Scope & Sequence* gives you some idea about the importance and complexity of scope and sequence in literacy instruction. When participating in workshops that augment meaning-emphasis instruction with phonics, course instructors will teach you how to use *Scope & Sequence* most profitably and demonstrate *Lesson-*

1971, 1976, 1981); and both the Spalding (Spalding and Spalding, 1980) and Herman (Herman, 1975) methods, as well as others. Additionally, the Lindamood (Lindamood and Lindamood, 1975) Auditory Discrimination in Depth (A.D.D.) training program was influenced by Orton and Gillingham.

[9] One such program is the Massachusetts General Hospital Boston Program of Education in Therapy for Specific Reading Disability, Boston, Massachusetts 02114. There are others throughout the United States as well. For information about other O-G programs contact the Orton-Gillingham Academy of Practitioners and Educators, P.O. Box 234, Main St., Amenia, New York 12501-0234.

Planner. For a more thorough foundation in multisensory, phonics-based instruction, Orton-based teacher education courses are recommended.[10]

School Administrators and Teachers Without Phonics

The fourth category includes educators with little or no training in phonics who are searching for ways to incorporate phonics into their schools or districts to meet state regulations, improve reading, and/or supply missing phonic elements, particularly to meaning-emphasis programs. If you are a school administrator or teacher without a background in phonics, a superficial review of *Scope & Sequence* will give you a fairly clear idea of what is required to augment your current reading programs with phonics that includes related strategies and techniques. By viewing the numerous tables sequentially you will appreciate the comprehensiveness of this textbook, the effectiveness of *LessonPlanner*, and the content and thoroughness of Orton-based instruction and training courses. For rationales and details that are interwoven throughout *Scope & Sequence*, a more careful reading is required.

---

[10] To give you an idea of the length of instruction, the introductory, summer Slingerland teacher-education course, or in-year or modules equivalents, are four weeks in duration, with an 8:00 a.m. to 4:00 p.m. daily schedule. The winter session of the Massachusetts General Hospital Program of Education in Therapy for Specific Reading Disability is a total of 335 hours. The practicum is approximately 255 hours and the seminars and conferences, 80 hours.

2

Handwriting

The Importance of Handwriting

Penmanship or handwriting is one of the most fundamental skills that children are taught in school. Especially during the primary and elementary school years, much of each school day is devoted to using a pencil to identify papers, to note the day and date, to study for and take spelling tests, to compute arithmetic problems, to fill in worksheets and quiz blanks, to write sentences, to compose stories, to label pictures, to copy a favorite poem, to record a friend's telephone number, and to write reports.

Even when students have access to computers in the upper grades for writing reports or for doing homework, personal computers are usually not available to them at their desks, so it is essential that they are able to automatically, quickly, and legibly write down homework assignments, take class notes, outline when studying, and take written tests and examinations. Handwriting remains important in adult life. During the next several days, note how often you and other adults pick up a pen or pencil to jot down a phone message, compile a shopping list, leave a note on the refrigerator, fill out a check, complete a medical or insurance form, compose a personal thank-you, or write comments on student papers you are correcting or grading. A person who lacks the ability to write legibly is at a distinct disadvantage that can affect daily organization, academic achievement, and employment opportunities and advancement.

The two main reasons the Slingerland handwriting program has been selected to be described in this chapter are similar to those for why this book is phonics-based: First, it advocates and reinforces the inclusion of direct or explicit instruction based on scientific research. Second, the author's training, experience, and success as a teacher of penmanship as a component of literacy instruction, is based on the respected, neurologically-based, successful Orton-Gillingham-Slingerland approach. Its evolution is explained more fully in the next several paragraphs.

Historical Perspective

Samuel T. Orton is widely known as America's Father of Dyslexia. His identification, study, and neurological understanding of what he termed *strephosymbolia*,[1] referred to as dyslexia today, led eventually to his enunciation of principles and procedures for instruction—principles which remain valid today: Instruction must begin with the smallest unit of sight, sound, and feel—a single letter; it must progress sequentially forward to more complex learnings after previous learnings are secure; teaching must be through the intellect to establish correct thought patterns; and simultaneous multisensory techniques—auditory, visual, and kinesthetic-motor—must be incorporated in all learning. In teaching handwriting, Dr. Orton's principles are particularly evident.

In the 1930s Orton employed Gillingham to develop a remedial approach to teach students with specific language disabilities (dyslexia) how to read, write, and spell. With the assistance of Stillman, Gillingham applied Orton's basic principles to develop the Orton-Gillingham-Stillman simultaneous multisensory instructional approach for the remediation of specific language disabilities.

In their pioneering instructional manual for teachers, Gillingham and Stillman (Gillingham and Stillman, 1956, 1960, 1997)[2] cite many causes for poor penmanship, including injury, poor and damaging penmanship instruction—for left-handers in particular, and causes related to specific language disability with several subgroup categories. Most teachers will find Gillingham's discussion of penmanship both pedagogically and historically informative.

Slingerland discusses handwriting instruction extensively in two of her three major textbooks. *Book 1* (Slingerland, 1971) provides manuscript handwriting instruction while *Book 3* (Slingerland, 1981) covers cursive instruction. Slingerland felt that much of

---

[1] *Strephosymbolia*, meaning "twisted symbol," was coined by Orton and is described in Orton's *Reading, Writing, and Speech Problems in Children*, published first in 1937. The *twisting* of the symbols pertains to the tendency of dyslexics to reverse, invert, and transpose letters and syllables.

[2] Two editions of *Remedial Training for Children with Specific Disability in Reading, Spelling, and Penmanship* were available from the publisher until recently. The 1956 fifth edition with a red cover—the "Red Manual"—is keyed to the pronunciation symbols in *Webster's New International Dictionary, Second Edition*. The 1960 seventh edition with a green cover—the "Green Manual"—is keyed to symbols in *Webster's Third New International Dictionary*. The 1997 edition, entitled *The Gillingham Manual: Remedial Training for Students with Specific Disability in Reading, Spelling, and Penmanship*, has just been released. It conforms to the pronunciation symbols of the tenth edition of *Merriam-Webster's Collegiate Dictionary*. This edition, which also has a green cover, but with a yellow stripe added, is intended to supplant previous publications.

Gillingham and Stillman's carefully developed penmanship instruction had been lost or altered because the procedures and techniques, with important rationales, had not been documented sufficiently. She did not want the same to occur to her own carefully honed handwriting programs that she adapted for classroom use from the original Orton-Gillingham-Stillman approach.

The Orton-based Slingerland approach has been taught since the early 1960s in approved Slingerland teacher education college courses.[3] Founded on sound pedagogical and neurological principles, it is recognized as having one of the most comprehensive and valuable handwriting programs in existence today.

Variations in Orton-Based Handwriting Programs

The various remedial instructional approaches derived from the original works of Orton, Gillingham, and Stillman differ in their emphasis on handwriting and how it is taught, especially to students with specific language disabilities. In contrast, other key Orton-based instructional techniques—for example, techniques for using alphabet cards and for decoding, spelling, and dictation—remain relatively constant. Variations in handwriting programs pertain mainly to:

- the size and kind of pencils used[4]

- whether students trace or merely copy introduced letters; if they do trace, whether they simultaneously name or give the sound of the letters

- the size of the letter patterns—if used at all—for tracing letters as they are introduced

- whether the patterns for left-handers are slanted back toward the left, have a forward slant as those for right-handers, or have almost no slant at all

- whether the initial tracing or formation of letters is on crayoned pat-

---

[3] The first two, graduate level courses are entitled "Adaptation for Classroom Use of the Orton-Gillingham Approach." They are taught throughout the United States, in Canada, and abroad. For further information write to the Slingerland Institute at One Bellevue Center, 411 108th Ave., N.E., Bellevue, WA 98004; Phone (425) 453-1190, fax: (425) 635-7762; email: Slingerland@aol.com; www.SlingInst.org.

[4] Slingerland recommends larger, easier-to-grasp, fat, primary pencils without erasers for the youngest children, then slightly smaller and slimmer eraserless pencils for older children, and finally, standard pencils for more advanced children. A favorite replacement for standard pencils are the newer, easy-to-grip triangular pencils. One currently popular brand is Jumbo Trirex.

terns on newsprint or also on chalk board, in sand or rice, on sandpaper, or even in shaving cream

♦ the sequence for introducing letters, and whether it is prescribed or recommended

♦ precisely how each letter is introduced—for instance, with or without a corresponding key word and/or letter sound (phoneme)

♦ which letters and how many are introduced per lesson; that is, what the scope of instruction is daily and also weekly, monthly, and throughout the school year

Why Use Slingerland's Handwriting Program?

There are several good handwriting programs available. Those developed by Slingerland are compatible with this book, and in the author's opinion, they are the best. The first of Slingerland's handwriting programs is intended for use with specific language disability students. Its procedures and techniques are imbedded in, and integral to, the Slingerland multisensory approach which is taught in Slingerland teacher-education in-year and summer school programs and in modules.[5] The second program, either for manuscript or cursive handwriting, was developed by Slingerland and her professional heir, Marty Aho. (Slingerland and Aho, 1985) This program is intended for students in regular classrooms and can be taught in separate units.[6]

Slingerland handwriting instruction clearly shows what is meant by simultaneous, integrated multisensory and direct (explicit) instruction. It is also an excellent way to begin to teach students to simultaneously incorporate multisensory strategies and techniques for all learning. Gradually, students and teachers gain a clear understanding of the importance of beginning with the smallest units of sight, sound, and feel, of teaching through the intellect, and for using a carefully planned scope and sequence. Handwriting instruction is the foundation for the development of many literacy skills.

---

[5] Slingerland *modules* are short courses that cover segments of the total Slingerland teacher training courses. One of the more popular modules is for handwriting instruction.

[6] Educators Publishing Service, Inc. publishes most of the books and materials used by the various Orton-based programs, including those for Slingerland instruction.

Preliminary Considerations for Handwriting Instruction

Practical scope and sequence choices will depend on whether instruction is to a class, a small group, or an individual tutorial student. The design of scope and sequence is also influenced by the age, maturity, motivation, and intelligence of the students—their grade level, previous writing instruction and practice, and the degree and type of learning disabilities they may have, including in particular, kinesthetic-motor and visual modality strengths and weaknesses. All these factors are important to the rationale upon which a scope and sequence for handwriting instruction can be recommended in order to ensure successful handwriting mastery.

Regardless of age or grade, there are several conditions that must be attended to before the actual introduction of letters begins:

1. Position right-handed students' chairs slightly to the left side of their desks, and position left-handed students' chairs slightly to the right side of their desks.

2. Place students' writing papers to the right side of the desks of right-handers and to the left side for left-handers.

3. Instruct students to hold their pencils so that the point of the pencil is showing at the tip between the thumb and first finger of the writing hand. The pencil should be set back in the hand so that the underside of the point can be pulled straight down and pushed straight back up. Elbows should be held parallel, toward the body so the pencil is positioned comfortably on top of the desk.

If students do not carefully position themselves, their papers, and their pencils in the same way every time they write, they will always be attempting to compensate for perhaps barely perceptible, but definitely distracting and detrimental, shifts in position that make it difficult to obtain handwriting automaticity. Ensuring correct positioning at the commencement of manuscript or cursive instruction allows greater focus on the key task of handwriting rather than on difficulties stemming from necessary adjustments in seating, placement of paper, and how pencils are held.

Considerations for a Manuscript Scope and Sequence in Grade 1

The Slingerland scope and sequence for handwriting presented here provides an overview of an exemplary handwriting program that is more detailed than the other literacy skills presented in this book. Even so, this overview does not replace the need for a comprehensive program for handwriting instruction. For instruction to non-SLD students, Slingerland and Aho's program (Slingerland and Aho, 1985) is recommended. For manuscript instruction to SLD students, Slingerland's *Book 1* (Slingerland, 1971) is recommended; for cursive instruction to SLD students, *Book 3* (Slingerland, 1981) is recommended. Enrollment in an introductory Slingerland teacher-education course will provide the most effective instruction in how to teach handwriting to students with specific language disabilities.

Manuscript instruction is often a painstakingly slow, lengthy, arduous, but hopefully joyful process, requiring patience and care. To summarize briefly how it is introduced to first graders using the Slingerland approach for SLD students, six steps for structuring new learning are followed. From the beginning the goal is to develop automatic memory for the sequential movements necessary to form letters through the use of gross motor movements that are simultaneously reinforced auditorily, kinesthetically, and visually.

Step 1.   The teacher teaches the students what letters are before introducing the name of the first letter to be taught—often the letter **h**—and then shows an **h** for the students to name.

Step 2.   The teacher forms a large **h** on a blackboard or chalkboard and explains its formation. With considerable guidance, the teacher aids individual students as they trace and name the letter **h** at the board.

Step 3.   Each student has the opportunity to trace and name his or her own **h** letter pattern at the board.

Step 4.   Large permanent letter patterns are given to the class for tracing and naming. This is done first with two fingers before moving to the next step. It could take one to three days to reach step 4.

Step 5. The children name and trace their permanent patterns with the eraserless, unsharpened ends of their primary pencils. All three modalities for learning are engaged simultaneously—auditory, visual, and kinesthetic-motor.

Step 6. The children are given expendable patterns on three-fold newsprint to trace and name as they did their permanent patterns. Then, with continued constant teacher supervision and guidance, the children copy their own **h** to be traced while simultaneously naming it. Lastly, they write an **h** from memory, again, while simultaneously naming it.

Approximately one-third of Slingerland's *Book 1* is devoted to *Learning to Write* because it is such a fundamental academic skill. To understand the complexity of teaching handwriting thoroughly and well, it is again recommended that you read the detailed coverage in *Book I.*

Concerning the scope and sequence for introducing manuscript letters, when *Book I* was first published in 1971, Slingerland stated that only eight to ten letters could be expected to be learned and put to functional use in the first grade by the beginning of the new year in SLD preventive classes. This was before year-round programs came into existence. With simple extrapolation, however, "the beginning of the new year" is approximately four months after the commencement of manuscript instruction.

The *preventive* classes Slingerland envisioned were usually slightly smaller, general education classes composed of first-graders who today would be considered "at risk" because of their specific language disability profiles. Since the publication of Slingerland's first textbook, many teachers discovered that they were either required to introduce letters more quickly than Slingerland recommends or they were able to do so quite easily because of the pre-writing training the children were given in kindergarten. In private schools, where parents often have more voice in how their schools are operated, parents often insist that children be moved forward at an accelerated pace even when it is not in the children's best interests. Parental requests may be prompted by the knowledge that their child's stay at the school will be brief or by other seemingly justifiable reasoning. Slingerland based her recommendations on an ideal continuum program that she developed wherein the establishment of solid academic skills in the first grade, including handwriting, were continued into the next two grades, and then supported in subsequent grades. At every grade level students were to be instructed by highly trained and skilled teachers in reasonably sized classes that were not so overwhelming as they often are today.

When considering how many and which manuscript letters should be taught, teacher judgment is crucial. Teachers must consider class size, age, intelligence, motivation, and the maturity of their students, as well as the quality and quantity of pre-school and kindergarten language and motor skill experiences the children were provided, and the degree and type of specific language disabilities present. The teacher's ongoing evaluation of children's handwriting performance and progress is also important, as well as subsequent modifications and adjustments to establish and maintain an appropriate scope and sequence. The key is for students to develop automatic writing skills.

The manuscript letters that Slingerland recommends to be taught at the beginning of a Slingerland or SLD first grade class are equally appropriate for non-SLD instruction. The letters are those that are formed similarly but are not easily confused, as well as those that can be combined readily to construct the first words children encode for spelling. For example, the manuscript letter **l** (ell) is best introduced before the more difficult letter **k** that requires more complicated letter strokes and lifting the pencil. Although **a** is a difficult letter to form, it is essential early because it provides the first vowel, a necessity for building words.

Not only are the usefulness, simplicity, and similarity of letters important. Equally important is ease or difficulty of the corresponding graphemes' phonemes.[7] For instance, **h** is taught before the more easily formed **l** (ell) because the /h/ phoneme is easier for children to feel and enunciate than /l/.

Introducing Letters that Look or Sound Alike

The greater the similarity between and among letters, the greater the possibilty for confusion. Letters that look alike—particularly those that can be easily reversed or inverted—should not be introduced too closely together, and certainly not in the same lesson. Be especially careful with the introduction of the following letters:

---

[7] A *grapheme* is a letter or more than one letter that represents a single sound or phoneme. A *phoneme* is the smallest unit of speech that distinguishes one utterance from another as /d/ in **d**uck and /oi/ in t**oi**l. Depending on the dialect, English is comprised of approximately 45 phonemes.

b and **d**

d and **p**

p and **d**

q and **p**

and sometimes

b and **q** and **d**

n and **m**

h and **n**

h and **y**

v and **w**

w and **u**

u and **v**

n and **r**

In Orton-based programs where the sounds or phonemes for letters or graphemes are introduced at the same time as letter names and formations, confusion can be avoided by separating the introduction of letters with similar corresponding phonemes by at least one lesson, if not several, and with precise instruction. The following letters have corresponding phonemes that are similar and must be taught carefully and separately:

f —/f/ and **v** —/v/

b —/b/ and **p** —/p/

k —/k/ and **g** —/g/

m—/m/ and **n** —/n/

i —/ĭ/ and **e** —/ĕ/

o —/ŏ/ and **u** —/ŭ/

The pairs of letters that cause the greatest difficulty are those that are both auditorily and visually similar. The introduction of these letters should also be well separated.

b —/b/ and **d** —/d/

m —/m/ and **n** —/n/

b —/b/ and **p** —/p/

e —/ĕ/ and **i** —/ĭ/

Regarding the usefulness of letters for reading, writing, and spelling, vowels are the most important. The consonants **b**, **c**, **d**, **f**, **g**, **h**, **k**, **m**, **n**, **p**, **r**, **s**, and **t** are more useful than **j**, **qu**, **z**, **y**, **x**, **v**, and **w** in the early grades.

First Trimester

As shown in table 2–1, the tall letters **h**, **t**, **l**, **f**, and **b**, and the vowel **a**, should be taught in the first three or four months. When **a** is introduced in the second month, encoding and spelling can begin shortly thereafter, using words made from just the few letters introduced to date (**bat**, **hat**, **lab**, **tab**, **fat**, **flab**, **blab**, etc.). Remember that the pace for introducing letters to SLD children will be slower than to non-SLD children.

Table 2–1. First Trimester: First Group of Letters	Definitely teach:	**h, t, l, f** **b** with special verbalization
	Maybe teach:	**a**
	Perhaps begin:	letter-size relationships

As you introduce letters, it is helpful to talk the children through *each* letter. For example, while a child or you form the letter **h** you should both say, "**h**—down all the way, up and around, and down." For letters that are easily reversed, the children should be taught to help themselves avoid confusions by repeating the special verbalizations developed by Slingerland and others. Similar verbalizations can be used with numerals as well, particularly when they are first introduced with patterns.[8]

The first special verbalization that children learn and say for a longer period of time than the initial verbalizations for all letters, is for the letter **b**. After talking through the formation of **b** (always taught considerably before **d**) right-handers should learn to say, "**b**—tall stem down, back up, turn *out* (*away*) from my body, and around (close to my body)." Alternatively they may say, "**b**—tall stem down, up, *out* (*away*) from my body, and around (close to my body)." Left-handers say, "**b**—tall stem down, turn *across (in front of)* my body, and around (close to my body)." Alternatively they may say, "... toward my other hand." To be consistent with the second alternative for right handers, left-handers say, "**b**—tall stem down, up, *into* my body, and around (close to my body)."

---

[8] For numerals, see page 65 of Slingerland's *Book 1*.

For the letter **a**, children should say before beginning to write, "**a** starts a little below the mid-line."

Instruction of letter-size relationships should also be started early.

As shown in table 2–2, the next group of letters include **f**, **k**, **c**, **a**, **g**, **m**, **s**, and the first consonant digraph, **ck**. Note that **f** and **a** may have been introduced in the earlier group. If **a** was not introduced earlier, it should be introduced in this group, after **c**, but before **g** and **s**. The prior introduction of **a** allows for two verbalizations that help children recall direction and formation: "**g**—round like an **a**, straight down below the line, under and up" and "**s** begins like an **a**."

Table 2–2. First Trimester: Second Group of Letters	Definitely teach:	**f, k, c** **a** with special verbalization **g** special verbalization **m** **s** special verbalization **ck** first digraph—introduced in visual cards a few numerals (with patterns) letter-size relationships
	Perhaps begin:	space reduction

Recall that **ck** is introduced in visual cards first, but only after **c** and **k** have been taught individually in handwriting. All single letters and **qu** are introduced when their formations are taught during handwriting instruction (*Learning to Write* in the Slingerland approach). Many words can be formed now that the children have learned three spellings for the /k/ phoneme.

Also teach spacing between letters. Spacing between the lines that the children use for writing should be reduced gradually when the children are ready.

Second Trimester

As shown in table 2–3, the vowel **i** and several more consonants, should be introduced within three months from the time manuscript instruction commences with an SLD class and within the first two months with non-SLD students. At the start of an SLD class beginning in September, this means January. In year-round programs, count four months forward to determine the month in which to introduce **i**. The other dotted letter, **j**, should be taught sometime after **i**. Both **d** and **p** are introduced in the second trimester, but never in the same lesson because of how readily they are confused. A few additional consonant digraphs such as **sh**, **ch**, and **th** (all introduced visually first) may be included. The digraph **th** is introduced early for reading and spelling because it is found in several important, high-frequency words that children are exposed to in the first grade (the, this, then, than, that, them, those, these, they, both, with, three).

Table 2–3. Second Trimester of an SLD Grade One and First Trimester of a Non-SLD Grade One		
Definitely teach:	space reduction more numerals letter-size **i** **d** with special verbalization **p** separated from **d** by several lessons; use verbalizations	
Maybe teach:	**sh** **ch** separated from **sh** by several lessons **th**	
Perhaps teach:	**j**, **w**, **wh**	
Practice:	letter groupings	
Maybe include:	the **ing** grouping	
Then maybe teach:	the first capital (perhaps **T**)	
Cautiously, if at all for writing:	**e** (no phoneme)	

In Chapter 4, *Auditory Presentations*, we discuss how the frequency of graphemes, such as **wh**, **th**, and **ph**, influences when they should be introduced. If an occasion necessitates teaching **w**, then the digraph **wh** can be introduced subsequently. Like **th**, **wh** should be introduced relatively early because of its frequency in important and useful words (where, why, when, who, and what). Other letter groupings commonly used in writing, encoding, and spelling include two-letter beginning consonant blends (bl, cl, fl, gl, sl, pl, br, cr, dr, fr, gr, tw, pr, tr, sc, sk, sm, sn, sp, st, and sw) and two-letter ending consonant blends (ld, nd, st, lf, lk, lp, lt, sk, mp, sp, ct, ft, nt, and pt). The first suffix, **ing**, can now be introduced. In her guide for teachers, Beverly Wolf (Wolf, 1982), recommends that **ing** be taught six months into the first grade. You can introduce the first manuscript capital letter as needed for writing. It could, for instance, be the capital at the beginning of your students' names, an address, or the name of their school.

When teaching **d**, to counteract visual confusion between **b** and **d**, both right-handers and left-handers create a multisensory differentiation as they say, "**d**—round like an **a**, tall stem up, straight (or pulled) down to the line."

When teaching **p**, to avoid confusion with **b** and **d**, right-handers say, "**p**—stem below the bottom (or writing) line, up (to the midline), *out* from my body, and around." Left-handers say, "**p**—stem below the bottom (or writing) line, up (to the midline), *into* my body, and around."

If needed, you can introduce the letter **e** for writing only, as explained in the following section.

Grade One SLD Third Trimester or Non-SLD Second Trimester

As shown in table 2–4, some of the remaining commonly used consonants may already have been introduced as needed. They include **n**, **m**, and **r**. If they were not introduced previously, introduce them now, as well as the vowel **u**, but during different lessons. Remaining consonants to be introduced as needed are **v**, **x**, **y**, and **z**. The digraph **qu** requires special teaching[9] and is sometimes not taught in a first grade SLD class, where the children are struggling with the automaticity of the other letters previously presented. When it is taught, the following verbalization is helpful.

Right-handed children say, "**qu**—goes round like an **a**, stem below the line, *out* (*away*) from my body to the **u**." Left-handers say, "**qu**—goes round like an **a**, stem below the line, *across (in front of)* my body to the **u**."

The next vowels to be introduced are **o**, first, and **e**, last. As noted, however, **e**, the most frequently used letter in the English language, *may* be introduced earlier for writing only—not for sounding out in spelling with SLD children. The letter **e** increases the number of suffixes that can be used, including **ed**, **er**, and **est**. Be reminded that **er** is a phonogram as well as a common suffix. In *Instructional Sequence for SLD Class-*

---

[9] Experienced Slingerland teacher, Barbara Sterling, finds that a nice way to teach little children to remember the **qu** formations—particularly the direction of the **q**—is to help them conceptually by explaining that since **q** and **u** are best friends, **q** is always reaching out to hold **u**'s hand.

rooms (Wolf, 1982), Wolf recommends that the suffix **er** be taught in April and **ed** in May. In year-round programs, this translates to the final few weeks of the first grade.

Table 2–4. Grade One SLD Third Trimester or Non-SLD Second Trimester		
If not taught previously:	**ch, sh, th, w, wh** letter groupings including **ing** first capital letter (perhaps **T**) **m** (keep separate from **n**), **n, r, u**	
Gradually teach:	**v, x, y, z, o**	
Perhaps for writing:	**e**	
Practice:	suffixes with **e** (**er, es, ed, est** for more advanced students)	
Practice combinations introduced visually:	**ing, ang, ung, ong**	
Perhaps practice:	**ink, ank, unk, onk**	
Practice phonograms introduced visually:	**oa or ee**	
Perhaps, if introduced, practice:	**oo, ai, ay, ar, ou, er**	
Practice other common groupings:	beginning and ending blends a word family (**old or ind**) non-phonetic spellings	
Maybe teach:	**e, eng, qu**	
And a few more common capitals:	**T, A, I, S**	

The phoneme for **e** should not be taught until all the other, less difficult short vowels have been introduced. However, definitely teach non-SLD classes the letter **e** with its corresponding key word and phoneme before the end of the first grade. You can also teach **e** to accelerated SLD classes.

Other letter groupings to be practiced in preparation for encoding and written spelling include the first phonograms[10] usually taught, **oa** and **ee**. The sequence for the

---

[10] Using Slingerland's definition, *diphthongs* and *vowel digraphs* are *phonograms*; a diphthong is a speech sound made by gliding from one vowel to another in a syllable, such as **oi** in **oil**. A vowel digraph consists of any two vowels adjacent to each that produce one phoneme (ai, ey, ee, etc.). A phonogram is a *diphthong* or *vowel digraph*.

presentation of phonograms is discussed more fully in visual cards where they are introduced. Capital manuscript letters should be taught as needed, especially when your children begin to write phrases and short sentences. Punctuation must be taught too. Patterns for teaching the formation of exclamation and question marks are optional. Capital manuscript letters that are often introduced first are **T, A, I**, and **S**. Manuscript capitals that children typically have more difficulty learning are **D, K, Y, Z**, and **Qu**. Less frequently used capitals are **Z, X**, and **Qu**.

In selecting capital manuscript letters to be taught, consider both their frequency or usefulness and similarity of formation compared to their corresponding lowercase letters. Capital **X**, although similar to its lowercase form, would not be one of the first capitals to be taught because it is not a capital that young children have occasion to use often, if at all. On the other hand, capital **S** is both useful and formed similarly to lowercase **s**. Other lower and uppercase formations that are similar are **w–W, c–C, k–K, o–O, p–P**, and **u–U**. Less frequent similar pairs are **v–V, x–X**, and **z–Z**. To a lesser degree of similarity are **f–F, m–M, n–N, j–J, t–T, y–Y, l–L**, and **i–I**. The remaining letter pairs of the alphabet are dissimilar.

Thus far there has been no discussion of letter combinations.[11] Wolf recommends that **ing** and **ang** letter groupings be taught shortly after the letter **i** is introduced, and likewise, **ung** after **u**, **ong** after **o**, and **eng** after **e**. The suffix **ing** is an especially useful letter grouping to practice. Interspersed in the introduction of letter combinations are the first phonograms.[12] Remember, phonograms and letter combinations are introduced visually. They can be practiced and reviewed as letter groupings in handwriting. The next letter combinations to include are **ink, ank, unk**, and **onk**.

Similar to letter combinations are word families.[13] In word family words, as used throughout this book, it is usually the vowel that has an unexpected phoneme. In one of the first word families introduced, **old**, it is expected that **o** would be short, /ŏ/, because

---

[11] A *letter combination*, as used here and throughout this book, is a group of letters which, when combined, makes a sound (phoneme) which differs from the individual sounds of its letters, as in **ink**, **ang**, and **tion**.

[12] Using Slingerland's definition, a *phonogram* is a *diphthong* or *vowel digraph*. A digraph is a combination of two letters that express a simple sound such as /th/ or /o͞o/.

[13] In word family words, usually the vowel has an unexpected phoneme. For example, in **ind** word family words, it is expected that the vowel **i** followed by two consonants in a closed syllable would be pronounced /ĭ/ instead of /ī/.

of the **vcc**[14] pattern forming a closed syllable. Contrarily, **o** is long, /ō/. Because of its frequency in common words (old, cold, hold), it must be introduced early and thus included as a letter grouping to be practiced and reviewed in penmanship.

Mention must be made about red flag or non-phonetic words discussed more fully in Chapter 4, *Auditory Presentations*. Such words are often copied and traced because they cannot be sounded out phonetically. More difficult letter groupings within these words should be practiced during handwriting instruction to ensure that when children study them for spelling they will be able to concentrate on spelling rather than on how the letters are formed. This is an example of what is meant by integration within the daily lesson plan.

Reviewing Manuscript Formations

There should be constant reviews of letters arranged in groupings that begin with similar strokes. For example, tall letters that begin with a downward stroke should be grouped: **l**, **h**, **b**, **k**, **t**, and perhaps **f**, with a special reminder about how it differs in formation from the other tall letters. Other letters that make a good grouping for review are: **g**, **j**, **p**, **y**, and, if taught, **qu**; for all these letters extend below the writing line. With capitals, children should be reminded that no manuscript uppercase letters have stems that go beneath the writing line, whereas some lowercase manuscript letters do (**g**, **j**, **p**, **qu**, and **y**).

In review, two- and three-letter groupings that occur in familiar words should be dictated by the teacher (**br**, **si**, **aut**, **ese**, etc.). Also, capital–lowercase letter pairs and lowercase–capital pairs (**C–c**, **M–m**, **a–A**) should be dictated as well as capitals with different lowercase letters (**Al**, **Ca**, **Th**). Whole words can be dictated too and then spelled aloud letter by letter (**will—w-i-l-l** or **laugh—l-a-u-g-h**) for children to write.

LessonPlanner records which letters a user has introduced to individual students or different classes for handwriting instruction, and provides the introduction status for all its graphemes and phonemes for each student or class.

---

[14] The **v** represents the word vowel and **c** represents the word consonant. When a vowel is followed by at least one consonant in a syllable, the vowel is usually short (cat, fish, box).

Continuum Manuscript Instruction

Throughout the first grade "scope and sequence" should be taught without hurdling or hurrying to reach unattainable and unreasonable goals. Such goals are too frequently based on preconceived ideas of what children should know and be able to do as they enter school and as they continue. You are now ready to continue manuscript instruction into the second half of a regular first grade or into a second grade continuum with SLD children. Included will be the following for review, practice, and new learning.

There will obviously be some overlapping between manuscript instruction in the first grade and that which will be taught in an SLD continuum second year program, or to non-SLD students in the second half of the first grade. Included in this continuum will be at least the following for introduction, practice, and review:

- review of letter-size relationships

- review of all consonants previously taught

- review of previously taught vowels

- introduction of short **e**, if not previously introduced

- introduction of **qu** if not taught before

- continued reduction of spacing between lines, down to the use of control paper[15] (by the end of the third trimester or earlier)

- use of standard sized pencils before the end of the first grade, or the slightly larger triangular pencils

- fewer special verbalizations for **a**, **s**, **b–d–p**, **g**, and **qu**

- review of the previously taught digraphs (**ck**, **sh**, **ch**, **wh**, and **th**) for the purpose of writing, and continuation of new digraphs and trigraphs as they are introduced visually. See the discussion of visual cards in Chapter 3.

---

[15] Control paper, sometimes referred to as split binder paper, is paper of varying sizes with dotted lines between the base writing line and the top line to assist students with sizing letters. The dotted line replaces a mid-line. Students write lower-case letters, such as **a**, between the base line and the dotted line and tall letters, such as **l**, through the dotted line, up to the top line, back down to the base line crossing at the dotted line.

- review of previously taught capital letters and continued introduction of new capital letter formations, as needed

- review of the previously taught letters in common suffixes (**ing**, **ed**, **s**, **es**, **er**)

- practice writing letter groupings in previously taught and new suffixes for use in spelling, such as **able**, **ful**, **est**, **less**, **ness**, **y**, **ment**, and **ly**, as needed

- review of letter groupings in common phonograms (**oa**, **ee**, and maybe **ai**, **ay**, **oo** or **ou**)

- addition of letter groupings in new phonograms such as **ar**, **er**,[16] **eigh**, **ey**, **ea** and **v–e** (**vce** or **vce** syllables)

- review of previously taught groupings in the letter combinations **ing**, **ang**, **ung**, **ong**, and for new ones (**eng**, **ink**, **ank**, **unk**, and **onk**)

- review of numerals

- review of letters grouped according to the similarity of their beginning strokes (two o'clock letters that begin where the "2" is on a clock, tall letters that are two spaces high, hill letters that curve like hills, etc.)

- punctuation marks, as needed in writing, and possibly quotation marks and comma formations

- practice of letter groupings with difficult formations for the study of word families (**old**, **ind**, **ign**) and non-phonetic words (**was**, **said**, **laugh**)

- review of letters with similar formations; for example, the 2 o'clock let-ters—**c**, **a**, **d**, **g**, **qu**, **o**)

- review of capitals or lowercase letters (**F**–**f**, **A**–**a**, and **G**–**g**) and capi-tals with lowercase letters (**Al**, **Ca**, **Th**)

For the preceding continuum instruction, Slingerland's second textbook, *Book 2*, (Slingerland, 1976) is recommended for its detailed instructional procedures, techniques, rationales, and more.

---

[16] In most Orton-based programs **ar** and **er** are distinguished from the other phonograms by being referred to as **r**-controlled syllables rather than phonograms. Slingerland includes all the **r**-contolled syllables (**ar**, **er**, **ir**, **or**, **ur**, **yr**, **ear**, and **our**) with the phonograms (**ai**, **oa**, **eigh**, etc.).

Considerations for a Cursive Scope and Sequence in Grade 3 and Beyond

In an ideal educational world, first grade children are taught manuscript handwriting so expertly that by the second grade they are ready to put to functional use their handwriting skills, as tools for spelling, dictation, and propositional and creative writing. Theoretically, all that is then required at the beginning of a second grade continuum is a review of handwriting from the previous year before new instruction begins. Finally, by the third year, cursive handwriting can be taught with alacrity because the students were provided such an excellent foundation.

The foundation includes the *Preliminary Considerations* for handwriting for students: how to position their chairs, where to place and slant their papers, and how to hold and use their pencils correctly. It also includes techniques for tracing new letters at the blackboard and tracing permanent patterns, first with two fingers and then with the blunt end of the pencil, while simultaneously naming the letters. If the students are secure with letter-size relationships and other techniques from their manuscript training, then they can begin immediately with expendable cursive patterns. Often, only a few permanent patterns are needed. Expendable patterns are large letter patterns that are traced and simultaneously named while being copied, and finally written from memory before new formations are practiced and reviewed. See Slingerland's *Book 3* (Slingerland, 1981) for a detailed description of cursive handwriting instruction.

If a solid manuscript handwriting foundation has been taught, cursive letters can be introduced with greater scope, i.e., with more letters introduced daily, and preferably using a sequence similar to that presented in this chapter. You must use your judgment as a teacher to determine how quickly to proceed. You will do this best if you weigh in the factors of age, intelligence, drive, maturity, the number of students in your class, grade level, quality and quantity of previous handwriting instruction, the degree and kind of specific language disabilities of your students, and most important, how quickly and well your pupils are learning handwriting based on their performance during handwriting instruction and during instruction of other subjects in which the focus is not on handwriting, but where handwriting is required.

If possible, at the beginning of cursive instruction, writing should be limited during the instruction of other subjects for at least the first month to allow all students time to secure new cursive skills correctly.

The Introduction of Cursive Handwriting

Cursive letters with similar formations, particularly similar beginning strokes, are often taught in the same lesson, and are put to functional use quickly. The simplest formations should be taught first. For example, the cursive letter *ℓ* should be introduced before the more difficult letter *f* that requires writing beneath the base (writing) line. The letter *h* should follow the letter *ℓ* because it is only slightly more difficult to form than *ℓ*.

First Three or Four Cursive Lessons

As shown in table 2–5, in the first lessons, plan to introduce, practice, and review similarly formed, two-spaced, tall, looped letters *ℓ, h, k, f,* or *b,* and the first vowel *a,* if the vowel is to be used soon in blending or spelling. If not, be cognizant that both *f* and *b* are more difficult to form than *ℓ, h,* or *k*. With some students and classes, depending on the factors previously discussed, you might wish to hold off teaching either *b* or *f* until the end of the first set of three or four lessons.

Table 2–5. First Three or Four Cursive Lessons

Definitely teach:	*ℓ, h, k*
Maybe teach:	*b* or *f,* with verbalizations
To begin encoding or spelling, teach:	*a*
Teach:	letter-size and spacing relationships

In Slingerland teacher training programs, at least four letters are usually taught daily. However, two of those are taught by the demonstration or master teacher while the other two are taught by the teacher participants to the student or students with whom they are practicing the techniques demonstrated earlier by the master teacher. Normally, you would introduce no more than two letters a day. In lengthy tutorial sessions, with students working at more advanced or sophisticated levels, all or most of the letters listed above might be introduced in one lesson. With larger classes, it might be possible to teach *ℓ* and *h,* or only *ℓ,* the first day; followed by *k* and *f,* or only *b,* the next day; and so on.

Before writing *b,* right-handers will be helped to avoid confusion with *d, f,* and *p* if they say, "*b*—tall loop up (like an *ℓ*), down, turn *out* from my body, up, and out."

Left-handers say, "*b*—tall loop up (like an *l*), down, turn *across* my body, up, and out." (For slight verbalization variations, see Slingerland's *Book 1* (Slingerland, 1971) and *Book 3* (Slingerland, 1981) verbalizations for avoiding handwriting confusions.)

It is not advisable to introduce *b, d,* and *f,* or *p* on the same day. To help avoid *b* and *f* similarity confusion, right-handed students benefit from saying, "*f*—up like an *l*, down below the line, turn *out* from my body, up, and out." Left-handers say, "*f*—up like an *l*, down below the line, turn *across* my body, up, and out." Refer to Slingerland's textbooks for other variations of verbalizations to help avoid letter confusions.

As shown in table 2–6, continue to introduce, practice, and review the looped, two-spaced letters. If you did not introduce *b* in the last lesson, teach students how to remind themselves about the formation of the letter *b* because it is not only easily confused visually with the letter *f,* but also with *d, p,* and *q.*

Table 2–6. Second Several Cursive Lessons	
Definitely teach:	*f*
Perhaps teach:	*b* with verbalization
Teach:	*c*
	a (if not previously taught)
	common connections (*ck, ll, ta*)
	difficult connections with patterns (*bl, ba*)
	d with verbalization
Perhaps teach:	*t*
	g (not with *d*)
Introduce with extreme caution:	*e* (for writing only—not spelling)

If *l, h, k, f,* and *b* have all been introduced, the next letters to consider for introduction should be *a* and *c,* ideally in the same lesson because of their similarity. Of the two, *c* should be introduced first in terms of letter formation, but *a* is often taught before *c* because it is needed to begin encoding and spelling. The letters *c* and *a* are often called two-o'clock letters because they start where the "2" is located on the face of a clock, and they are formed counterclockwise. Other two-o'clock letters to introduce soon thereafter, but on different days, are *q* and *d*.

The letters *b* and *d* should not be introduced in the same lesson because they are easily reversed by both younger and older students. Similarly, it is advisable not to teach *q* and *d* together; they are easily reversed and/or inverted. When teaching *d*, Slingerland recommends another verbalization to help avoid reversing *d* with *b*. Both right-handers and left-handers say, "*d*—round like an *a*, straight up, down, and out."

With students who will soon begin to encode and spell, the one remaining tall, but not looped letter, *t*, might now be introduced to increase the number and kind of words that can to be encoded or spelled containing only the letters taught to date.

Introduce the letter *e* if your students are in an Orton-based continuum program. The letter *e*, the most frequently used letter in the English language, is needed for writing. The cursive *e* formation is similar to that of *l* except it is half its size. If, however, key words and phonemes are being taught at the beginning of instruction, *e* should definitely not be introduced until your students are secure with the other, less difficult to learn single vowels. You will be able to introduce *e* earlier to non-SLD students—as previously discussed.

Finally, teach and practice letter connections. Use common connections, particularly letter connections that are required when writing at other times throughout the day. Patterns are recommended for the more difficult connections, such as *ba* and *bl*, after *b* is taught.

Second and Third Weeks of Cursive Instruction

If *l*, *h*, *k*, *b*, *f*, *a*, *c*, *d*, and *q* have been introduced, practiced, reviewed, and integrated into encoding or spelling, the letter *i* is the next vowel to be taught in most Orton-based programs, as shown in table 2–7. With the introduction of the letter *i* the beginning upward stroke that is used to start the cursive letters *j*, *r*, *s*, *u*, *t*, *w*, the easier, unlooped *p* formation, and the *y* formation that begins like *u*, is introduced. The letters *r* and *s* occur more frequently than *j*; therefore, they are good choices at this point. If there is time for only *s* or *r*, remember that *s* increases the number of words that can be spelled more than *r*, for *s* is used both as a plural and third person singular inflection.

Table 2–7. Second and Third Weeks of Cursive	Definitely teach: *t, g, s, i*
	Perhaps teach: *r, j, ck* (first digraph, introduced visually first)
	Teach: common and difficult connections such as *bs, br, bi* – some with patterns.

It is important to try to integrate the day's handwriting instruction with what is expected to be written at different times during the day. Referring again to the ending *s*, if it had been recently noted or discussed in reading, then including it in spelling would be timely, and the choice between teaching *r* versus *s* would be intelligently confirmed.

The first consonant digraph *ck* is usually taught around this time. Recall that *ck* is introduced in visual cards first, and that all single letters, including *qu*, are introduced when their formations are taught during *Learning to Write* in the Slingerland approach. When *ck* has been introduced, more words can be formed, for now you have given your students three spellings for the /k/ phoneme. The *ck* connection requires penmanship practice and review.

Third or Fourth Week of Cursive Instruction for an SLD Class or Slightly Earlier for Non-SLD

As shown in table 2–8, during this period the third vowel, *u*, is usually introduced as well as the remaining letters that begin with the same upward stroke as *i* and *u*.[17] At the same time, introduce a few easier digraphs—*sh* and *ch* in separate lessons, and *wh*—each with only one key word and phoneme provided. Teach *th* with two key words—one to represent the unvoiced phoneme, as in *thimble,* /th/, and the other for the voiced /th/ phoneme as in *these.* (Remember, digraphs are usually introduced in visual cards and practiced in handwriting.) The digraph *th* is introduced early for reading and spelling because it is found in several important, high-frequency words that children are exposed to at the beginning of reading (the, this, then, than, that, them, those, these, they, both, with, and three). The digraph *wh*, like *th*, should also be introduced early because of its fre-

---

[17] Phyllis Bertin and Eileen Perlman, authors of the Orton-based program entitled *Preventing Academic Failure* (Bertin and Perlman, 1980), use the descriptive term *rocket letters* for these letters; they look as if they are taking off.

quency in important, useful words (where, why, when, who, and what). Penmanship practice and review of these digraph connections is essential.

Table 2–8. *Third or Fourth Week of Cursive Instruction for an SLD Class or Slightly Earlier for Non-SLD*	Teach letters perhaps not introduced previously:	*j, n*
	Definitely teach:	*ck* (visually first), *u, w*
	Perhaps teach:	*sh, p* (verbalization)
	Practice and review digraph connections:	*ch, th, wh*
	Practice:	easy and difficult connections such as *bu, wh, wa, wr, wi* – some with patterns

See further discussion for scope and sequence of digraphs and trigraphs in Chapters 3 and 4 on visual and auditory cards, respectively, and in *LessonPlanner*. Refer to visual cards for how *ck*, often the first digraph to be taught, is introduced as the third spelling for the /k/ phoneme.

When teaching *p*, right-handed students should say, "*p*—up to the midline, down below the writing line, up to the midline, round *out* from my body, and out." For slight variations refer to the manuscript instructions of this chapter. Left-handers should say, "*p*—up to the midline, down below the writing line, up to the midline, round *across* my body, and out."

End of the First and Start of the Second Month of Cursive for an SLD Class or Slightly Earlier for Non-SLD

As shown in table 2–9, during this period, you should introduce the fourth vowel, *o*, as well as *qu*, that begin with the same two-o'clock formation as the previously taught *a, c, d,* and *g; qu* requires careful teaching. The *q* is not taught without *u* following it, for *q* does not appear in English words without *u*. The adjacent *u* acts as a consonant (most frequently with the /w/ sound rather than the short /ŭ/ phoneme). When teaching the digraph *qu*, remind right-handed students that both *qu* and *f* have stems below the writing line that turn *out* from their bodies. For left-handers, *qu* and *f* have stems that turn *across* their bodies.

Right-handed students say, "*qu*—round like an *a*, stem below the line, turn *out* from my body, up, and out." (Again, consistent variations are acceptable.) Left-handed students say, "*qu*—round like an *a*, stem below the line, turn *across* my body, up, and out."

At this point, or even a bit earlier, you can review in writing additional digraphs and even a trigraph—*ph* and *tch*, respectively—after they are introduced visually.

Also, begin to gradually introduce cursive capital letters, especially to students in Orton-based programs that require writing sentences to put to functional use, words that are encoded or spelled. One of the earliest capitals to introduce is *T*, followed by perhaps *A* or *W* or *H*, again, as needed. *L* requires careful instruction since its beginning stroke, to the left and upward, is unusual. The only other capital that begins in the same direction is *J*. More manuscript upper- and lowercase letters are formed similarly than cursive letters because most cursive capitals, excepting for *D*, *L*, *S*, and *J*, begin on the top writing line while all lowercase letters begin on the base writing line. Only cursive *a*–*s* are somewhat similar, both beginning on the base line. Therefore, similarity cannot be used to help determine which cursive capitals to teach as it does in manuscript instruction.

Table 2–9. End of First and Start of the Second Month of Cursive for an SLD Class or Earlier for Non-SLD		
Practice grapheme connections remaining from previous lessons:		*sh, ch, th, wh*
Definitely teach:		*p, o, qu* (verbalization)
First capitals:		*T, A, W,* or *H*
Gradually add more capitals.		
Lowercase difficult connections:		*bo, oi, ot, ob, oo, od,* etc.
Uppercase with lowercase connections:		*Al, Wh, Th, Ho,* etc.
If introduced visually first, practice and review digraph connection:		*ph*
and trigraph connection:		*tch*

Capital connections must also be taught at this time (*Th, Al, Ho,* etc.) Be sure to point out that *J, Z,* and *Y* all go beneath the writing line in cursive. Other capital cursive letters that are typically introduced early are *D, L, F, S,* and *M.* Cursive capitals that students often have the most difficulty learning are *D, E, G, I, J, Qu,* and *Z.* Less frequently used capitals, introduced later, are *Z, Qu, U,* and *X.*

Completing Lowercase Cursive by the End of the Second Month or Earlier for Non-SLD

As shown in table 2–10, cursive instruction in the first month with students who are responding with relative ease, or well into the second month for slower moving classes, should include letters that begin the way *n* begins—referred to as hill letters in some programs. Both *m* and *n* could have been introduced earlier if there had been a need for more words with them in encoding and spelling. For example, the addition of the letter *n* gives the possibility of introducing the first letter combinations in visual cards, the digraph *kn,* and the suffix *ing* in spelling. The letter *m* increases the number of available one-syllable words that end in two or more consonants (limp, bump, stamp). Other letters you can introduce that begin like *n* and *m* include *v, x, z,* and one of the two accepted *y* formations. (The other common *y* begins like a *u.*)

Table 2–10. Completing Lowercase Cursive by the End of the Second Month or Earlier for Non-SLD	Definitely teach:	*n, m, e*
	Gradually teach:	*v, y, z, x*
	Teach, practice, and review:	letter connections bridge connections, some with patterns (*on, vi, ws,* etc.) letter combinations (*ing, ong, ang, ung*)
	Perhaps practice and review:	more advanced letter combination connections (*eng, ink, ank, onk, unk, kn*)
	Practice:	phonogram connections (v-e, *oa, ou, eigh,* etc.) letter connections for affixes and non-phonetic spellings
	As needed, teach:	more capitals and punctuation

Students should be taught that the cursive letter *m* has three downstrokes whereas *n* has two. This helps avoid the confusion that occurs when students attempt to count the number of humps when identifying or forming an *m* or *n*. Counting humps works most of the time but not when *m* is connected with a preceding *o*, one of the four cursive letters that end on the midline (*b, o, v,* and *w*). The most common of these are the letter connections *om* and *on*, where the first hump is not really distinguishable as such.

Mention must be made again regarding red flag or non-phonetic words that are learned by copying and tracing them. The more difficult connections in these words should be practiced during handwriting instruction. This ensures that when students study spelling they can focus on how the words are spelled rather than on how the letters in the words are formed and connected. This is an example of the importance of integration within the daily lesson. Integration is equally important as letter combinations (*ing, ang, ung, ong, eng, ink, ank, unk, onk, tion, sion, ture*), phonograms (*oa, ee, ai, ay, oo, ou, ar, er, eigh, ey, ea,* **v-e**), and affixes (*ed, s, es, er, able, ful, est, less, y, ment, ly* and *re, dis, un, il, con, pre, pro, de,* etc.) are included for writing, as well as capitals, capital connections, and common connections in blends, starting with two-letter beginning and ending consonant blends, as follow: *bl, cl, fl, gl, sl, pl, br, cr, dr, fr, gr, tw, pr, tr, sc, sk, sm, sn, sp, st, sw,* and *ld, nd, st, lf, lk, lp, lt, sk, mp, sp, ct, ft, nt,* and *pt*. In brief, integrate!

Definitely introduce the vowel *e* for spelling as well as writing.

Finally, remember that the pace will be far swifter in non-SLD classes or in individual tutoring than it will be in SLD classes or some tutoring sessions.

Review of Cursive

As with manuscript, you should constantly review letters arranged in groupings that begin with similar strokes. For example, all the letters that begin with the two o'clock stroke should be grouped together for review: *c, a, g, o,* and *qu*. Remind your students that every stroke begins on the writing line and most go toward the right as they are formed; just four letters end on the midline (*b, v, w,* and *o*); and few uppercase cursive letters go beneath the writing line (*g, y,* and *z*).

In review, dictate two- and three-letter connections that occur in words (*br, sm, aut, een,* etc.). Also review mixed capitals and lowercase letters (*F-f, A-a, G-g*) and capitals with lowercase letters (*Al, Ca, Th*). Whole words can be dictated and then spelled aloud letter by letter; for example, "**will—w-i-l-l**" or "**laugh—l-a-u-g-h**" for students to write.

What Else to Teach with Patterns

Patterns may be used when teaching musical notations, arithmetic signs, geometric figures, shorthand notations, scientific symbols, abbreviations, typical key-board symbols, or any other two-dimensional figures that students must write or draw for various subjects, as well as letter formations, numbers, and punctuation.

Handwriting Practice and Review (Manuscript and Cursive)

Practicing new letters occurs in Slingerland instruction immediately after all the letters in a given lesson have been introduced. Practice is for the kinesthetic feel, rhythmic flow, alignment, correct use of letter-size relationships, and correct groupings in manuscript and connections in cursive. Letters are most frequently practiced on the back of expendable patterns, on newsprint folded in the same way, and then on nine-fold newsprint. All letters introduced in a day's lesson are practiced before moving on to Review of Letters.

Reviewing letters occurs after Practice of New Letters in Slingerland and after the introduction of letter formations in other handwriting programs. It includes the review of previously taught lowercase and uppercase letters with letter groupings in manuscript and connections in cursive. Integration is especially important: letters that will be written elsewhere during the day in blends, digraphs, letter combinations, phonograms, non-phonetic words, affixes, and as numerals and punctuation should be reviewed in handwriting instruction.

To incorporate Slingerland's Practice of New Letters and Review of Letters into a handwriting program for SLD students, teachers should use her *Book 1* for manuscript and *Book 3*.cursive. For non-SLD students, Slingerland and Aho's *Learning to Use Manuscript Handwriting and Learning to Use Cursive Handwriting* is recommended as well as the accompanying duplicator masters. The detailed coverage of every aspect of teaching handwriting, including practice and review, in these books is impressive.

3

Visual Presentations

What Are Visual Presentations?

Visual presentations begin with alphabet cards and are followed by decoding and then reading. Movement progresses from the smallest units of sight, sound, and feel in visual cards to slightly larger units, words for decoding, and finally to the largest units, text for reading.

Visual cards provide a time for students—and teachers—to learn and practice with simultaneous visual-auditory-kinesthetic association graphemes that are put to functional use in acquiring the skills of language, including decoding and reading. Visual card introduction, review, and practice are essential in establishing the foundation for the sequential development of subsequent visual presentations.

A Comparison of Orton-Gillingham and Slingerland Use of Visual Cards

In many Orton-based instructional programs, consonants and vowels are introduced with cards visually. In Slingerland, the name and formation of each consonant, including the digraph **qu** and single vowels, are introduced in the section of the daily lesson called *Learning to Write*, described in Chapter 2. In most Orton-based programs, including Slingerland, digraphs (**ch**, **kn**, **wr**, etc.), trigraphs (**tch**, **dge**, **sch**, etc.), letter combinations (**ang**, **ink**, **tion**, etc.), phonograms (**ai**, **oi**, **a-e**, etc.), consonant-le syllables (**ble**, **gle**, **stle**, etc.), and ligatures (**du**, **tu**, etc.)[1] are introduced as graphemes on visual cards before they are identified in words to be decoded.

---

[1] A *ligature* is two letters together (tu, du, di) that make a sound which is different from the expected blend of their individual sounds; for example, /jo͞o/ in graduate rather than gra**d-u**-ate.

The terms used to identify the different types of graphemes differ somewhat from program to program. For instance, in Slingerland, **tle**, **gle**, and **stle** are referred to as *silent-e* syllables whereas in most other Orton-based programs they are called *consonant-le* syllables. This book uses the abbreviated term **C-le** syllables.

Precisely how each grapheme is introduced differs, too. A Slingerland teacher exposes a card showing the grapheme to be introduced and says, "This is the letter (phonogram, letter combination, etc.)" and names it; then names the key word and the sound the grapheme makes. For example, when introducing the digraph **ch**, the teacher says, "This is (the digraph) **ch** - chair - /ch/." With older students, the term *digraph* is included.

While looking at the card, students form the letter(s) in the air while simultaneously naming it, name the key word, and then the corresponding phoneme (sound). For example, after the teacher introduces the digraph **ch**, students form the letters **c** and **h** in the air while saying, "**ch**", and then, "chair - /ch/."

In traditional Orton-Gillingham instruction, the teacher introduces **oa** to a slightly more advanced student by saying, "This is the diphthong **oa**; it says /ō/ as in boat." The student then says, "**oa** - /ō/ - boat" and often writes **oa**, or the student says, "**oa** - boat - /ō/" before writing it.

An Orton-Gillingham Program

Table 3–1 through table 3–6 show the sequence for the introduction of graphemes used in the Massachusetts General Hospital Boston Program of Education in Therapy for Specific Reading Disability. This program adheres more to the original instructional program developed by Orton, Gillingham, and Stillman than those that have been augmented or adapted from the original and are referred to as *Orton-based* in this text. Individual graphemes are listed together with key words for the corresponding phonemes that are then carried over into decoding and spelling. The order of introduction is prescribed within several *Levels*. Students progress gradually from one level to the next.

Table 3–1. Orton-Gillingham Level I—Group I			
	a - apple	h - hat	m - man
	b - boy	i - Indian	p - pan
	c - cat	j - jam	t - top
	f - fun	k - kite	

Letters and other graphemes are introduced with visual cards in two groups, as shown in table 3–1 and table 3–2.

Table 3–2. Orton-Gillingham Level I— Group II			
	g - goat	ch - chin	y - yes
	o - octopus	e - elephant	v - van
	r - rat	s - sun	z - zebra
	l - lamp	sh - ship	a-e safe, lake
	n - nut	d - dog	e-e these, Eve, Pete
	th - thumb	w - wind	i-e pine, pipe
	u - umbrella	wh - whistle	o-e home, cone
			u-e mute, cube

Sequencing Differences in Orton-Based Programs

The Slingerland program differs only slightly from the Orton-Gillingham program at Boston Mass General Hospital or from most Orton-based programs, with respect to its sequence for the introduction of graphemes. The letters **l**, **d**, **s**, and **g** are usually introduced slightly earlier in Slingerland because they are taught in *Learning to Write*, where there is greater emphasis on *how* letters are formed. Other differences are logical consequences. For example, once **l** is introduced, it is logical to follow with the introduction of similarly formed letters (**h**, **b**, **k**, etc.). Once **c** is introduced, it is logical to follow with the introduction of **d** and **g**.

Once individual letters have been introduced, Slingerland and Orton-Gillingham instruction become much more alike in their progression for the introduction of graphemes. Some of the Level II graphemes shown in table 3–3 may just as easily be introduced later, while several of the Level III graphemes shown in table 3–4 may be introduced slightly earlier, depending on need. For example, in Orton-Gillingham Level II, **ey** - valley - /ē/, could be introduced later, whereas **oi** - oil and **oy** - boy might be introduced earlier in Slingerland.

Finally, the graphemes which remain to be taught using visual cards have been compiled into an Advanced Gillingham Checklist by Helaine M. Schupack, as shown in table 3–6. This list is given to teacher trainees in the Boston Mass General Program, and is used by Schupack in her own advanced Orton-based training course offered at the Center for Neuro-psychology and Learning Disorders in Rhode Island.[2]

Table 3–3. Orton-Gillingham Level II

e - he	ay - play	oe - toe
o - go	ee - feed	ow - snow
ang, ing, ong, ung	ea - eat	ed - rented
ank, ink, onk, unk	ck - black	ed - jumped
y - my	ar - car	ed - sailed
x - box	or - horn	oo - food
qu - queen	ind, old, ost, ild	oo - book
tch - catch	oa - boat	ow - plow
y - candy	er - her	ey - valley
ai - sail	ur - burn	ou - out, ouch
all - all family	ir - bird	

Table 3–4. Orton-Gillingham Level III

oi - boil	ea - steak	tion - station
oy - boy	a - baby	sion - mission
igh - light	e - erase	sion - television
ie - piece	i - spider	c - /s/ before e, i, y
ie - pie	o - pony	g - /j/ before e, i, y
ph - phone	u - music	au - August
ea - bread	a - Alaska	aw - saw
		ou - soup

Table 3–5. Orton-Gillingham Level IV

consonant-le	eigh - eight	dge - fudge
ew - few	ue - rescue	ei - ceiling
ew - grew	ue - true	ei - vein
eu – Europe		

---

[2] 475 Lloyd Ave., Providence, RI 02906.

Table 3–6. Advanced Gillingham Checklist

ear - /ər/	ligature d - /j/	**endings**
our - /ər/	ligature t - /ch/	-ary, ory, ery
ard - /ərd/	ci - /sh/	-able
rr	ti - /sh/	-ible
ough - /ô/	-cian - /shən/	-al, -el
ough - /o͞o/	-ive	-ant, -ance
ough - /ou/	-ine	-ent, -ence
ough - /ō/	-ce, -ise	-ic, -ics, -ical
ough - /ŭf/	Greek medial y	-icle
ough - /ôf/	-gue - /g/	-cede, -ceed, -sede
augh - /ô/	-que - /k/	-ist, -est
ou - /ə/	-mb, -mn	-ess
ui	-th/the	-ous, -us
eo	wr	
ai - /ĕ/ or /ŭ/	kn	
i - /ē/	gn	
-age - /ĭj/	**homonyms**	
-ion - /yən/		

Rationale for Visual Card Scope and Sequence

The scope and sequence presented here is compatible with most Orton-based programs, including Slingerland, and is also implemented in *LessonPlanner. LessonPlanner*, initially developed specifically for Slingerland teachers, was strongly Slingerland based and thus immediately applicable to the Slingerland approach. Subsequent versions of *LessonPlanner* were developed for a broader audience of teachers and are adaptable for use by most Orton-based instructors. If you are a whole language or meaning-emphasis teacher with phonics training, you will find the scope and sequence presented herein beneficial when developing phonics and spelling programs tailored to augment and enhance your own reading program or other similar, current programs.

The purpose here is to recommend an order (sequence) for introducing graphemes, with cards, as well as to recommend how many graphemes (the scope) should be introduced and reviewed during instruction. Scope and sequence depends on whether instruction is to an individual student in tutoring, to a small group, or to a class. Variations in scope and sequence are also influenced by student grade level, age, maturity, educational background, degree and extent of any learning disabilities—especially within the visual modality—intelligence, and current achievement levels, particularly in reading and spelling.

All of these factors are important to the rationale upon which a scope and sequence for visual cards can be recommended to ensure success. Visual cards contain the smallest units of sight, sound, and feel that lead to the next larger units—words for decoding—and to yet larger units—phrases, sentences, paragraphs, a page, a chapter, and ultimately, books with stories, poetry, news articles, recipes, jokes, fiction and non-fiction, and biographies. Beginning with the introduction of the smallest grapheme units and continuing gradually to larger and more complex units, reading mastery is the goal.

Rationale for Visual Card "Levels"

Slingerland was reluctant to provide teachers with a definitive, inflexible sequence for the introduction of graphemes and phonemes because she felt that so much depends on the many factors discussed previously. If, for example, a class is required to use a reader where **vce** (or **v-e**) words are introduced almost immediately and occur frequently, then Slingerland would recommend that **a-e**, **e-e**, **i-e**, **o-e**, and **u-e** be taught early in the school year. In the same vein, Slingerland introduces **ey** - they - /ā/ earlier than in most Orton-based programs even though **ey** words, particularly with **ey** pronounced long /ā/, do not appear frequently. However the word **they** does appear often and early in reading, causing considerable frustration, especially for SLD children, unless its difficulty is prevented by early and careful introduction.

In this book, "Levels" analogous to the preceding Orton-Gillingham Levels are presented because one of the most frequently asked questions in any Orton-based teacher education course is, "How will I know what to teach next or not to teach next?" Encouraging teachers to rely on logic and instinct, to scour a myriad of references, or wait a year or more to obtain additional training, is not the solution. Teachers today have too many added responsibilities that often prevent them from an ideal and scholarly approach in trying to determine how much of what to teach next. If they are asked to "wait" they may seek a different, easier, or more accessible instructional approach that often is not as comprehensive or effective.

Teachers today frequently have not been provided with as adequate a foundation in phonics and other related language skills as were teachers of Gillingham, Stillman, and Slingerland's era. Those carrying on the work of these pioneers have a responsibility to give newer teachers all the help they need and to prevent them from becoming so overwhelmed by the scope of what they must learn that they resist further training. Only with quality instruction, support, and guidance can teachers become effective literacy instructors who will, over the course of many years, help students with and without specific language disabilities learn to read, write, and spell. With this in mind, Levels corresponding to the Orton-Gillingham Levels have been compiled. Furthermore, the Levels are based on years of experience teaching, observing, and talking to Slingerland teachers intent upon mastering skills for effective literacy instruction.

---

ck Generalization

ck comes directly after one short vowel at the end of a one-syllable word.

For younger children it is sufficient to say, "**ck** comes at the end" when introducing it. When children are a little further along in the program they can learn the entire generalization.

When exposing the **ck** card, first teach "**ck** - jack - /k/ comes at the end of a word." (In some Orton-based programs, the verbalization might be "**ck** - /k/ - jack.")

Later you may instruct students to say, "**ck** - jack - /k/ comes directly (or immediately) *after one short vowel* at the end of a word."

Finally the children say, "**ck** - jack - /k/ comes directly (or immediately) after one short vowel at the end *of a one-syllable word.*"

Visual Card Scope and Sequence for First and Second Grades

If you are a manuscript grade one or grade two Slingerland teacher, you can skim over much of the discussion and tables that pertain to the introduction of vowels and consonants. Instead, you will want to follow the scope and sequence for teaching manuscript handwriting outlined in Chapter 2. For how to introduce the phonemes for vowels and consonants, simply apply the techniques you learned in your Slingerland training. However, carefully note the ***ck** Generalization* sidebar on page 45.

If you are not a Slingerland teacher, or if you do not intend to follow the manuscript handwriting scope and sequence described in Chapter 2, carefully read the following discussion and tables that focus on the initial introduction, scope, and sequence of graphemes using visual cards, including letters of the alphabet.

Graphemes for the First Trimester in a Beginning First or Second Grade

As shown in table 3–7, in a beginning first or second grade class, teach the graphemes **h**, **l**, **s**, **b**, **t**, **a**, **c**, **m**, **k**, **f**, and **g**. Perhaps introduce **ck** with its corresponding spelling generalization described in the ***ck** Generalization* sidebar on page 45.

Table 3–7. Level I—Group I Graphemes for the First Trimester in a Beginning First or Second Grade	Definitely teach:	**h***, **l**, **s**, **b***, **t**, **a**-/ă/, **c**, **m***, **k**, **f**, **g**
	Perhaps teach:	**ck** with generalization
	Subsequently teach:	**i**-/ĭ/, **j**, **d***, **p***
	Perhaps teach:	**sh**
		ch (separate from **sh**)
	Maybe teach:	**th** with both phonemes
	Teach the second phoneme for:	**s** /z/
	Teach for writing only:	**e**

Do not introduce, within the same lesson, graphemes that are easily confused visually or those with similar phonemes that may be auditorily confused. Those that are visually confusing are noted in the preceding and following tables with asterisks (*). Refer to *Introducing Letters that Look or Sound Alike*, beginning on page 18, for a list of letters that are frequently confused due to visual or auditory similarities.

In the next several months, you will introduce **i**, **j**, **d**, and **e** for writing only, **p**, **ch**, **sh**, and **th** with both sounds or *phonemes*—/th/ and /t̶h̶/. The unvoiced phoneme, /th/, occurs more frequently; however, it is recommended that the less common, voiced phoneme, /t̶h̶/, be introduced first because it is contained in several essential, common, high-frequency words (the, this, then, than, that, them, those, these, and they). Perhaps a better solution is to introduce both phonemes at the same time.

You should teach the second phoneme for **s**, /z/, as well. Remember that how quickly you introduce graphemes will depend on whether you are working with SLD or non-SLD students.[3]

Graphemes for the Second Trimester in a Beginning First or Second Grade

As shown in table 3–8, within the last several months of first grade you can introduce **u**, **w** as a consonant, **wh**, **n**, **r**, **m**, **v**, **x**, **y** as a consonant, **z**, **o**, **oa**, **ee**, **ing**, **ang**, **ung**, **ong**, **ink**, **ank**, **unk**, **onk**, and maybe **ai**, **ay**, **oo** with two sounds, /o͞o/ and /o͝o/, and **ou**. Depending on what your first graders are reading, you may choose to introduce fewer phonograms and instead introduce **a-e**, **e-e**, **i-e**, **o-e**, and **u-e**.

Table 3–8. Level I— Group II for the Next Trimester in a Beginning First or Second Grade SLD Class or Earlier for Non-SLD		
	If not taught:	**m**, **sh**, **ch**, **th**, the second phoneme for **s**
	Teach:	**u** /ŭ/*, **w***, **wh**, **n***, **r***, **v***, **x**, **y***, **z**, **o**-/ŏ/
	Definitely Teach:	**ck** generalization with verbalization
	Teach:	**oa**, **ee**
		ing, **ang**, **ung**, **ong**
		ink, **ank**, **onk**, **unk**
	Maybe teach:	**ai**, **ay**
	Teach:	**oo** with 2 phonemes, **ou**
	If needed:	**v-e: a-e**, **e-e**, **i-e**, **o-e**, **u-e**
	Maybe teach:	**e**, **qu**

In Orton-based programs, **v-e** is referred to as one of six syllable types. Slingerland includes **v-e** in her phonogram chart and other phonogram lists.

Sometimes in an SLD class with more severe disabilities, you will not be able to teach all the vowels in a first year program—especially short **e** except for writing—nor the less frequently used and difficult digraph **qu**. This means, too, that you will not be able to introduce as many letter combinations and phonograms with a slower paced class. However, non-SLD students progress more quickly.

Be sure not to introduce graphemes that are easily confused visually, auditorily, or both visually and auditorily within the same lesson.

---

[3] Appendix A contains a list of the graphemes found in *LessonPlanner* together with their corresponding key words and phonemes.

Graphemes for a Continuum Second Grade SLD Class or Earlier for Non-SLD

After considerable review of all the previously introduced material, introduce any remaining phonograms and letter combinations listed in table 3–8 (**oa**, **ee**, **ai**, **ay**, **ou**, and **oo** with two phonemes).

As shown in table 3–9, teach **ai** and **ay**, **e**, and **qu** if you did not teach them before. The same applies to **a-e**, **e-e**, **i-e**, **o-e**, and **u-e** with both phonemes, long /ū/ and long /o͞o/. Additional phonograms include **oi**, **oy**, and **ow** with both sounds, long /ō/ and /ou/; **igh**, **ar**, **or**, **er**, **ir**, and **ur** with one phoneme for each; **ea** with all three phonemes, long /ē/, long /ā/, and short /ĕ/; **ie** with two sounds, long /ī/ and /ē/; perhaps **eigh**; and more slowly and cautiously, **aw** and **au** before **ew**, with both phonemes, /ū/ and /o͞o/. When **ew** is introduced, students should be taught that **oo** is usually found in the middle of a word while **ew** is usually at the end of a word.

Table 3–9. For a Continuum 2nd Grade SLD Class or Earlier for Non-SLD	Definitely teach:	e-/ĕ/, **qu** **ai, ay, oo** with 2 phonemes, **ou** **a-e, e-e, i-e, o-e, u-e** with 2 phonemes **ing, ang, ung, ong** **ink, ank, onk, unk**
	Gradually teach:	**oi, oy, ow** with 2 phonemes **igh, ar, or, er, ir, ur** **ea** with 3 phonemes **ie** with 2 phonemes
	Perhaps teach:	**eigh**
	Teach cautiously:	**au, aw, ew** with 2 phonemes

As designated in table 3–10, introduce the letter combinations **eng**, **tion** with one phoneme, /shən/, and **sion** with two, /shən/ and /ɪhən/, with care. The digraphs **kn**, **wr**, and **gh** can easily be added if they were not taught previously.

It is recommended that **ph** be taught cautiously; **ph** appears frequently in reading, but not in many first and second grade readers. It occurs more commonly in multisyllabic words. The trigraph **tch** should definitely be taught now. See the *tch Generalization* sidebar on page 50. Hold off longer for **dge** unless you have a very fast paced class.

The second pronunciation for the vowel **o**, **scribal-o**[4], in closed syllables may be introduced around this time to non-SLD students definitely, and perhaps to more capable SLD students. It is **o** - honey - /ŭ/. The main reason to not wait too long to teach **o** - honey - /ŭ/ is that so many common words (some, come, love, month, Monday, mother, brother, another, other—to name just a few) contain a **scribal-o**. It is perfectly acceptable to teach some of these as sight words initially, if you prefer.

Table 3–10. For a Second Grade Accelerated SLD Class or Earlier for Accelerated Non-SLD	
Teach more readily:	**eng, tion, sion** with 2 phonemes
Teach easily:	**kn, wr, gh** with 2 phonemes
Teach carefully:	**ph**
Definitely teach:	**tch** with verbalization
Teach to a slightly accelerated class:	**dge** with verbalization, **scribal-o**
Teach:	**ce** and **ge**, at least, for soft **c** and soft **g**
To an accelerated class, teach:	**ce, ci, cy, ge, gi, gy**
Teach with cards:	**tle, ple**
Without cards:	**ble, dle, fle, gle, kle, zle**
Teach only to an accelerated class:	**ue** with 2 phonemes, and/or **eu** with 2 phonemes

Another concept appropriate for a faster group of non-SLD first graders or SLD second graders, usually after the **dge** verbalization is introduced, pertains to "soft **c** and soft **g**." Refer to the ***dge*** *Generalization* sidebar on page 58.

If introduced at all to young children, use individual cards and key words, including: **ce** - cent - /s/, **ci** - city - /s/, **cy** - fancy - /s/, **ge** - gentle - /j/, **gi** - ginger (giraffe) - /j/, and **gy** - gypsy - /j/ to teach soft **c** and soft **g**. Likely you will only be able to introduce **ce** and **ge** at this stage. Later, individual cards may or may not be necessary, as explained later in this chapter. Earlier EPS Slingerland cards,[5] did include separate cards for **ce, ci,**

---

[4] See the story in the Gillingham-Stillman Manuals, and in the *Scribal-o* sidebar on page 56 of this chapter, for why early scribes changed the letter **u** to an **o** but retained the short /ŭ/ sound. It is suggested that you not relate the story to very young or immature children as it may cause confusion.

[5] Teacher's Hand Pack for Classroom Use. Cambridge, Massachusetts: Educators Publishing Service, Inc.

and **cy**. However, they do not now, which reflects Slingerland's change in view as to how to teach soft **c** and soft **g** without individual cards. In the yellow Slingerland cards, discussed in *Chapter 4: Auditory Presentations*, a card with **s**, **ce**, **ci**, and **cy** is included, but a corresponding one with **j**, **dge**, **ge**, **gi**, and **gy** is not. The latter can be added to a hand-made yellow card and then attached to the other half of the EPS **j** - **dge** yellow card.

With SLD second graders or non-SLD first graders who are progressing nicely and beginning to decode two-syllable words, some of the **C-le** syllables may be introduced: **ble**, **dle**, **fle**, **gle**, **kle**, **ple**, **tle**, and **zle**. In the EPS teacher's hand pack, cards for only **tle** and **ple** are provided. Usually

> ## *tch Generalization*
>
> **Tch** comes directly (or immediately) after one short vowel at the end of a one-syllable word. This is similar to the **ck** generalization. Older students can learn the entire generalization, but younger students must learn it gradually as they acquire the concepts governing the generalization.
>
> Second graders should only say, when **tch** is exposed, "**tch** - match - /ch/ comes at the end of a word."
>
> Later, or if your students are particularly capable, you may choose to change the ending to, "**tch** comes directly (or immediately) after one short vowel at the end of a one-syllable word." Whether you use "directly" or "immediately" be consistent and do not use both.

when students understand the concept of **C-le**, introduced with just two visual cards, but taught with much discussion and practice in decoding, they generalize correctly when encountering other **C-le** syllables where only the first consonant is different.

The frequency of usage for various graphemes and corresponding phonemes is discussed in greater detail in the section entitled *Decoding* later in this chapter.

If your students are extremely adept, you may teach **ue** or **eu**, or both, each with two phonemes, /ū/ and /o͞o/, but with extreme caution. Students will benefit if they are taught that **ue** is found only at the end of words; **ue** and **eu** occur less frequently than **ew**.

As an interesting aside, there are several graphemes in table 3–9 and table 3–10 that some educators recommend not be taught as phonetic elements to young pupils.

Their reason is that these phonograms, **ie** and **ue**, appear in fewer than ten single-syllable, common words. The same applies with the digraph **gh**. They recommend instead that words such as p<u>ie</u>, ch<u>ie</u>f, bl<u>ue</u>, c<u>ue</u>, <u>gh</u>ost, and lau<u>gh</u> be taught as sight or learned words. Some Orton-based teachers contest this position because of the frequency and usefulness of the words that contain these graphemes. The decision rests in your hands.

Rationale for More Vertical than Horizontal Instruction

In a non-SLD first grade or continuum SLD second grade where Orton-based instruction has been provided for at least a year, at times it is better to focus more on horizontal teaching with practice and review than vertical teaching with new skills and concepts. In other words, the letters, digraphs, trigraphs, letter combinations, and phonograms already taught throughout the first year should be put to greater functional use and practice in handwriting, decoding, reading, encoding, spelling, and in writing phrases, sentences, and paragraph dictations. The increase in the number of visual cards, compared to auditory cards, comes from the addition of new phonograms for decoding, including **v-e**.

Visual Card Scope and Sequence for Third Grade and Above

A third grade SLD class might well be composed of students who are continuing their Slingerland instruction from the first and/or second grades, or they might be new to the program. Additionally, some students may have begun cursive instruction while others may have had none. The following discussion parallels the sequence for the introduction of graphemes for cursive instruction in *Learning to Write*, described in Chapter 2. It also provides the recommended scope and sequence for the introduction of graphemes using visual cards for students in the third grade and above. The instructional pace is swifter than it is with first and second grade children.

If you are a third grade Slingerland teacher teaching cursive, you will be able to skim over some of the discussion and tables that pertain to the introduction of vowels and consonants because you will want to follow the scope and sequence for teaching cursive handwriting outlined in Chapter 2. For how to introduce the phonemes for vowels and consonants, simply apply the techniques you learned in your Slingerland training. However, carefully note the accompanying *ck and tch Generalizations* sidebar on page 53.

If you are not a Slingerland teacher or do not intend to follow the cursive handwriting scope and sequence described in Chapter 2, carefully read the following discussion and tables that focus on the initial introduction, scope, and sequence of graphemes, including letters of the alphabet, using visual cards.

Since visual cards are printed in manuscript, it is important to heed the discussion on page 18 in Chapter 2, *Introducing Letters that Look or Sound Alike*, listing graphemes that should not be introduced in the same lesson because of how easily they are confused due to their visual or auditory similarities.

Graphemes for Third Grade and Above

Table 3–11 summarizes the Level I, Group I scope and sequence. It will be helpful when you work with a group of new students rather than with continuum students.

Table 3–11. Level I Graphemes for Third Grade and Above	First, definitely teach:	**l, h, k, b** or **f, a-/ă/**
	Next, depending on which was taught first, teach:	**b** or **f, c, g, d**
	Maybe teach:	**e** for writing only
	Perhaps teach:	**t**
	Next teach:	**i-/ĭ/, s, r, t**
	Maybe teach:	**j**
	Definitely teach:	**ck** with verbalization
	Continue by teaching:	**w, p, u, sh, ch, wh**
	Maybe teach:	**th** with 2 phonemes
	Teach second phoneme for:	**s-/z/**
	Gradually teach:	**o-/ŏ/, qu, tch** with verbalization
	If not introduced, teach:	**ph**
	Continue by teaching:	**n, m, v, y** as a consonant, **z, e-/ĕ/**
	Perhaps teach:	**kn, oa, ee, ai** and **ay**
	Add:	**ing, ang, ung, ong**
		ink, ank, unk, onk
	Maybe teach:	**eng**

Within the first three or four days, introduce and/or review **l**, **h**, **k**, maybe **b** or **f**, and **a**. Refer to the more detailed *Scope and Sequence for Teaching Cursive Handwriting* in Chapter 2 for guidance when introducing consonants and vowels. It is comparable primarily to the Orton-Gillingham Level I, Group I and II categories, and to the beginning of the Orton-Gillingham Level II, with several readily detectable differences. It also parallels the sequence for the introduction of vowels and consonants in Slingerland's cursive *Learning to Write*.

Within the next several days, moving into the second week, teach either **b** or **f**, **c**, **g** and **d** on separate days, maybe **e** for writing only, and perhaps **t**.

Within the second and third weeks, teach either **b** or **f**, **i**, **s**, **r**, **t**, and maybe **j**. Around this time also teach **ck** with its generalization. Refer to the accompanying *ck and tch Generalizations* sidebar on this page.

Within the third and fourth weeks, or earlier for non-SLD, teach the graphemes not taught within the second and third weeks, plus **w** as a consonant, **p**, **u**, **sh**, **ch**, and maybe **th** with its voiced and unvoiced phonemes, and **wh**. Also teach the second phoneme for **s**, /z/, at this point or earlier with more skilled or advanced students. It should be introduced shortly after the letter **z** is introduced.[6]

> ### *ck and tch Generalizations*
>
> **Ck** comes directly (or immediately) after one short vowel at the end of a one-syllable word.
>
> Slightly older students can easily master the entire **ck** generalization. Teach them to say, "**ck** - jack - /k/ comes directly (or immediately) after one short vowel at the end of a one-syllable word." (In some Orton-based programs, the verbalization is "**ck** - /k/ - jack.")
>
> **Tch** comes directly (or immediately) after one short vowel at the end of a one-syllable word. Third graders and older students can learn the whole generalization. When **tch** is exposed, students say, "**tch** - match - /ch/ comes directly (or immediately) after one short vowel at the end of a one-syllable word."

At the end of the first month and beginning of the second, teach **o** and **qu**. You may teach **ph**, and **tch** with its special verbalization at this time, too, if not introduced earlier. Refer to the accompanying *ck and tch Generalizations* sidebar on this page.

---

[6] For the list of graphemes found in *LessonPlanner* with corresponding key words and the phonemes for each grapheme, see Appendix A.

Within the second month or slightly earlier for non-SLD students, teach **n**, **m**, **v**, **y** as a consonant, and **z**. Also teach **e**. Perhaps teach **kn**, **oa**, **ee**, **ai**, and **ay**. Now that **n** has been taught, you can introduce the letter combinations **ing**, **ang**, **ung**, and **ong**. At this level, key words are usually not essential for the letter combinations. Students respond to the **ang** card by saying, "**a-n-g** -/aŋ/." Soon you can also introduce **ink**, **ank**, **unk**, **onk**, without key words, and maybe **eng**, with a key word because of its difficulty.

Rationales for Deciding What to Teach Next

Level II graphemes for the third grade could conceivably be taught by the start of the new year, or four months from the start of cursive instruction in a year-round program of a *continuum* third grade class or with non-SLD students. Level II could also be covered in a new Slingerland SLD fifth grade class or with a new fifth grade tutorial student in another Orton-based program. With a new fourth grader or class, the pace, scope, and sequence will obviously be slower; whereas, in non-SLD classes the pace will be faster.

When deciding which phonogram to introduce next, check to see whether the phonogram you have in mind appears frequently and if it usually represents only one vowel sound, in one-syllable base words.[7] Thus far, most of the introduced phonograms appear in common, everyday, mostly one-syllable base words that spell only one, long vowel sound, usually: (1) /ā/ in **ay** words, (2) /ē/ in **ee** words and (3) /ō/ in **oa** words. Remember, part of your decision for what to introduce will also be determined by the readers you use.

Apply similar checks when selecting digraphs or letter combinations for introduction. Note that the first digraph, **ck**, occurs frequently, is found mostly in one-syllable words, and spells only one relatively easy, consonant sound, as do **sh** and **wh** which you should also introduce early. The digraph **sh**, found in many common words, is pronounced /sh/ nearly always; **wh** is pronounced /hw/ less frequently than expected, but its frequency is still significant; **kn** appears infrequently, especially in young children's reading, but its phoneme is not difficult and is usually pronounced as expected. Also, **kn** is visually easy to recall. The two sounds of **th** are more difficult, but **th** appears far more frequently in reading than, say, **gn** or other digraphs not yet recommended for introduction.

---

[7] One excellent resource for grapheme frequencies is *Direct Instruction Reading* (Carnine, et. al., 1990).

The rationale for introducing the first letter combinations (**ing**, **ang**, **ung**, and **ong**) is similar: Each of the designated letter combinations appears frequently in common words and each represents only one, not difficult phoneme. Because **ing** is a suffix or inflection, too, it is particularly frequent. As we continue in our scope and sequence, try to determine why certain graphemes are introduced, and why the introduction of others is postponed. For example, **ay**, **er**, and **oa** are good phonogram candidates for early introduction because of their regularity and frequency: **ay** is pronounced /ā/ in over 100 words nearly one hundred percent of the time; **er** is pronounced /ᵾr/ in nearly 300 words, also nearly one hundred percent of the time, and **oa** is pronounced /ō/ ninety percent of the time (Carnine, et. al, 1990).

Graphemes for Third Grade and Above

As shown in table 3–12, digraphs and trigraphs should now definitely include **ph**, **wr**, **kn**, **tch**, and perhaps **dge** if **tch** was taught and mastered, as well as **gn**, and **gh** with one or both pronunciations—/f/ often at the end of words and /g/ often at the beginning. You may also introduce the less common graphemes **mb** and **mn**. The second phoneme for **ch**, /k/, found often in Greek-based scientific and medical words, should be taught at this time, if not a bit earlier. See the ***dge** Generalization* sidebar on page 58.

Table 3–12. Level II Graphemes for Third Grade and Above	Probably teach from the previous table:	**ph, kn, eng, tch** with verbalization
	New:	**wr**
	Perhaps teach:	**gn, gh** with 2 phonemes
		dge (see the ***dge** Generalization* sidebar on page 58)
	Maybe teach:	**mb, mn**
	Teach the second phoneme for:	**ch** /k/
		a-e, e-e, i-e, o-e, u-e with 2 phonemes
		tion, sion with 2 phonemes
	With faster classes:	**ture**
	Those that could be taught previously:	**oo** with 2 phonemes
		ou, ar
	New:	**scribal-o**

With slightly more advanced students, many teachers prefer not to make and use individual cards for **gn**, **gh**, **mn**, or **mb**. Instead they include them only in yellow auditory cards and, of course, in spelling, decoding, and reading. See further discussion in Chapter 4 in the section on auditory cards.

The **v-e** graphemes should be introduced; they include **a-e**, **e-e**, **i-e**, **o-e**, **y-e**, and **u-e** with both pronunciations, /ū/ and /o͞o/. Since **y-e** occurs most frequently in more advanced, multisyllabic words, do not teach it at this time. Also, do not teach **u-e** yet because it is difficult and has two phonemes. You should introduce **u-e** in a separate lesson.

Letter combinations should certainly include **eng**, and **tion/sion**, and maybe **ture** with faster moving or non-SLD classes or students. Although **eng** appears infrequently, students will generalize from learning the other similar letter combinations and quickly be on their way to reading and spelling **length** and **strength** with proficiency. The introduction of **tion**, **sion**, and **ture** implies that your students have begun decoding two-syllable words or will soon. (Slingerland teachers might want to make a **ture** card.)

> ## *Scribal-o*
>
> With more mature students it is helpful to use the story from the Gillingham-Stillman Manual, or a slightly altered version, that explains why early scribes changed the letter **u** to an **o**: The scribes saw that too many of their quill-penned letters were almost indistinguishable from each other, especially **m**'s, **n**'s, **w**'s, **u**'s, **r**'s, and **v**'s, made with similar, beginning, flourishing strokes—readily illustrated on the blackboard for the enjoyment and benefit of your students. Therefore, the wise scribes, when copying, changed the vowel **u** to **o** when **u** appears adjacent to one of the offensive letters just listed. The scribes, however, obviously could not alter the pronunciation of the words that were affected by the changes they made in writing. Therefore, the letter **o** in words like **month**, **brother**, **love**, **some**, and **wonder**, is pronounced /ŭ/.

Phonograms other than **oa**, **ee**, **ai**, and **ay** might include **ou**, and **oo** with two phonemes. Note that **ai** is pronounced /ā/ most of the time, especially in one-syllable words. In two-syllable words, **ai** is frequently pronounced /ĭ/ or /ə/ (**mountain**, **bargain**). The phonograms **ou** and **ar** could be introduced in Level II now, or Level III later.

The second phoneme for the vowel **o**, scribal-o, in closed syllables, may be introduced around this time: **o** - honey - /ŭ/. (See the *Scribal-o* sidebar above.)

As shown in table 3–13, digraphs and trigraphs may include **gn**; **gh**, definitely with two phonemes; perhaps the three phonemes for **ch**—the third being /sh/ in French-based words; and **dge**. Any of these can wait until Level IV, or even later, or they can be introduced earlier.

Most of the **C-le** or **silent-e** syllables may be introduced here or in Level IV: **ple** and **tle** (with published cards), and **kle** (with a handmade card) usually at the end of two-syllable words, plus **ble**, **dle**, **gle**, **zle**, and **fle**—not to be confused with the word **full** or the suffix **ful**.

Table 3–13. Level III Graphemes for Third Grade and Above		
	Definitely teach from the previous table:	**gn**, **gh** with 2 phonemes **dge** with verbalization **a-e**, **e-e**, **i-e**, **o-e**, **u-e** **tion**, **sion**, **ture**
	Begin to teach the easier **C-le** syllables:	**ple**, **tle**, and **kle**—usually at the end of two-syllable words **ble**, **dle**, **gle**, **zle** **fle**—not to be confused with the word **full** or the suffix **ful**
	Teach the third phoneme for:	**ch** /sh/
	New:	**y-e**, **oi**, **oy**, **igh** **ow** with 2 phonemes
	Perhaps teach:	**ie** and **ey** both with 2 phonemes
	Teach second phoneme for **c** and **g**:	soft **c** /s/ and soft **g** /j/ with the verbalization on page 58
	With less capable students, teach:	**ce**, **ci**, **cy** and **ge**, **gi**, and **gy** with key words and verbalization
	Perhaps begin to teach phonemes for the vowels in accented, open syllables:	**a**, **e**, **i**, **o** (all long vowel sounds)
	Perhaps teach:	**y** as a suffix

If **u-e** with both phonemes was not introduced earlier it should be now, along with **y-e**, found more frequently at the end of multisyllabic, Greek-based words. Also, if **y** has been introduced as a suffix, include its corresponding phoneme in visual cards.

Additional phonograms to include that do not appear as frequently in reading as others introduced earlier are: **oi**, **oy**, and **igh**; **ow**, pronounced /ō/ is more common than

ow pronounced /ou/. Both phonemes should be introduced at the same time. You can also introduce **ie** with two separate phonemes, /ī/ and /ē/, carefully; **ey** might have been taught earlier because of the frequency of the word **they**. If not, teach it at this Level with both phonemes, /ā/ and /ē/.

The concept of "soft **c**" and "soft **g**" may be taught at this point with a fast-paced SLD student or class, without individual cards, or in Level IV. You can also teach "soft **c** and soft **g**" readily with most non-SLD students at this time. Instruct your students not only to say, "**c** - cake - /k/" but also "**c** - followed by **e**, **i**, or **y** says /s/" when exposing the **c** card. For **g**, have your students say, "**g** - followed by **e**, **i**, or **y**, *sometimes* says /j/." Remember, however, that the task at hand is not to teach students to merely memorize meaningless words. To emphasize concept instead when teaching soft **c**, relate another tale found in the Gillingham-Stillman Manuals about poor, sad, little letter **c**, that has no sound of its own and must borrow the /k/ from letter **k** or the /s/ from letter **s**.

> *dge Generalization*
>
> With visual cards, students initially say, "**dge** - bridge (fudge) - /j/ comes directly (or immediately) after one short vowel, at the end of a one-syllable word." (**dge** is slightly more difficult to learn than **ck** and **tch** for decoding; **dge** is definitely more difficult than **ck** and **tch** for spelling.)

With more disabled students, it is advisable to follow the procedures using hand-made individual cards described in the continuum, second grade Level II section. The hand-made cards include one for each of the following: **ce** - cent - /s/, **ci** - city - /s/, **cy** - fancy - /s/, **ge** - gentle - /j/, **gi** - ginger (giraffe) - /j/, and **gy** - gypsy /j/.

Depending on how well decoding progresses, you can introduce the second phoneme for each of several vowels, as shown in table 3–13 on the previous page: **a**, **e**, **i**, and **o**, but not for **u** or **y**. The second phoneme for each vowel occurs when the vowel is at the end of an accented, open syllable. This will require careful instruction before your students respond to an exposed vowel card by: first, naming the vowel, giving the key word, and then the short vowel sound found in closed syllables, and, second, repeating the following for the second vowel phoneme: **a** - baby - /ā/ at the end of an accented syllable; **e** - meter (secret) - /ē/ at the end of an accented syllable; **i** - tiger - /ī/ at the end of an accented syllable; and **o** - pony - /ō/ at the end of an accented syllable.

It is perfectly acceptable to choose a slightly different response for your students as long as you are consistent. What is not acceptable is to allow your students to respond one way one time and a different way another time. Consistency is essential. In Slingerland textbooks, "**o** at the end of an accented syllable, pony, /ō/," is given alternatively as a way to respond to open syllable - **o**, and likewise with the other long vowels. In some other Orton-based programs, the response is, "**o** as in pony, /ō/."

When a vowel card (**a**) is shown, Slingerland students now respond by saying, first, "**a** - apple - /ă/" or "**a** - *consonant* - apple - /ă/." The word *consonant* is sometimes added for awhile to emphasize the difference between an open (**a** at the end) syllable and a closed (**a** followed by a consonant) syllable or the difference between a vowel - consonant - **e** (**v-e**) syllable and a closed syllable or an open syllable.

Second, students say, "**a** - baby - /ā/ - at the end of an accented syllable" or even "at the end of an open accented syllable." In several other Orton-based programs, students say, "**a** - /ă/- apple" and "**a** - /ā/ - baby" or "**a** as in baby – **a**."

Referring to table 3–14, if the digraphs **gn**, **gh**, **mb**, and **mn** were not taught before, you can introduce them now as well as the trigraph **dge**. In Level IV, definitely introduce both phonemes for **gh** at the same time.

Table 3–14. Level IV Graphemes for Third Grade and Above		
	Definitely teach from the previous table:	**gn, gh, mb, mn, eng, tion, sion, ture, ar, ie,** and **dge**
	New:	**or, eigh, er, ur, ir, ea** with three phonemes, **au** and **aw**
	More cautiously:	**ew** with two phonemes
	For non-SLD students only:	**ue** with two phonemes
	Very carefully if at all:	**eu**
	Definitely teach, likely without individual cards:	soft **c** and soft **g** with verbalization
	Continue teaching vowels at the end of accented, open syllables:	**a, e, i, o**
	A bit later, teach open syllable:	**u** with two phonemes
	If **y** has been taught as a suffix, then teach:	**y** as /ĭ/
	Perhaps teach open syllable:	**y**
	Teach as needed:	new phonograms

As you use the tables in this chapter, it is important to remember that although you might introduce and review the more difficult and less common graphemes, such as **gh** and **gn**, you would usually not include **gh** or **gn** words for spelling this soon. However, you would teach **dge** for spelling, for it occurs frequently in common one-syllable words (fudge, badge, judge). This becomes clearer once you study Chapter 4, *Auditory Presentations*.

If not taught previously, teach the last couple of common letter combinations, including **eng** and **ture**. You would likely have already taught **tion** and **sion**, but if not, introduce both phonemes for **sion**, /shən/ and /zhən/, in Level IV.

Several phonograms usually taught in Level IV could just as well have been introduced in Level III if needed. They include **ar**, **or**, **eigh** (infrequent), **er**, **ir**, **ur**, **ea** with all three phonemes, and **au** and **aw**. More cautiously, teach the less frequently occurring phonograms **ew**, **eu** and **ue** with their respective two phonemes to non-SLD students. The phonogram **ue** pronounced /ū/

> ## *Structuring the Introduction of a New Learning: Soft c and Soft g*
>
> The steps for teaching new concepts, designed by Slingerland, are beneficial when teaching the generalization governing soft **c** and soft **g**.
>
> In Step 1, explain and demonstrate (model) what governs the hard and soft sounds of **c** and **g**. Then instruct your students how to respond when the **c** and **g** cards are exposed henceforth.
>
> In Step 2, guide one of your students to repeat your instructions. Have the class repeat, before you call upon several other individual students to respond to the **c** and **g** cards as newly taught.
>
> In Step 3, after your students have learned how to decode soft **c** and soft **g** words, they should be able to respond to the visual cards without additional guidance.
>
> In Step 4, they should be able to differentiate between the phonemes for **c** or **g** when reading independently. By mentally reviewing the **c** or **g** card and the related decoding techniques, they will apply the soft **c** and soft **g** generalization to decode successfully.
>
> In Step 5, students apply the soft **c** and soft **g** generalization in spelling.

occurs at the end of words (hue, rescue, revenue) except in the word **fuel** that, theoretically, may be considered a two-syllable word (fu/el).

You can also teach **ie** with two phonemes, /ī/ and /ē/.

The phonograms **ar**, **er**, **ir**, **or**, **ur**, **yr**, **ear**, and **our** are often referred to as **r-controlled**.[8] Of these, **ur** and **ir** are most reliably pronounced /ʉɾ/; **ur** is twice as common as **ir**; **ar** is the most common but not as reliable in its pronunciation since it has three phonemes, /är/, /ər/, and /ăr/. The phonogram **or** is slightly less common, but again not as reliable because it has two corresponding phonemes.[9]

The concept of "soft **c** and soft **g**" should be taught without individual visual cards, if possible. (See the preceding level, Level III.)

Depending on how many vowels were already introduced with their long vowel sounds, you can teach all of them now. As discussed previously, the second phonemes occur at the end of accented open syllables and require careful instruction before students respond to an exposed vowel card in the following way:

> *Two Phonemes for **tion**:*
> */shən/ and /chən/*
>
> It is debatable whether to teach both phonemes for **tion** with cards. There are only a handful of words with the /chən/ sound spelled **tion**. They *usually* follow an **s**: **question**, **digestion**, **combustion**, **suggestion**, **congestion**, **bastion**, and **exhaustion**. Not after an **s** are: **attention**, **contention**, and **mention**.
>
> If you decide to teach /chən/ with its few memorizable words, then you might also want to teach **cion** - /zhən/ or /shən/ in the two words **coercion** and **suspicion**.

1. The student names the vowel (while forming it in the air or writing it), gives the key word, and enunciates the short vowel sound; for example, "**a** - apple - /ă/."

2. The student renames the vowel (while forming it in air or writing it), gives the second key word, enunciates the second, long vowel sound, and adds, "at the end of an accented (open) syllable"; for example; "**a** - baby - /ā/, at the end of an accented (open) syllable."

---

[8] An **r-controlled** phonogram or syllable is one with an **r** at the end that alters the sound of the vowel that precedes the **r**; thus, the **r** *controls* the vowel sound so that it is neither purely long nor short, as in th**ir**d, **ear**th, and ch**ur**ch.

[9] As discussed more fully in Chapter 4, some instructors teach that in spelling, when in doubt as to which grapheme to use for /ʉɾ/, the best choice is **er**. Strictly speaking, **er** does not appear to be as common as some of the other **r**-controlled phonograms because it is given the /ʉɾ/ pronunciation mainly in the middle of words (h**er**d). As the extremely common suffix **er** (hott**er**) or in an unaccented syllable in the middle of a word (refrig**er**ator), many dictionary diacritical notations reflect that **er** is contained in an unaccented syllable and use the /ər/ notation—thus making the frequency of **er** as /ʉɾ/ seem less that it is.

Students in other Orton-based programs say "**a** - /ă/- apple" and "**a** - /ā/ - baby" or "**a** - baby - at the end of an accented, *open* syllable - /ā/." Although verbalizations differ somewhat among Orton-based programs, it is important to be consistent within specific programs and schools.

Previously, the key words accompanying **a**, **e**, **i**, and, **o** (baby, meter or secret, tiger, and pony) were given in Cursive Level III. For **u**, there is a slight important variation in that **u** spells *two* long vowel sounds: **u** - music - /ū/ at the end of an accented syllable and **u** - lunar - /o͞o/ at the end of an accented syllable. The vowels **a**, **e**, **i**, and **o** have just one long vowel phoneme at the end of an accented open syllable.

The Greek medial **y** with its short **i**, /ĭ/, phoneme is now taught. Since, in some programs, **y** would already have been introduced as a suffix in spelling—found mostly in multisyllabic words—students would now have learned at least two phonemes for **y**, short **i**, /ĭ/, and long **e**, /ē/. They might have also learned the third phoneme, /ī/, that **y** spells at the end of little words—mostly one syllable—as in **my**, **cry**, **shy**, etc. and in a few slightly longer words (**reply**, **deny**, **supply**, and **July**). Usually teach **y** - cycle /ī/ at the end of an accented syllable a bit later.

Either at this level, or the next, students' response to the usually salmon-colored **y** vowel card should follow the response order of all the vowels (short sound in a closed syllable, first; long vowel sound at the end of an accented open syllable, second; unaccented vowel sound at the end of an open syllable, third): **y** - myth (gym) - /ĭ/, **y** - cycle - /ī/ at the end of an accented syllable, and **y** - candy - /ē/. Since **y** does not quite follow the pattern of the other vowels, some teachers add nothing about accenting at the end while others add, ". . . in an unaccented syllable." Remember, too, never rely on **i** or **y**.

Note that the handling of **y** is similar to that for the second **ar** and **or** phonemes that some teachers have their students verbalize: **ar** - dollar - /ər/ *in an unaccented syllable* and **or** - doctor - /ər/ *in an unaccented syllable.*

In some Orton-based programs, especially in the southern part of the United States, the pronunciation of **y** as a suffix or inflection, as in candy, is /ĭ/. This corresponds to the phoneme for **y**'s twin **i** in an unaccented syllable: **i** - Tibet - /ĭ/ at the end of an unaccented syllable.

Rationale for Slight Differences in the Advanced Checklists

You may notice that the suffixes and endings in Schupack's Advanced Gillingham Checklist (table 3–6), are not included in the advanced checklists in this book. They are omitted because common suffixes and endings are presented auditorily in spelling first, while word families (**ind**, **ild**, **old**, and **ost**), homonyms, advanced suffixes, and Latin and Greek roots are usually presented visually without cards. In accordance with Slingerland instruction, common suffixes and endings are introduced in spelling first. More advanced suffixes and endings are commonly taught first in decoding. They are explained more fully at the end of Chapter 3 and in Chapter 4.

Teachers who still have an older edition of the EPS Slingerland teachers' hand pack will have a suffix **ed** card. Indeed, **ed** was contained in the hand pack until Slingerland realized that it was not helping teachers teach their students the concepts for the application of suffixes. Misconception regarding the purpose of including the **ed** card led to the overuse and overmemorization of numerous hand-made suffix cards with excessive accompanying verbalizations. (This writer was among a group of well intentioned teachers who tried to teach affixes with hand pack cards before grasping the underlying rationale for their application and before understanding that **ed** had been included in the cards because it is the only common suffix with three phonemes.) The suffix **ed** is discussed again in this chapter.

Scope and Sequence for Fifth and Sixth Grades

Regarding scope, if you are working with a new fifth or sixth grade class, you can expect to cover most of the hand pack cards and concepts contained in Grapheme Levels I through IV. In some cases the pace will be slower, and in others it will be faster. Much will depend on whether you are working with continuum or new students and whether your students are SLD or not SLD. The way to ensure appropriate pacing is to constantly observe and evaluate the performance of your students as they begin to put to functional use each new learning.

In more advanced programs, the same care should be used as recommended throughout. That which determines how quickly you introduce and put to functional use advanced graphemes will be your own teacher judgment. As expected, working with SLD students demands slower pacing and more review than when teaching non-SLD students, but at times, especially when a solid foundation has been established, you should be pleasantly surprised by how quickly bright, motivated, diligent SLD students learn. Again, your good professional judgment is crucial. This is what the art of teaching is all about.

Advanced Group I Graphemes

As shown in table 3–15, of the phonograms already taught, the second phoneme for **ar** and **or** in unaccented syllables, /ər/, should definitely be introduced, for your students will have already begun work on accenting. In the second **ar** and **or** response, some teachers have older students add, after the respective key words **dollar** and **doctor** are named, ". . . in an unaccented syllable." Additionally, inform students that **ar** often follows an **l** (poplar, granular), and **or** often follows **ct** (factor, doctor).

Table 3–15. Advanced Group I Graphemes		
	Teach second phoneme for:	**ar, or** /ər/ **ai** /ĭ/ or /ə/
	Or, teach the ending:	**ain**
	Gradually teach di/trigraphs:	**sc**, **rh**, **gu** or **gue**, **que**
	Plus new phonograms:	**ei, ear, our** **oe** (perhaps with two phonemes)
	Teach second and third phonemes for:	**ou** with verbalization
	Teach with one or two phonemes:	**ui**
	Continue **C-le**:	**stle, sle, cle**
	Maybe teach the ligatures:	**du, tu, su, di**
	Perhaps teach:	**augh**
	Teach initially with one or two phonemes only:	**ough**

Other phonograms for which a second or third phoneme should be taught include **ai** as /ĭ/ or /ə/, usually in an unaccented syllable (foun'tain, moun'tain). Some teachers prefer to teach **ain** as an ending instead of **ai** - mountain - /ĭ/ or /ə/ in an unaccented syllable.

Teach the next digraphs and trigraphs—**sc** and **rh** are found in Greek-based scientific words, **que** and **gue** in French words. It might be preferable to include them only in yellow cards, discussed in greater detail in Chapter 4. Without putting less common digraphs and trigraphs on visual cards, they can still be learned and included in decoding and spelling. In Slingerland, **gu** as in **guest** is taught before **gue**. However some teachers prefer not to teach **gu** as a digraph but rather as a concept: The **u** is inserted sometimes to keep the **g** hard (g**u**ess, g**u**ide) before e, i, and y.

New phonograms can include: **ei** with its /ā/ phoneme; **ear** and **our** as /ur̸/, and **oe** as /ō/. Recall that some teachers recommend that **oe** not be taught as a phonetic element. Two common words that provide both of **oe**'s phonemes are **toe** and **shoe**. Students can easily remember: Put your **toe** in your **shoe**. If not taught previously, teach the second and third sounds for **ou**, /o͞o/ in French-based words, and /ə/ in unaccented syllables—particularly in the suffix **ous**. The short /ŭ/ sound of **ou** is really the same as schwa, /ə/,[10] in unaccented syllables (fam**ous**). To recall **ou** as /ŭ/, remember: A **couple** of **tough**, **young**, **country cousins** were in **double**, **rough trouble**.

The phonogram **ui** is taught differently in different parts of the country. Certainly in California, **ui** spells only one sound, /o͞o/ and not /ū/—no one says /sūt/ for **suit** in most parts of the country anymore. To remember the most common **ui** words, the following should help: On our **cruise** we sat in our **swimsuits** (playsuits, jumpsuits) and drank **juice** made from **bruised fruit**. Although **ui** with its /o͞o/ phoneme could easily have been presented in an earlier Level, because it appears in several relatively common one- and two-syllable, everyday words, **ui**, as in **build** and **guild** with the /ĭ/ sound and **ui** in **biscuit** and **circuit** with the /ə/ sound, are usually not introduced until the Advanced Level, or as discussed earlier, not presented at all as phonetic elements. See further discussion on grapheme Oddities in the last section of this chapter.

The problem with graphemes such as **ui** and **ue** is that they appear less frequently as phonograms than they do in other forms. If you conduct a dictionary word search for **ui** words, you will find **u** and **i**, indeed, adjacent to each other, but in different syllables (**acu/ity, circu/itous**). You will also find the **u** in the second letter of the digraph **qu** adjacent to **i** in v-e syllables (**acquire, beguile**) or before an ending consonant (**acquit**); **ue**, too, is found frequently in forms or positions other than as a phonogram, as an analysis of the following shows: **afflu/ent, antique, fatigue, bequest,** and **cru/elty**.

---

[10] The schwa (ə) is used frequently to represent the vowel sound in unaccented syllables made by **a** and **o** especially (c**a**det, p**o**lite), sometimes **e** (r**e**gard), and less frequently **u** and **i** (s**u**perb, clar**i**ty).

The last, more difficult **C-le** syllables can now be taught, beginning with: **stle**—more common than **sle** but sometimes problematic because its **t** is silent. Teach **sle**, and **cle** (found mostly in words of three or more syllables) with the following four exceptions: **uncle**, **circle**, **cycle**, and **chicle**. The **cle** requires special teaching to avoid confusion with **cal** in numerous words like **musical**, **historical**, **electrical**, and **cubical**, which are all adjectives. **Cubicle**, **article**, and **particle** with **cle** are all nouns.

The ligatures **du**, **tu**, and **su** may also be taught, but usually not with cards; **di** is considered a ligature, too, as in the words **soldier** and **cordial**.

How **augh** and **ough** are introduced differs from program to program and within programs. You may teach **ough** with several phonemes using hand-made visual cards, and **augh** at this time. Refer to the sidebar on this page for teaching **aught** versus **ought**.

---

augh/aught *and* ough/ought

A favorite way for many teachers and students to remember when to use **augh/aught** instead of **ough/ought** is to memorize the following **aught** sentence (also found in *LessonPlanner's* Grapheme Information): The (**distraught**) farmer **caught** his **haughty**, **naughty daughter** and **taught** her not to **slaughter** with **laughter**. **Laughter** should be pronounced with an exaggerated British accent, and you should explain why **laughter** does not quite fit with the other **aught** words. When students hear /ôt/ in a word they can use a process of elimination to decide whether the spelling will be **augh(t)** or **ough(t)**. The same applies when **augh(t)** or **ough(t)** appear in reading. You can teach the remaining **ough(t)** words with different phonemes as sight words. Expect to progress more quickly with non-SLD students than with SLD students.

Advanced Group II Graphemes

As viewed in table 3–16, new digraphs should include **ti**, **ci**, **si**, **xi**, **ce**, **su**, which all spell /sh/, as well as the trigraph **sch**; **que** and **qu** that provide the fifth and sixth spellings for /k/; **sc** and **ps** for the third and fourth ways to spell /s/, and **pn** for the fourth spelling for /n/. It is not recommended that you make cards for any of these graphemes. They should, however, be included in auditory yellow card exercises described in Chapter 4.

Table 3–16. Advanced Group II Graphemes	Definitely teach from the previous tables:	**ough**, **augh** or **aught**, **ought**
	Also possibly introduced previously:	**ear**, **our**, **al**
	Gradually teach:	**ti**, **si**, **ci** (as /sh/, not /s/)
	Less frequent:	**xi**, **su** /sh/ **ce** (as /sh/, not /s/) **sch**
	Teach:	**que**, **sc** and **ps**, **pn**
	Maybe teach:	**yr**, **et**, **é**
	Teach second phonemes for:	**ir**, **er**, **ei**
	Teach second and third phonemes:	**z** - /s/, **x** - /gz/ and /z/ **u** /o͞o/ and /w/ **su** as a ligature
	Teach second and/or third phonemes:	**ei**, **ar**
	Maybe not for:	**ie**
	Teach using Choice I or II:	**w(a)** and **qu(a)** **w(ar)** and **qu(ar)** **w(or)**
	If not yet introduced, teach second phoneme:	**qu** /k/
	Begin to teach vowels at the end of unaccented, open syllables:	**a** and **o** /ə/
	Continue:	**e** and **i** /ĭ/
	Definitely all three phonemes for:	**y**
	Another one or two phonemes:	**i** /ē/ and /y/

How **ough** is taught differs among Orton-based programs. Note that in the Advanced Gillingham Checklist (table 3–6), **ough** is given six sounds whereas in this book, it is given four (table 3–15 and table 3–16).

Here, and in Schupack's Advanced Checklist, **augh** is designated as having just one phoneme. Schupack's six phonemes for **ough** include four that many Slingerland and other Orton-based teachers use as well: /ô/ as in **ought**, /ō/ as in **although**, /ou/ as in **drought**, and /o͞o/ as in **through**. In the last two of Schupack's list, the final **gh** is pronounced /f/. One contains words such as **tough** and **rough**, which advanced Slingerland students decode by isolating the **ou** as /ŭ/ and recognizing **gh** as one grapheme representation for /f/, especially at the end of several common words (**enough, tough, laugh**). Words such as **cough** and **trough** can be included in the same category as the **ought** words without the ending **t**, or perhaps as sight words. As an informed teacher, you decide.

A few teachers teach **ght** (**drought**) as another spelling for /t/. This is perplexing because **igh** has already been presented as a spelling for /ī/ and **eigh** as /ā/. In both instances the **gh** may be considered silent. Thus, **ght** - /t/ is not recommended. Because **bt** - /t/ and **pt** - /t/ appear infrequently, it is better to include them also with sight words (**debt, doubt, subtle,** and **receipt, ptarmigan, pterodactyl, Ptolemaic, ptomaine**).

Other new phonograms to be taught if not introduced previously include those that are **r-controlled**: **ear** (earth), **our** (journey), and **yr** (zephyr) with the phoneme /ur̶/. Found primarily in French words, **é** and **et** provide the ninth and tenth ways to spell long /ā/. You can teach **al** with its /ôl/ sound as a phonogram if you have not done so earlier. Certainly you would have taught **al** as a word family or with sight words for the most common **al** or **all** words (halt, malt, ball, call, fall).[11]

Teach the second phoneme for **ir**, the second and third for **ei**, and the third phoneme for **ar**. The respective phonemes are /ĭr/; /ī/ and /ē/; and /ăr/. Consider carefully whether you wish to teach the third phoneme for **ie**. Some teachers prefer not to apply more than two key words and phonemes because the third, short /ĭ/, is found in so few, although relatively common words: **mischief, mischievous, kerchief, handkerchief,** and **sieve**. Including **ie** as the fourth or fifth spelling for /ĭ/ in yellow cards only, is usually sufficient (**i, y, ai, ie,** and **e** at the end of an unaccented syllable). You should also introduce the second phoneme for **er**, /ĕr/.

Single consonants requiring additional instruction include **z** and its second phoneme, /s/, and **x** as /gz/ (**exam** and **existence**). Later, or at this point, you can teach **x** pronounced /z/ (**xerox** and **xylophone**) from the Greek, also.

Gradually teach students to understand the influence of letters that follow **w** and **qu** in the same way that they learned the influence of **e, i,** and **y** upon **c** and **g**. Since the **u** most frequently acts as the consonant **w** when it follows **q**, teach your students to respond to the **w** and **qu** cards with either *Choice I* or *Choice II* (See table 3-17).

---

[11] A vowel followed by an **l** (l-controlled) is affected similarly to a vowel followed by an **r** (r-controlled).

With **er**, **ar**, and **ir**, there are dictionary diacritical and spoken differences similar to those described for **w** and **qu** followed by **a**. With careful discussion, students rarely have difficulty accepting and learning such differences.

Referring again to table 3–16, you can introduce another spelling for **u**, as **u** - full - /o͞o/. Also, **u** with its corresponding /w/ sound can be introduced, and the second or third phoneme for **su**, as /sh/ or a ligature, can be given, if not introduced previously. It is not recommended that a visual card be made for **su**.

Table 3–17. Choices for Teaching w and qu	***Choice I***	***Choice II***
	w - wagon - /w/	**w** - wagon - /w/
	w followed by **a** often says /wŏ/[12]	**w-a** - watch - /wŏ/
	w followed by **ar** says /wôr/	**w-a-r** - war - /wôr/
	w followed by **or** says /wᵤᵣ/	**w-o-r** - world - /wᵤᵣ/
	qu - queen - /kw/	**qu** - queen - /kw/
	qu followed by **a** often says /kwŏ/	**qu-a** - quad - /kwŏ/
	qu - followed by **or** says - /kwôr/	**qu-a-r** - quart - /kwôr/
	qu - quiche - /k/ (in French words)	**qu** - quiche - /k/ (in French words)

Now that the second long vowel phonemes for all the vowels have been introduced, it is time to introduce the third phonemes. The third occurs at the end of unaccented, open syllables and requires careful instruction before students respond to any visual vowel card by (1) naming the vowel, (2) giving the key word, (3) giving the short vowel sound in closed syllables, (4) renaming the vowel, (5) naming the second key word, (6) giving the long vowel sound at the end of accented (open) syllables (ex: **a** - baby - /ā/, at the end of an accented syllable), (7) renaming the vowel, (8) giving the third key word, and (9) for **a**, **e**, **i**, and **o**, giving the unaccented vowel sound (ex: **o** - polite -

---

[12] Different dictionaries use different diacritical notations for the pronunciation of **wa** (and **qua**). Furthermore, some dictionaries distinguish between the **wa** pronunciation in words such as **wad**, **wallet**, **want** and **walker**, **walrus**, **water**. If you discuss these differences, after perhaps having your students discover them themselves, **wa** words should not pose as much difficulty.

/ə/, at the end of an unaccented syllable). For **a**, the third response is: **a** - cadet - /ə/, at the end of an unaccented (open) syllable; for **e**, it is **e** - sedan - /ĭ/ or /ə/, at the end of an unaccented syllable; for **i**, **i** - Tibet - /ĭ/, at the end of an unaccented syllable. For **u**, recall that **u** says /ū/ or /o͞o/ at the end of an accented syllable. Often the unaccented **u** is simply not taught because it occurs so infrequently, as in the word **superb**. (The response to vowel **y** has already been discussed at the end of the previous Level.) All three vowel phonemes for **y** should usually have been introduced by now.

The letter **i** spells two additional sounds that are usually not introduced until an advanced level of instruction. They are /y/ and long /ē/. An excellent warning to students is: **i** can do anything **y** can do, and **y** can do anything **i** can do, but never rely on **i** (therefore also **y**). Eventually, your students should respond confidently to the **i** card in the following ways:

> **i** - inch - /ĭ/
>
> **i** - tiger - /ī/, at the end of an accented syllable
>
> **i** - Tibet - /ĭ/, at the end of an unaccented syllable
>
> **i** - million - /y/ (**i** acting as the consonant **y**)
>
> **i** - maniac - /ē/ (**i** before another vowel often says /ē/ when the syllabification occurs between two vowels, and also in French-based words such
> as **boutique** and **machine**.)

You will likely choose not to teach unaccented **u**, or **ght** as /t/, for the reasons already given. They are thus not included in table 3–16. The digraphs **bt** (debt) and **pt** (receipt) representing /t/ and **gm** representing /m/ are not included because of their infrequency and because it is recommended that they be included in the instruction of sight words instead. Refer to the prior discussion when deciding the number of corresponding phonemes to teach.

A Note About Visual Card Verbalizations

Verbalization for the use of visual cards (hand pack) will vary somewhat in different Orton-based programs. The preceding, strongly Slingerland influenced verbalizations have been provided as a guide. Adaptation is expected and encouraged providing the verbalizations are kept consistent within each program.

Rationale for Changes in Pronunciation of Graphemes

It should be noted that the pronunciations—particularly of unaccented vowels—are not always the same as those found in the Gillingham-Stillman Manuals or in Slingerland's textbooks. It is not just a matter of dictionary preferences and styles. It stems, too, from the fact that our beautiful English language is constantly changing. The first published Green Manual reflects changes that occurred since the publication of the earlier Red Manual, and Slingerland's work reflects changes that she noted since the publication of the first Green Manual.[13] In one of this writer's last conversations with Beth Slingerland, shortly before her death in 1989, the question was posed whether the time had come to change the designated pronunciation of "the half-short, half-long **e**"[14], since so many modern dictionaries indicate the pronunciation of unaccented **e** with /ĭ/ or /ə/. She responded by saying that she was happy that she no longer had to make such decisions and could leave those and similar responsibilities to the many good teachers she had trained. Her response was accepted as both a challenge and compliment.

Advanced Oddities

Under the category of Advanced Oddities (table 3–18) are the most advanced, less common phonemes that may or may not be introduced with cards visually, auditorily, or in decoding or spelling, or not introduced at all. You can place several of the already presented graphemes into the Advanced Oddities category if you so choose. For instance, **ui** as in **build** and **guild**, and also in **biscuit** and **circuit**, discussed in Advanced Group I, might be better placed in Oddities, or presented in a different way completely. With **gui** or just **gu**, instead of **ui**, explain that the **u** is inserted to prevent the soft /j/ pronunciation that occurs frequently when **i** follows **g**, at least in **guild**, **guilt**, **guide**, and **guitar** and several other common words. Then treat the other **ui** words (built, biscuit, etc.) as non-phonetic (learned) words to be copied, traced, and memorized. Also, **su** with the /sh/ and /zh/ sounds, might be best taught as oddities and not included in visual cards at all. The same applies with **sia** (Asia) and **sc** (science) that spell /zhə/ and /s/, respectively.

---

[13] The most recently published Gillingham Manual also has a green cover, but with a yellow band which distinguishes it from the earlier publication. Revised and published by Educators Publishing Service, Inc., it reflects changes that have occurred over the course of time and since the publication of the earlier Manuals in 1936, 1940, 1946, 1956, and 1960.

[14] as in **event**, **depend**, **reply**, **sedan**, etc.; often represented by "e" with a macron and dot above that.

Other Oddities in Schupack's Advanced Gillingham Checklist (table 3–6), include how the pronunciation of **th** changes from the unvoiced /th/ enunciation (**breath** and **bath**), when an **e** is added to the end, to the voiced /th/ enunciation (**breathe** and **bathe**). (Note that the **e** changes the sound of the vowel graphemes **ea** and **a** from short to long.) She includes **eo**, with possibly three phonemes, as a phonogram in words such as **people**, **luncheon**, and **leopard**, and also in **bludgeon**, **pigeon**, and **surgeon**, where the **e** in the **eo** retains the soft /j/ sound of the **g**. Many of the advanced oddities are discussed further in the main discussion of yellow cards for spelling in Chapter 4, and in the decoding discussion of this chapter.

When you teach at an advanced level, you will certainly come across oddities that have not been included in this book, but with a solid foundation, you will know how and when to include them for the benefit and enjoyment of your students. One might be **uy** as in **buy** or **ae** in **algae** and **aesthetic**. How would you teach **oe** in **Phoenix** or in **amoebae**? And what about that **ae** ending on **amoebae**?

Table 3–18. Advanced Grapheme Oddities	If not taught previously, teach:	**yr, et, é** the last phoneme for **i**, /y/
	Complete the introduction of the unaccented vowels in open syllables:	**a, e, i, o, y** with slight differences (usually not **u**)
	Perhaps teach a second or third phoneme for:	**ui** /ĭ/ and /ə/
	Maybe teach:	**sia, th(e)** where **e** changes the **th** phoneme, **eo** with three phonemes
	Teach affixes and Latin and Greek roots with or without cards:	See discussion in decoding in Chapters 3 and 4.

Rationale for Eliminating Prompts in Visual Cards

Students must be extremely automatic in their responses to visual card review and practice before key words can be dropped. Certainly, in the first grade, key words should not be eliminated at all, and in the second grade continuum, only key words for the consonants with not more than one corresponding phoneme should be eliminated. In a third grade continuum and beyond, the objective should be for students to establish such automaticity that they are eventually able to pronounce only the phoneme or phonemes for each grapheme, in what is often referred to as "sound only" card review. Again, the easiest graphemes will be those with only one corresponding phoneme, beginning with consonants, consonant digraphs, letter combinations, **C-le** syllables, phonograms, and so on. Graphemes that require additional verbalization to reinforce generalizations, such as **ck** at the end of a word, **ar** in an unaccented syllable, or verbalizations for any of the single vowels, should be the last that you present in "sound only" card review.

Rationales for Differences in the Introduction of Graphemes in Different Grades

Assuming that manuscript instruction is confined to first, second, and perhaps the beginning of the third grade, and that cursive instruction is for third grade and above, the differences in scope and sequence for the presentation of graphemes stem from several sources. First, the older cursive-level students learn more quickly than younger manuscript-level students. Second, especially in cursive instruction, the introduction of letters is determined to some extent by letter formation similarities and dissimilarities. Third, younger children are frequently not conceptually ready to acquire some of the more advanced skills and concepts that older students learn capably.

Table 3–19 and table 3–20 compare manuscript and cursive scope and sequences. They differ slightly from those presented in Chapter 2, and are compatible with most Orton-based programs where graphemes are introduced visually with cards or in Slingerland's *Learning to Write*.

Before moving on to the next comparison table, remember that scope and sequence differences also depend on the factors previously discussed: the number of students being instructed at one time, age, motivation, intelligence, previous schooling, achievement levels, as well as the degree and kind of their disabilities—particularly those related to visual modality strengths and weakness.

Specific graphemes may be introduced legitimately at any of several levels depending on the many factors discussed, and particularly on the performance, progress, and success of the students.

In grade three and above, Level II and Level III graphemes are gradually introduced with visual cards.

Table 3–19.
Manuscript and
Cursive Com-
parison–Level I

Manuscript Level I

First trimester
l, h, s, b, t, a, c
m, k, f, g, ck

Second trimester
i, j, d, p, sh, ch, th
maybe **w** and **wh**

Third trimester
u, w, wh, n, r, m
v, x, y, z, o, oa, ee
ing, ang, ong, ung
ink, ank, onk, unk
ai, ay, oo
a-e, e-e, i-e, o-e, u-e
maybe **qu**
e for writing at least

Cursive Level I

First three or four lessons
l, h, k, b or **f, a**

Next several lessons
b or **f, c, g, d,** maybe **t**
e for writing only

Second and third weeks at least
i, s, r, t, j, ck

Third week—end of month or earlier
w, p, u, sh, ch, th, wh

Before start of second month
o, qu, maybe **ph** and **tch**

Before end of second month
n, m, (e), v, y, z, x
ing, ang, ong, ung
maybe **kn**
perhaps **ink, ank, unk, onk, eng**
several phonograms: **oa, ee, ai, ay**
a-e, e-e, i-e, o-e, u-e, etc.
second phoneme for **s** - /z/

Table 3–20.
Manuscript and
Cursive Com-
parison–Level
II

Manuscript Level II

Second Year
Review of first year including
oa, ee, ai, ay, ou, oo
Definitely **qu, e,**
a-e, e-e, i-e, o-e, u-e
Plus **oi, oy, ow, igh, ar, or, er,**
ir, ur, ea, ie, eigh, aw, au, ew
Maybe **ue, eu, eng, tion, sion,**
kn, ph, wr, gh, tch, dge,
o - honey - /ŭ/
ce, ci, cy, ge, gi, gy,
or only **ce, ge**
ble, dle, fle, gle, kle, ple, tle, zle
with only **ple** and **tle** on card
ey

Cursive Level II

Second or Third Month
Possibly **ph, wr, kn, tch,**
dge, gn, gh, mb, mn,
but not all with cards
The second phoneme for
ch - /k/
oa, ee, ai, ay, oo, ar, etc.
All **vce**'s except **y-e**
eng, tion, sion, ture
Maybe **o** - honey - /ŭ/

Table 3–21. Cursive Continuum–Level III and IV

Cursive Levels III

Continuing in the first year—Level III

Certainly **gn**, **gh**, **ch** - /sh/, **dge**

ble, **dle**, **fle**, **gle**, **kle**, **ple**, **tle**, **zle**, **u-e y-e**, **oi**, **oy**, **igh**, **ow**, **ie**

ey (both phonemes)

Soft **c** and soft **g** with or without individual cards

Maybe open syllables for: **a** - baby - /ā/, **e** - meter-/ē/, **i** - tiger - /ī/, **o** - pony - /ō/, all at the end of accented syllables

Cursive Levels IV

First Year or Continuum—Level IV

y - /ĭ/ and **y** - /ī/ (my, shy, etc.); **y-e** for sure, and most of the following: **gn**, **gh**, **mb**, **mn**, **dge**, **gh**, **eng**, **ture**, **tion**, **sion**, **oo**, **ar**, **or**, **eigh**, **er**, **ir**, **ur**, **ea**, **aw**, **au**, **ui**, **ew**, **eu**, and **ue**

maybe **ei** as /ā/

soft **c** and soft **g** definitely

all open syllables including **u** - music - /ū/, and **u** - lunar - /o͞o/, plus **y** - cycle - /ī/

ar and **or** in unaccented syllables, /ər/

The phonogram **ey** with both phonemes, shown in table 3–20, may be introduced at any point in the manuscript continuum. In an exceptionally fast-paced class, a few of the following graphemes might *conceivably* also be introduced with great care: **y** as /ĭ/, **sc**, **gn**, **mb**, **mn**, **gu**, **que**, **gue**, **ture**, **cle**, **stle**, **sle**, **y-e**, **ui**, **su** as /sh/, **al**, **ei**, **rh**, **ear**, **oe**, **our**, **augh**(t), and **ough**(t). Presentation depends on relevance to every area of instruction.

Table 3–22 contains the graphemes that may or may not be included in your own teachers' hand pack. Corresponding to the graphemes are key words and phonemes. Key words can be easily changed if your school or language arts program uses different key words, or if you want to change key words because of personal preferences. It is important, however, to be consistent within programs. Once you select a key word, do not change it, or your students will become confused.

The grapheme **ght** is not included because it is not recommended that it be taught as a spelling for /t/ since, as discussed before, it is too easily confused with **igh** and **ight**.

Table 3–22. Advanced Graybeme Checklist

Group I

unaccented **ar** and **or** as /ər/

ai as /ĭ/ (or /ə/) in mountain, or taught as the ending **ain**

sc, **rh**, **gu**, **gue**, **que**

ei with all three phonemes (/ā/, /ē/, /ī/)

ei with one, two, and three phonemes (/ā/, /ē/, /ī/)

ear and **our** as /ur/, **ui**, and **oe** with two phonemes

ou as /o͞o/ and /ə/

stle, **sle**, and **cle** versus **kle** (also **cal**)

ligatures **du**, **tu**, **su**, **di**

augh, **ough** or **aught**, **ought**

Group II

ti, **si**, **ci**, **xi**, **ce**, **su**, all as /sh/

a bit later, **sch** as /sh/, and **que** and **qu** as /k/

definitely **ps** and **sc**

maybe **pn**

ough, **augh** or **ought**, **aught** if not taught previously

definitely **ear** and **our**, and **al** as a phonogram

maybe **z** with its second phoneme, /s/

x with its second and third phonemes, /gz/ and /z/

é and **et**, and perhaps **yr**

the second phonemes for **er** and **ir** and the third for **ar**

w, **wa**, **war**, **wor** and **qu**, **qua**, **quar**, plus **qu** as /k/

the second and third phonemes for **u**, /o͞o/ and /w/

ligature **su** as /zh/

unaccented open syllables:

    a - cadet - /ə/

    e - sedan - /ĭ/ or /ə/

    i - Tibet - /ĭ/

    o - polite - /ə/

    i - /ĭ/, /ī/, /ĭ/, /ē/, and /y/

Table 3–22 is intended for use with students beyond the third grade in a continuum program, and not as a guide for the instruction of first and second grade students. Table 3–23, Advanced Grapheme Oddities to Ponder and Perhaps Teach, is most useful for instruction of continuum students in at least the fourth grade and beyond.

Table 3–23. Advanced Grapheme Oddities to Ponder and Perhaps Teach	**al** as a phonogram /ôl/ (although) if **al** was not introduced previously in a different context
	ui as /ĭ/ in **build** and /ə/ as in **circuit**
	gu to maintain the hard /g/ sound in words like **guitar** and **guest**
	ge to maintain the soft /j/ sound in words like **pigeon** and **gentle**
	u as /w/, not only in **qu**, but also in words such as **suave** and **languish**
	w sometimes as a vowel (like **y**) as in **saw** (and correspondingly play)
	sia as /zhə/ (**Asia**)
	i-n-e as /ēn/ (**machine**)
	x as /gz/ (**exist**) if not introduced before
	z as /s/ (**waltz**) if not introduced
	age not only as the suffix or ending pronounced /ĭj/ but also /äzh/ in French-based words (**mirage**, **camouflage**, **bon voyage**)
	perhaps **bt** (**debt**) and **pt** (**receipt**) as /t/
	- the change from the unvoiced to the voiced **th** phoneme when **e** is added (**breath - breathe**)
	- not in *LessonPlanner,* **eo** as in **people**, **luncheon**, and **leopard**, and also in **bludgeon** where the **e** maintains soft /j/

The reverse of the *grapheme* table in Appendix A is that for *phonemes*, key words, and graphemes in Appendix B.

Decoding

Research indicates that poor decoding skill in the first years of school correlates significantly with poor comprehension and decoding in the higher grades. Thus, it is crucial that decoding be taught and that teachers learn effective decoding techniques (Brady and Moats, 1997). In Orton-based instruction, the smallest units of sight, sound, and feel are presented first for their introduction, practice, and review in visual cards. Next, slightly larger visual units, words, are presented for decoding. The words contain the graphemes introduced or reviewed in visual cards.

Decoding involves the application of skills to *unlock* words in order to name or pronounce them correctly. These skills include the systematic identification of graphemes with corresponding phonemes, syllabification, and accenting. Decoding is not reading. Reading occurs only when students read and derive meaning from sentences, paragraphs, and pages from a variety of texts. However, the inclusion of explicit decoding instruction and practice is supported by research as an essential prerequisite to reading if we want all children to learn to read.

When a student makes a mistake or miscalls a word in decoding, it is important to *print* the misnamed word or word approximation, so that the student can compare it visually with the miscalled decoding word. If a teacher simply *pronounces* the correct word for a student, the student is suddenly presented with an auditory stimulus that prevents him from detecting a visual error visually within the visual task of decoding. Although responses are ultimately multisensory, i.e., visual (seeing), auditory (hearing), and kinesthetic-motor (saying and writing), simultaneously, the initial stimulus and the techniques for decoding are visual. Sudden auditory interference causes a breakdown in the visual process of decoding.

In Orton-based programs, graphemes are first introduced with visual cards and decoding follows. In most programs students decode across words from the beginning of each word, left to right. In Slingerland, a student first underlines the vowel unit (**a**) of a word (**f<u>a</u>t**), then names it (**a**), before giving its corresponding phoneme (/ă/). Finally the student sounds out or decodes the word from left to right. The techniques for decoding are not the main focus here. Instead, the purpose is to provide the rationale behind the recommended order for the presentation of decoding words. From the rationale and the sequence, it is easier to determine how many words and word types you can introduce daily and throughout the school year with success to accommodate scope.

When decoding begins, reference to the visual card grapheme sequence will be helpful. The first words to use in decoding are the same or similar to those that are first encoded or spelled. Decoding, therefore, begins with one-syllable short **a** words (closed syllable) that contain only the letters that have been taught. When using *LessonPlanner*, you can select words from the 1-syllable, short vowel pull-down menus in Decoding.

Decoding should be limited to one-syllable short **a** words until the techniques for decoding become automatic. The first words selected from the numerous short **a** options should follow a specific sequence that begins with the easiest word pattern and continues to the next slightly more difficult pattern. The easiest are **cvc** words, where **a** represents the first vowel. In some reading and spelling programs, further distinction is made regarding the difficulty of the first consonant in <u>c</u>vc word, as discussed following table 3–24.

Table 3–24. Beginning Decoding with cvc (- a -) One-Syllable Words	**- a –** words In *LessonPlanner,* select from the one-syllable, short vowel pull-down menu and the vowel **a**, in Decoding.	hat, fat
	- a - - words	cast, hand
	- a — words (with digraphs)	back, mash
	- - a – words	glad, flap
	— a - words (with digraphs)	shad, than
	- - a - - words (also with digraphs)	blast, grant, whack
	- - - a - or **- - - a - -** words	sprat, scrap, splash
	Review: words with **x** having two consonant sounds—/k/ and /s/-/ks/, and **s** with two corresponding phonemes—/s/ and /z/	wax, has
	Be sure to include words that begin with the recently introduced vowel **a**.[15]	at, ask

Some educators feel that a consonant represented by a phoneme with a continuous sound is easier than one made with a stop sound consonant. A *continuous sound* is one that can be pronounced and maintained for several seconds without distortion; a *stop sound* is one that can be pronounced (spoken, said, or enunciated) only for an instant. The *continuous sound consonants* are **f, l, m, n, r, s, v, w, y** (yellow), and **z**. The more difficult *stop sound consonants* are **b, c, d, g, h, j, k, p, q, t,** and **x**. This distinction is helpful for understanding why young children, or those with severe specific language disabilities, might falter more on a word beginning with a **b** than an **m**. Stop sound consonants should

---

[15] In most word lists, **vc** words are not listed separately because of their infrequency. They are often included in the **cvc** lists.

be avoided initially when working with students who have phonemic awareness weakness and/or significant specific language deficits.

Decoding word lists may be extracted as needed from *LessonPlanner* or from published word books intended specifically for that purpose (Akin, 1941; Slingerland and Murray, 1987; Bowen, 1980). How and where to retrieve them in *LessonPlanner* is noted in the tables. Another source is from the day's reading, from which decoding words are selected for reinforcement of previous learning or the acquisition of new learning.

Table 3–25. Decoding with cvc (- i -) One-Syllable Words	**- i –** words In *LessonPlanner,* select from the one-syllable, short vowel pull-down menu and the vowel **i**, in Decoding.	wig, kid
	- i - - words	tint, milk
	- i —— words (with digraphs)	dish, lick
	- - i - words	clip, slid
	—— i - words (with digraphs)	ship, chin
	- - i - - words (also with digraphs)	twist, thick
	- - - a - or **- - - a - -** words (with digraph)	sprig, script, thrift
	with **i** at the beginning and with **s -** /z/	is
	with **x**	fix
	ff, ll, ss, and **zz** words	sniff, grill, miss, frizz
	- i - - -, - - i - - -, or **- - - i - - -** (also with di- and trigraphs)	pinch, clinch, stitch, wrists
	Review: Mix one-syllable short **a** words for discrimination with one-syllable short **i** words. Adherence to the **- v -, - v - -** sequence need not be as strict.	rapt, rift, grass, fifth, scratch, snitch

Including Nonsense Words

Nonsense or pseudowords should frequently be included in your students' decoding. You can use your own favorite resources or create your own nonsense decoding word lists. Be sure to create words that look like real words, but are not. If, for instance, you are teaching **cvc** decoding, then include words that follow the **cvc** pattern (**fam**, **bip**) or **cvcc** pattern (**fint**, **samp**) and so forth. Many should be real syllables such as **sis** in the word **sister**. It is not suggested that you combine letters that will not look like real words.

Rationale for Introducing the Vowel "a" Before "i"

Discriminating the difference between the easiest to pronounce vowel phoneme /ă/ and the slightly more difficult /ĭ/, is easier than among the other short vowels because there is greater distinction or variation in their sounds than between any other pair of vowels. Short /ĕ/ and /ĭ/ are the closest in sound and therefore taught far apart from each other. Also, there is more difference in how /ă/ and /ĭ/ are formed and feel as they are enunciated, another reason they are not as difficult, and thus taught first.

Table 3–26. Decoding with cvc (- u -) One-Syllable Words	- **u** - words In *LessonPlanner,* select from the one-syllable, short vowel pull-down menu and the vowel **u**, in Decoding.	sun, lug
	- **u** - - words	hunt, duct
	- **u** — words (with digraphs)	gush, luck
	- - **u** - words	smug, spun
	— **u** - words (with digraphs)	thug, chug
	-- **u** - - **words** (with digraphs)	thump, stuck
	- - - **u** - or - - - **u** - - words (with digraph)	crutch, thrust, thrush, struck
	- **u** - - -, - - **u** - - -, or - - - **u** - - - words	hutch, crunch, scrunch
	with **u** at the beginning	up
	with **x**	flux
	with **s** - /z/	bugs

	Review:
	   mixed double **f**, **l**, **s**, and **z**
	   mixed **short a**, **i**, and **u**
		stuff, still, crass, whizz
		yam, film, stuff, splash, script, brunch

	Be sure to include words that begin with the recently introduced vowel (**i**).	it, itch

Decoding is much like weaving, for one must constantly review words and concepts while carefully intertwining new concepts and words for added shade and texture. Three categories of words should be presented almost daily from the sources mentioned: (1) words that introduce new graphemes or concepts, (2) review words, (3) and words from the day's reading. Words from the day's reading may be considered separately or included in the "new" and "review" lists.

Words with suffixes, usually introduced in Spelling, may now be included for decoding. In *LessonPlanner*, use the pull-down suffix prompt menus in Decoding to recall which suffixes were introduced and which can be added to base words. Type the new word into the User Entry window and add it to the Selections decoding list. As digraphs are introduced visually, they are included in the decoding lists. If you just want a list of one-syllable words ending in **ck** or that contain **sh**, **ch**, or **th**, select them from the one-syllable, di/tri pull-down menu in Decoding.

Table 3–27. Decoding with cvc (- u -) Suffixes and Digraphs	words with **suffixes**	jump, thrill, jumps, thrills, jumping, thrilling
	include words with **digraphs**	**ck** - duck, trick, whack **sh** - ship, shack, shush **ch** - chap, crunch, chinch
	voiced and **unvoiced th** Depending on the abilities of the children, just one phoneme might be presented for **th**.	**th** - thud, with, that, thin

If the double f, l, s, z spelling generalization was introduced in Spelling, use one-syllable short **i** words ending in **ff**, **ll**, **ss**, and **zz** initially to reinforce the generalization. In *LessonPlanner*, words of this type can be retrieved in Spelling under Rules and Generalizations, designated as "f, l, s, z" in the menu. After they have been placed in the Spelling Selections, they can be brought over for decoding by selecting them from Spelling in the Other Sources pull-down menu, in the Decoding panel.

A Note About the Suffix "ed"

Although the **ed** suffix was introduced for decoding in table 3–28, it is easier to teach after short **e** has been introduced, as shown in table 3–29. The **ed** suffix requires special instruction because it has three corresponding phonemes: /d/, /t/, and /ĕd/. In *Lesson-Planner*, **ed**, pronounced /d/, and /t/ can be retrieved from the "Phoneme Spelled As" panel in Blending and then brought over to Decoding by using the Other Sources pull-down menu on the Decoding panel and Blending. Pronounced /ĕd/, the suffix **ed** can be retrieved by searching multisyllabic /ĕ/ and /ĭ/ words in Decoding.

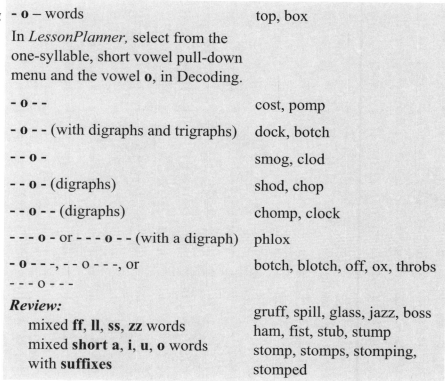

Table 3–28. Decoding with cvc (- o -) One-Syllable Words	- **o** – words In *LessonPlanner,* select from the one-syllable, short vowel pull-down menu and the vowel **o**, in Decoding.	top, box
	- **o** - -	cost, pomp
	- **o** - - (with digraphs and trigraphs)	dock, botch
	- - **o** -	smog, clod
	- - **o** - (digraphs)	shod, chop
	- - **o** - - (digraphs)	chomp, clock
	- - - **o** - or - - - **o** - - (with a digraph)	phlox
	- **o** - - -, - - **o** - - -, or - - - **o** - - -	botch, blotch, off, ox, throbs
	Review: mixed **ff**, **ll**, **ss**, **zz** words mixed **short a**, **i**, **u**, **o** words with **suffixes**	gruff, spill, glass, jazz, boss ham, fist, stub, stump stomp, stomps, stomping, stomped

Adding Soft c and Soft g Words

Words with soft **c** and soft **g**, depicted in table 3–29, may be included for decoding soon after the vowel **e** has been taught with second grade continuum students or beginning third or fourth grade students. In *LessonPlanner*, use the pull-down "soft c; g" prompt menus in Decoding to obtain separate lists for **ce**, **ci**, **cy**, **ge**, **gi**, **gy** words. Perhaps begin only with **ce**, and then **ge**.

Note that table 3–29 shows the introduction of the first homonyms. In *Lesson-Planner*, use the pull-down Special Words menu to find Homonyms, in Spelling. Select the homonyms you wish to include in your decoding lesson, and then return to Decoding to retrieve them from Spelling in Other Sources.

Table 3–29. Decoding with cvc (- e -) One-Syllable Words	**- e -** words	net, vex
	In *LessonPlanner,* select from the one-syllable, short vowel pull-down menu and the vowel **e**, in Decoding.	
	- e - - words	next, kelp
	- e — words	deck, mash
	- - e - words	sled, step
	— e - words	them, shed
	- - e - - words	crest, dwelt
	- - - e - or **- - - e - -** words	stress
	- e - - -, **- - e - - -**, or **- - - e - - -** words	depth, wrench, elf, hex, sheds
	Review: mixed **ff**, **ll**, **ss**, **zz** words mixed **short a**, **i**, **u**, **o**, **e** words	staff, spell, loss, fuzz, hiss jam, list, wrap, quest (with care), splotch
	1-syllable phonetic homonyms several with **suffixes**	its, it's
	Introduce words with other common suffixes that have been introduced in Spelling by this time. Include: **est**, **ful**, **ly**, **ness**, **y**, and **ment**. Endings **s**, **es**, and **ed** require careful instruction.	stretch, stretching, stretches, stretched, stretcher, stretchless, stretchable (for more advanced students)
	ce and **g e**	cent, cell, since, chance, gent, gem, fringe, lunge

More sophisticated students will be interested in knowing that **c** is the most common spelling for /k/, and that less frequently (twenty-five percent of the time in words in which it appears) **c** has the /s/ pronunciation, especially when followed by **e**, **i**, or, **y**. The letter **g**, on the other hand, represents the /j/ sound with somewhat greater frequency than **c** as /s/ (Carnine, et. al., 1990).

Table 3–30. Beginning Decoding with Letter Combinations	**letter combination** words In *LessonPlanner,* select from the one-syllable, letter combination (l.comb) pull-down menu in Decoding.	
	ang	sang, slang
	ing	sing, string
	ung	sung, swung
	ong	song, thong
	with **suffixes**	fangs, thronging, longed, stronger, stingless, singable, twangy

Rationale for Letter Combination and Phonogram Sequences in Decoding

Once decoding is secure with several vowels, then decoding one-syllable letter combination words (table 3–30) and one-syllable phonogram words (table 3–31 through table 3–38) can be included, even before short **e** decoding (table 3–29). The first phonogram is usually **oa**.

Table 3–31. Decoding with Phonogram oa	**oa** phonogram words In *LessonPlanner,* select from the one-syllable, phonogram **oa** pull-down menu in Decoding.	boat (- **oa** -) coast (- **oa** - -) poach (- **oa** —) (digraph) float (- - **oa** -) throat (— - **oa** -) (digraph) oath (**oa** at the beginning) hoax (with an **x**)
	with **suffixes**	groans, poaches, roasting, toaster, moaned, foamy (if suffix **y** has been introduced), coatless, floatable (perhaps)
	A few prefixes would also have been introduced in Spelling by this time, including the common ones such as **un, mis, tri, bi, dis,** and **re**.	unclip, misspell, tripod, bisect, dislike, retoasted
	Review: mixed **short a, i, u, o,** and **e** words, **digraphs, trigraphs, letter combinations,** and **oa** with new and review **suffixes**	graphs, wrenches, twisted, fussing, splotchy, shifty, thumping, blackness (if suffix **ness** has been introduced), bringing, soapless

Recall that for the introduction of graphemes, the following are usually taught by the end of the first grade and included in decoding:

- all the vowels except perhaps **e**

- all the consonants except perhaps **qu**

- the phonograms **oa**, **ee**, and maybe **ai**, **ay**, **oo**, and **ou**

- letter combinations **ing**, **ang**, **ung**, **ong**, **ink**, **ank**, **unk**, and **onk**

- digraphs **ck**, **ch**, **sh**, **th**, and perhaps **wh**.

In the first trimester of a third or fourth grade class, additional graphemes are usually taught. These may include **wh**, **tch**, **kn**, **eng**, **ar**, **er**, **eigh**, **ey**, **a-e**, **e-e**, **i-e**, **o-e**, and **u-e**. Very quickly more graphemes are added that can be included in decoding one-syllable words. They are: **ph**, **wr**, and maybe **dge**, **gn**, **gh**, **mb**, **mn**, and **eng**.

Table 3–32. Decoding with Phonogram ee	**ee** words In *LessonPlanner,* select from the one-syllable, phonogram **ee** pull-down menu in Decoding.	feed (- ee -) weeds (- ee - -) teeth (- ee —) greet (- - ee -) speech (- - ee —) screech (- - - ee —)
	with **suffixes** It is important that suffixes be added only to words where no spelling rule (1-1-1-**V**owel, Consonant-**Y**, Silent-**E**) is applicable first. (See Chapter 4.)	jeeps, queens, speeches, screening, weeded, greener, greenest (if suffix **est** has been introduced), needful (if suffix **ful** has been introduced), cheerless, greedy, sweepable, meekly (if suffix **ly** has been introduced), sheepish (if suffix **ish** has been introduced), deepness
	Review: **short vowels, digraphs, trigraphs, letter combinations**, with **double f, l, s,** and **z;** also **oa** and **ee** with **suffixes**	tracks, quenches, quickly, flossing, patchy, French, crushing, thinness, graphable, whiffing, knits, strongest, tweeter, poaches

Choosing Which Phonograms to Introduce Next

After decoding at the level depicted in table 3–33, there are options for what to introduce next, depending on all the factors discussed previously. With both manuscript continuum and beginning cursive SLD students, you may continue to introduce new phonograms gradually. These include any of those previously listed (**oo**, **oi**, **oy**, **ou**, **ow**, **igh**, etc.) in the Level II categories.

Table 3–33. Decoding with Phonograms ai and ay	**ai** words In *LessonPlanner,* select from the one-syllable, phonogram **ai** pull-down menu in Decoding.	rain (- ai -) faint (- ai - -) faith (- ai —) (with a digraph) claim (- - ai -) sprain (- - - ai -) (with a digraph) aim (**ai** at the beginning)
	ay words	say, sway, stray
	ai and **ay** words with **suffixes**	pails, stains, draining, chained, painful, airless, grainy, waistless, trainable, faintly (if suffix **ly** has been introduced), plays, player, playing, playable
	Challenge: As a challenge to more advanced students, **ai/ay** words with **prefixes** and two **suffixes** may also be included.	replay, misplayed, unplayable, underplayed, displayed, dismayed, dismayingly
	Review: 　**short vowel** 　**digraphs** 　**trigraphs** 　**letter combinations** 　**double f, l, s, z** 　**oa, ee, ai, ay** 　words with **suffixes** **homonyms**	wrist, less, elf, staff, fetched, dredge, crunchable, scratches, knocker, scriptless, thrushes, hinge, glanced, sprayable, hairy, gents, centless, junky, singing, singe, soapy, greeted, ailment, shrunken, blanket, impish, wishfully, blackest, sadness be and bee

Phonogram **ay** and **ai** words are often introduced at the same time. Note that the less common **ay** occurs most frequently at the end of one-syllable base words whereas **ai** is usually found at the beginning or middle of one-syllable words, often followed by **n** or **l**. Words with **ai** in unaccented syllables will be introduced later.

Several additional digraphs could also be introduced, particularly at the cursive level to non-SLD or to more adept SLD students. The same applies for the introduction of soft **c** and soft **g** words for decoding. Some teachers teach how to decode words that end in **y** with its corresponding long /ī/ phoneme, first (table 3–34). There are a handful of common, one-syllable **y** - /ī/ words. You may also introduce **v-e** words around this time.

Decoding V-Consonant-E Words

First and second grade students should be instructed that when (magic) **e** is added to words like **hat**, **pin**, **tap**, **cup**, and **hot**, the pronunciation of the first short vowel will change. It becomes long or says its own name. It is called a silent-**e** because the **e** has no sound. For further discussion review the lesson plans in Chapter 5.

Table 3–34. Decoding with y - /ī/ and v-e Words	**y** - my - /ī/ with **suffixes** In *LessonPlanner,* select from the one-syllable, long vowel **y** pull-down menu in Decoding *Review*: Constantly review words with the already taught **short vowels**, **di- tri-graphs**, **letter combinations**, **phono-grams**, the double **f**, **l**, **s**, and **z** spelling generalization, soft and hard **c** and **g**, and words with **affixes**, as well as **homo-nyms**.	cry, why shyness, trying
	vcv or **v-e** words In *LessonPlanner*, select from the one-syllable, phonogram pull-down menus in decoding with only **a-e**, **i-e**, **o-e**, and **e-e**, at first.	gave, trace (soft **c**), craze (hard **c**), rage (soft **g**), glade (hard **g**); write (twisty **wr**), scribe; chrome (with the /k/ phoneme for **ch**); stoke, core
	Although **e-e** appears less frequently in one-syllable base words than the other **v-e**'s listed, **here** and **these** are common.	here, these, mere, eve, theme, breve, scene, sphere, we've (with punctuation)
	with **suffixes**	blameless, merely, spiteful, choked

At this early stage of decoding, when trying to decide which letter combination or phonogram to teach next, ask yourself whether the grapheme you have in mind appears frequently, if it spells only one, easy sound, if it occurs frequently in one-syllable base words, and whether your students are sufficiently prepared to learn them without difficulty. You should use the same type of questioning when deciding which digraphs and trigraphs to include in decoding.

You again have several options. You might choose to continue with phonogram words and introduce several from table 3–35 and table 3–36. In *LessonPlanner*, select from the one-syllable, phonogram pull-down menu in Decoding.

Table 3–35. Decoding with More Phonograms		
	ou words	loud, round
	oo words with the long /o͞o/ phoneme	swoop, tooth
	oo words with the short /o͝o/ phoneme	cook, shook
	ow words	cow, scowl, brown, vowel, tower, how, snow, thrown
	oi and **oy** words	toil, choice, joy, Troy
	igh words	sight, knight
	ar words	spark, march
	or words	force, north
	er words	nerve, merge
	ir words	shirt, squirt
	ur words	burst, church
	ea with the long /ē/ phoneme	eat, wheat
	ea with short /ĕ/	spread, breadth
	ea with its long /ā/ phoneme	great, swear
	mixed **ea** list with **affixes**	realms, real, unreal, tear, weakling, steady, unsteady, greatness, creamer, deafen, treatment, retreat, wearable

The **ow** words can be taught at the same time as **ou** with only the /ou/ phoneme and noting, perhaps, that **ou** is usually found at the beginning or middle of words; **ow** is at the end of base words or when followed by a *single* l, n, el, er. If **ow** is not introduced with **ou**, then **ow** should be introduced with both corresponding phonemes, /ou/ and long /ō/.

The long /ā/ phoneme for **ea** is the least common. Some educators claim that **ea** spells /ā/ in only four words, contained in the following: **Yea**, we enjoyed a **great steak** at our **break**. If **ear** words pronounced /ār/ or /ăr/ are included, then the list lengthens (pear, bear, tear, wear, swear).

Table 3–36. Decoding with Yet More Phonograms		
	ie with the long /ī/ phoneme	pie, cries
	ie with long /ē/	thief, shriek
	eigh	sleigh, eighths
	aw and **au**	law, drawl, dawn, squawk, fault, Paul (an exception because **au**—not **aw**—is followed by a single **l**)
	ew words with the long /ū/ phoneme	few, skew
	ew words with the long /o͞o/ phoneme	grew, shrewd

Phonograms **aw** and **au** are taught together or closely. Note that **au** is usually found at the beginning or middle of words; **aw** is at the end of base words or when followed by a *single* **l**, **n**, or **k**, always with exceptions, of course.

Phonogram **ew** is usually not taught at the same time as **eu** because of how frequently **eu** is confused with **ue** and **ew.** The spellings for long /ū/ and /o͞o/ are difficult, even for teachers.

You again have options for what to introduce next. You can continue with some or all of the preceding phonograms in words, or, as shown in table 3–37, you can introduce **u-e** and the letter combination **eng** into decoding as well as several new digraphs and trigraphs and/or soft **c** and soft **g**. You may also introduce **scribal-o** for decoding. In *LessonPlanner*, all are selectable from the one-syllable, pull-down menus in Decoding.

Constantly review words in decoding that were introduced previously. Include words with several short vowels, digraphs, trigraphs, letter combinations, phonograms, doubled **f**, **l**, **s**, and **z**; **ck**, **tch**, **dge**; soft and hard **c** and **g**; **scribal-o**; **homonyms**; and words with a variety of **affixes**.

Table 3–37. Continuing Mixed Decoding	new digraph **ph**	graph, phone
	u-e words with the long /ū/ phoneme	mule, pure
	u-e words with /o͞o/	crude, spruce
	eng words	length, strength
	soft **c** and soft **g** words	cinch, gist, fancy, stingy
	scribal-o words	ton, month, and love, not as a **v-e** word, but instead with the final **ve** acting as a consonant ending[16]

Decoding Word Families and Homonyms

Continuing with the options you have for what to weave into decoding, new homonyms can be added or the first selection from Word Families, as shown in table 3–38. In *LessonPlanner*, use the pull-down Special Words menu to find Homonyms or Word Families in Spelling. You can select the homonyms you wish to teach from one lengthy list of 420 words, and then return to Decoding to retrieve them from Spelling in Other Sources.

Table 3–38. Decoding Homonyms, Word Family Words, Phonograms, and Plurals	**homonyms**	son (containing the newly introduced **scribal-o**) and sun
	ind word family	mind, kind
	al phonogram or **word family**	mall, stall, ball, call, fall, hall, tall
	oo word family (or **phonogram**)	blood, bloodless, flood, flooded
	-s plural or **third person singular**	strings, loves
	-es after the sibilants s, x, z, ch, and **sh**	hisses, taxes, fizzes, branches, dishes
	irregular plurals	oxen, feet, teeth, sheep

For Word Families there are several choices (**ol**, **old**, **ind**, **ost**, **ild**, **ign**, and **oo** pronounced /ŭ/) before selections can be made and brought into Decoding. Word Family

---

[16] In English, **e** is usually added to words that end with the consonant **v**.

words are not difficult. As used in this textbook, the vowel in word families usually is represented with an unexpected phoneme. For example, in **ind** words, it is expected that the vowel **i** followed by two consonants in a closed syllable would be pronounced /ĭ/ instead of /ī/.

Students will not have difficulty decoding word family words if they are carefully taught to recognize word families. For example, when decoding the word **blind**, from the **ind** word family, students should identify **ind** first and then pronounce it before pronouncing the whole word, **blind**.

Although **al** is designated as a phonogram in *LessonPlanner*, it could just as easily be taught as a word family—**all** or **al**—especially in common one-syllable **all** words. The **l** is actually doubled because of the double **l, f, s, z** generalization. When treating **al** as a phonogram, do not introduce it too soon. In this book, it is included in the most Advanced Oddities list. However, the smaller, easy **al/all** words can be taught much earlier (salt, waltz, alter). Decide for yourself how and when to teach **al** or **all**. Remember that many **al** words are more sophisticated and multisyllabic (although, almhouse, antiballistic) and that **l** in each word controls the preceding vowel.

In *LessonPlanner*, **oo** is designated as a phonogram with two common phonemes, /o͞o/ and /o͝o/, and in Word Families with its least common phoneme, /ŭ/. Some teachers prefer to teach **oo** only as a phonogram with all three phonemes in visual card drill. Most teachers find that middle and junior high students enjoy, and have no difficulty with, the **oo -/ŭ/- blood/flood** words of which there are more than expected. They are retrievable from the Spelling Word Family pull-down menu.

Another appropriate option to weave into decoding is the introduction and review of plurals. Although plurals might have been introduced elsewhere in a lesson, to help your students understand when plural **s** is used instead of plural **es**, words from each category can be brought from Spelling into Other Sources of Decoding. Plurals are found in Spelling in the pull-down Rules/Gen's menu. **S**, **es**, and **irregular** plurals are entitled "add-s"; "s,x,z,ch,sh-es" and "irreg. plural," respectively.

Depending on what you decide to teach from the various options, review now includes the newer teachings from those options (**plurals**, perhaps **all** as a word family, and **ind**). Include words with **short vowels**, some **digraphs**, **trigraphs**, **letter combinations**, **phonograms**, double **f, l, s,** or **z, ck, tch, dge**, soft **c** and soft **g, scribal-o**, some **homo-**

nyms, and words with a variety of **affixes**. The task of weaving new and review material into decoding is becoming more complex, but not less important. Also, visual instruction will notably outpace what you are presenting auditorily for encoding and spelling.

But Where Do You Teach Vocabulary and Grammar?

It should be clearly understood that once decoding begins, vocabulary must be included, too. It is useless for students to decode and pronounce words that have no meaning for them. You can teach vocabulary at almost any time during your instructional day and in any part of your daily plan. For example, you often teach vocabulary in math lessons, even though you might not be fully cognizant that you are doing so. You can also teach it in specific lessons during or after a decoding exercise. As you teach vocabulary, you will find *LessonPlanner's* homonym list in Special Words beneficial. At a more advanced level, the word lists for advanced suffixes and endings, in Decoding, are useful. In particular, suffixes often indicate parts of speech, an important factor in vocabulary development. Other *LessonPlanner* sources for words that expand vocabulary are the Latin and Greek roots, also found in Decoding. You can begin teaching them to fourth and fifth graders as well as to older students.

An important component of vocabulary development is the instruction of dictionary skills. The development of dictionary skills usually begins with instruction for alphabetization and continues gradually to the study and use of synonyms, antonyms, idioms and colloquialisms. It also includes etymology, the study of words and their origins, and morphology, the study of the meaningful units in words (morphemes), and how they are combined. How to use a thesaurus must also be taught. No matter where you introduce these skills, they should constantly be reviewed and reinforced throughout the day in reading, speech, composition, and in other subjects.

Learning to read, itself, broadens students' opportunities to build vocabulary. Research indicates that the majority of new words that students learn yearly are learned by encountering them while reading (California Department of Education, 1996a). Thus, the more that children read, the more their vocabularies will expand and improve.

Grammar instruction is similar to teaching vocabulary: Teachers need not set aside only one specific segment of a lesson to teach grammar exclusively. Since grammar is such an integral part of language and communication, it can and should be taught and reinforced where and when it will be learned most effectively and meaningfully. At times this might be when reading phrases in *Preparation for Reading*, when reading aloud directly from text, or, auditorily, when writing phrases and sentences from dictation. Grammar should not only be integrated throughout language arts instruction, it should also be reinforced in other subject areas. For example, parts of speech can be identified from, say, a science textbook just as readily as from a reader. Or, grammar can be taught and reinforced in oral discussions when speaking in complete sentences should be mandatory.

The study of grammar, like that for many subjects, is cumulative. It must begin with the smallest units and gradually progress to larger, more complex units. This progression or sequence should begin with the identification and definition of parts of speech, beginning with concrete nouns, and continuing with instruction and acquisition of the following, and beyond:

- concrete nouns

- nouns as simple subjects

- singular and plural nouns (number)

- the first irregular plurals

- action verbs

- present tense (using the **ing** suffix)

- past tense (using the **ed** suffix)

- regular verbs

- introduction to irregular verbs

- proper and common nouns

- verbs as nouns, too (test, dock, trust)

- verb endings to designate the time of an action

- simple sentences

- definition of a phrase (already familiar because of those written in dictation)

- beginning punctuation (period and capital letter to begin a sentence)

- subject and predicate

- use of ? and !

- adjectives (to tell which, what kind of, how many)

- adjectives (to describe color, size, and shape)
- the use of an apostrophe to designate possession for nouns
- irregular verbs (begin with the most common—to be)
- punctuation for abbreviations
- helping verbs
- quotation marks
- irregular "to have"
- base predicates
- verb phrases
- irregular "to do"
- future tense (with *will* and *shall*)
- first person (the speaker)
- second person (one spoken to)
- third person (one spoken about)
- informal language
- formal language (especially for writing)
- pronouns
- possessive pronouns (always without an apostrophe)
- pronoun number
- first, second, and third person pronouns
- indenting
- past, present, and future
- subject, object, and possessive pronouns
- prepositions that tell when
- use of *could* and *would*
- direct and indirect object (answering whom? or what?)
- sentences with compound subjects
- sentences with compound predicates
- the use of ; and :
- compound sentences
- structure of paragraphs

- compound words for decoding, spelling, and vocabulary
- moving prepositional phrases to vary and enhance writing
- adverbs (beginning with words ending with **ly**)
- adverbs to designate when, where, how, how much, how often
- adverbial prepositional phrases
- comparative and superlative adjectives and adverbs
- active voice
- passive voice
- use of hyphens
- learning to proof using proofers' symbols
- more irregular plurals
- the apostrophe in contractions (representing the missing letter or letters)
- clauses
- dependent and independent clauses
- common Anglo-Saxon suffixes
- inflectional endings that change a verb's form (**ed**, **es**, **ing**)
- inflectional endings that change an adjective's form (**er** and **est**)
- inflectional endings that change a noun's form (**s** and **es**)
- Latin suffixes (**ist**, **age**, **ible**, etc.)
- derivational suffixes that change a word's function (**great**, an adjective, becomes a noun when **ness** is added)
- the use of commas to set off clauses
- commas in lists
- relative clauses (usually beginning with a relative pronoun—who, which, what, that)
- complex sentences
- continued study and use of semantics
- form versus function
- **ize** and **ify** as verbal functions
- present tense and present progressive tense
- more uses of commas
- conjunctions in sentences
- punctuating conjunctions
- sentence patterns
- compound and complex sentences
- sentence combining to vary sentence patterns

- using commas in direct quotes
- many more uses for commas (in direct address and to set off independent clauses, dates, addresses, geographical names, introductory phrases and clauses, appositives, restrictive phrases and clauses, and with salutations)
- punctuation with quotations
- past participles
- theme development in reading and writing
- continued study and use of syntax
- Greek combining forms for vocabulary, decoding, and spelling
- writing formal and informal letters
- indefinite pronouns
- reflexive pronouns
- intensive pronouns
- case (nominative, possessive, objective)
- similes
- figurative language
- metaphors
- dialogue in reading and writing
- other pronouns (interrogative, demonstrative, and reflexive)
- oral and written paraphrasing

As grammar skills are gradually introduced, they must be put to functional use as soon as possible; previous skills must constantly be reviewed and reinforced in language arts lessons, and in other subjects whenever feasible. Within the visual presentations, many grammar concepts and skills can be introduced and reinforced in decoding, in Slingerland's *Preparation for Reading,* and when reading. Within the auditory presentations, grammar must be put to functional use as writing skills are introduced, practiced, and reviewed.

Two-Syllable Decoding

Two-syllable decoding can begin either earlier or later than at this point. Begin two-syllable decoding when students appear ready to learn the letter combinations **tion**, **sion**, and **ture** (for older students), and when they are able to learn the **C-le** or **silent-e** syllables (**ble**, **tle**, **zle**, etc.) Some teachers prefer introducing two-syllable decoding using words that end in **C-le** (sim/ple and rum/ble). Others prefer doing so with words where the division or syllabification is between two dissimilar consonants (cac/tus). Wolf[17] recommends the following sequence when introducing syllabification for the first seven word types:

1. short vowel, like consonants (muf/fin)

2. second syllable ends in **er** (ham/mer)

3. short vowel with unlike consonants (cac/tus)

4. short vowel and **silent-e** syllable (bat/tle)

5. phonograms and **silent-e** or **C-le** syllables (mar/ble)

6. short vowel with **v-e** (stam/pede)

7. phonogram and short vowel (seam/stress)

In *LessonPlanner,* two-syllable words for syllabification can be retrieved by selecting from the 2-Syllable menus in Decoding. The first pull-down menu identifies the four ways in which words can be syllabified, designated for easy identification for teachers, as Rule I, Rule II, Rule III, and Rule IV. The second pull-down menu lists the syllable combinations for each rule that is used when searching the database. The order in *LessonPlanner* is slightly different from Wolf's for syllabification between two consonants, and the computer searches provide more variation. For example, if you want a list of two-syllable words with like consonants or a list with unlike consonants, you can select them from the *LessonPlanner* category designated as "v or ə:v or ə" that contains words from Wolf's 1 and 3 types, above. On the other hand, in *LessonPlanner* it is possible to search for two-syllable words with a short vowel in one of the syllables and a letter combination in the other. You can, within the broader range of syllabification between two consonants, use your own judgment for the sequence to present. Either Wolf's or the *LessonPlanner* two-syllable decoding sequence can be used comfortably by both Slingerland and other Orton-based teachers, as well as whole language teachers with phonics training.

Often in Orton-based programs, including Slingerland, emphasis is placed on the importance of vowels for syllabification, accenting, and pronunciation. In the decoding sequence presented in this book, it is recommended that students be encouraged to focus

---

[17] Beverly Wolf worked closely with Beth Slingerland when writing her *Instructional Sequence for SLD Classrooms* (Wolf, 1982).

upon where the action is or where the division (syllabification) is made for Rules I, II, and III: **between** (table 3–39), **before** (table 3–44), and **after** (table 3–43) consonants in medial positions, and **between** vowels (table 3–45) for Rule IV.

Decoding with Double-Duty *g* and *k*

To decode words like **jungle** is more challenging than decoding other **C-le** words because the **g** provides two phonemes. The first is the final sound in the **ung** letter combination, and the second is the beginning sound of **gle**, a **C-le** syllable. Similarly, when decoding **wrinkle**, the **k** is what is often referred to as a "double-duty" **k**. It is amusing to observe students, on their own, cleverly divide the **k**, or **g**, carefully down their centers instead of underlining the letter combination first and then slightly below it, the **C-le** syllable. (The **k** or **g** then have two lines with the second line extending to the end of the **C-le** and beginning slightly

> ### *Learn: Word Division*
>
> **Rule I: The most common way to divide a word is *between* two consonants. (C/C)**
>
> Although many instructors begin decoding of two-syllable words with those that contain like consonants, others find that because one of the "like" consonants—the one in the unaccented syllable—is usually silent, this can be perplexing (muffin - /muf' in/); therefore, they prefer beginning with two-syllable words containing "unlike" consonants.

beneath the one underscoring the letter combination in the first syllable.) This is often trickier for teachers than for children. Other examples include **shingle** and **twinkle**.

Pronunciation and Accenting Two-Syllable Words with Short Vowels in Both Syllables

Younger children, while decoding two-syllable words, usually pronounce each syllable as an accented syllable or one-syllable word. Then they pronounce the whole word as spoken in normal speech with one syllable more heavily accented or stressed, and the short vowel sound in the accented or stressed syllable more distinct. In the unaccented syllable the vowel sound is less distinct for most of the vowels. The vowels **a** and **o** in unaccented syllables are pronounced /ə/, and **e**, **i**, and **y** are pronounced /ĭ/. Unaccented **e** and i are sometimes pronounced /ə/ as well.

Table 3–39. C/C Syllabification	**Divide *between* 2 unlike consonants with a single vowel in each (closed) syllable.**	vel/vet, campus, pastel
	***between* 2 like consonants with a single vowel in each (closed) syllable**	rab/bit, muffin, success (a bit more challenging for students who are secure with soft and hard **c**), and suggest (equally challenging)
	***between* 2 consonants—like and unlike—with a single vowel in the first (closed) syllable and a C-le second syllable**	lit/tle, hum/ble
	***between* 2 consonants with a single vowel in the first (closed) syllable and a letter combination in the second syllable**	fic/tion, vulture
	***between* 2 consonants with a phonogram in the first syllable and C-le in the second**	mar/ble, gurgle
	***between* 2 consonants with a single vowel in either the first or second (closed) syllable and a letter combination in the other syllable**	thank/less, ginseng
	***between* 2 consonants with a single vowel in either the first or second (closed) syllable and a phonogram in the other syllable**	duct/work, journal 3 consonants are together in ductwork. Usually, the division is between the first 2 consonants, but in ductwork, the **ct** is a consonant blend that is not separated.
	***between* 2 consonants with a single vowel in the first (closed) syllable and v-e in the second syllable**	sin/cere, expose, and distaste (vowel, consonant, consonant, **e** or **v- -e**)
	***between* 2 consonants with a phonogram in one syllable, and in the other syllable, a single vowel, letter combination, v-e, another phonogram, or C-le**	mar/gin, weakling, vouchsafe, saunter, dawdle, dollar, thankless, graveyard, eastern

It is not necessary for students to refer to how words are syllabified or divided by rule numbers. It is more important that they learn that syllabification between two consonants (Rule I) is the most frequent, that syllabification between two vowels (Rule IV) is the least frequent, and that when they have a word with a single consonant (or consonant digraph or blend) in a medial position, they should try syllabifying before the single consonant (or consonant digraph or blend) in the medial position (Rule II) first, and after the single consonant (or consonant digraph or blend) in the medial position (Rule III) second.

Syllable pronunciation is determined by the rules, generalizations, and accenting hints that govern decoding. The first two accenting hints are discussed in table 3–40.

Table 3–40. Accenting hints 1 and 2

Accenting hint 1	
In two-syllable words, the accent will *usually* fall on the first syllable (three-quarters of the time). Now go back and accent the preceding two-syllable words (table 3–39) and note that, indeed, approximately 75% of the words are accented on the first syllable.	**cam**pus, **vel**vet, **hum**ble, **dol**lar, pas-**tel**
Accenting hint 2	
Affixes are usually not accented; **silent-e** or **C-le** syllables never are; Latin and Greek roots frequently *are* accented.	**thank**less, mis**spell**, **bub**ble, suc**cess**, ex-**pose**

If you are working with older or more advanced students, you can begin teaching accenting as soon as initial two-syllable decoding techniques are secure. Teach the first two accenting hints, shown in table 3–40, first.[18]

Since we have not discussed "roots" yet, only the first part of hint 2 can be applied. Soon, however, and especially with students in the upper elementary grades and beyond, the second part of hint 2 is beneficial.

Typical Review of Two-Syllable Word Decoding, Beginning with One-Syllable Words

Daily decoding review, as shown in table 3–41, should now include, initially at least, one-syllable words with several short vowels, a variety of digraphs, trigraphs, phonograms, double **f**, **l**, **s**, and **z**, as well as **ck**, **tch**, and **dge** immediately after one short vowel at the end of a one-syllable word, soft **c** and soft **g**, **scribal-o**, homonyms, and affixes.

---

[18] Another resource that covers syllabification and accenting in depth is *Patterns for Reading* (Hoover and Fabian, 1975).

Table 3–41. Review One and Two-Syllable Word Decoding	beginning with **consonant-vowel-consonant (cvc) words**	hat (- **v** -) fist, can't (- **v**- -) bath (- **v** —) (a digraph) grid (- - **v**-) thin (— **v** -) (a digraph) trust (- - **v** - -) splash (- - - **v** —) or (- - - **v** - -) fifth, drench, crutch (- **v**- -) and (- - **v** - - -)
	ce and **ge**	cell, binge
	homonyms	seen and scene
	letter combinations	slang, trunk
	with **suffixes**	thronging
	phonograms and **letter combination** words with more **suffixes**	strings, sweltering, conked, boasted, foamy, blackness, bringing, meanest, sweepable, greedy, meekly, sweetish, knits, draining, chained, replayed, toothless, powerfully, hoisted, northern, merged, thirty, curling, breached, pears, tries, chiefly, weighty
	y - /ī/ words	dry
	more **phonogram** words with **affixes**	crawlers, vaulted, strewed, mews
	v-e (phonogram) words	grace (soft **c**), stage (soft **g**), blameless, merely, spiteful, choked, puled, fluted
	scribal-o	lovers
	alk family	talk, walk, calk—also spelled caulk, chalk, stalk
	al or **all**	wall
	irregular plural	child – children

Additionally, weaving in new and review material should include two-syllable words with short vowels, soft **c** and soft **g**, double-duty **g** and **k**, scribal-**o**, v-e, C-le, letter combinations, phonograms, affixes, as well as homonyms, word family words, and vocabulary development. Confusables are words that are readily "confused," particularly by students with learning disabilities. In *LessonPlanner*, Confusables are retrieved from the Special Words menus in Spelling, as are Homonyms and Word Families. They must then be moved to Decoding.

If you are teaching accents, include hint 1 and hint 2 words for review too. A good review exercise at this point is to go back and accent some of the words in table 3–41 and table 3–42, where either hint 1 or hint 2 is applicable. Applying hint 1: **flood**light, **frac**ture, and **sys**tem are accented on the first syllable, whereas sin**cere** and com**piled** are accented on the second syllable. Applying hint 2: **gym**nast is accented on the first syllable—not on the affix. Also, **hum**ble is not accented on the **C-le** syllable (hint 2). The word suc**cess** is accented on the second syllable or on the Latin root **cess** but not on the prefix **suc**.

Table 3–42. Two-Syllable C/C Decoding		
	between unlike consonants	ban/dit
	between like consonants	tun/nel
	between consonants with a C-le second syllable	bub/ble, pimple
	between consonants with a phonogram and C-le	tur/tle
	between consonants with a letter combination in one-syllable	trac/tion, juncture
	Note that **juncture** has a letter combination in both syllables. In *LessonPlanner*, **unc** is found in the same letter combination list as **unk**.	
	mixed **C/C**	junc/tion, miscall, disband, unjust trickle, system, suppose, comply, accuse, gardener, harpooned, version
	singular possessive	Jor/dan's, gymnast's
	contraction	did/n't
	plural possessive	gym/nasts'
		ac/cess, gypsy, cygnet, fracture, factoring
	double-duty g and k	single, sprinkler
	2-syllable homonyms	as/cent and assent
	word family	blood/sucker, floodlight
	confusables	com/p<u>ie</u>d, compl<u>ie</u>d

Syllabification — Rules II, III, and IV

Rule III should be taught before Rule II because students have fewer new techniques to learn when syllabifying with Rule III than they do when decoding Rule II words. The only decoding difference between Rule I and Rule III occurs with the actual syllabification. Students syllabify, or divide, *after* a single consonant, digraph, or consonant blend (**C/**) rather than *between* consonants (**C/C**). Then they decode or unlock the separate closed syllables that resemble closed one-syllable words, as shown in table 3–43.

Table 3–43. C/ Syllabification	**Divide *after* a single consonant in a medial position.**	sol/id, famish
	or *after* a consonant digraph	with/er, plumber
	or *after* a consonant blend	front/age, pointer
	Review: Beginning with one-syllable decoding, review should now also include two-syllable decoding with Rule I and III words. Constantly weave into both the one- and two-syllable lists a variety of words with short vowels, digraphs, trigraphs, phonograms, letter combinations, doubled **f, l, s,** and **z, ck, tch,** and **dge,** hard and soft **c** and **g, scribal-o,** homonyms, word families, confusables, and words with affixes. If you are teaching accents, include hint 1 and hint 2 words.	

In *LessonPlanner*, words for Rule III syllabification can be retrieved by selecting from the third of the Decoding 2-Syllable menus. There are three categories of words:

- short vowel or schwa in the first syllable and "arb"[19] in the second

- phonogram in one syllable and "arb" in the other syllable

- letter combination in one syllable and "arb" in the other

When Rule II decoding begins, syllabification occurs *before* a single consonant (or consonant digraph or blend) in a medial position, as depicted in table 3–44. Now stu-

---

[19] "Arb" is an abbreviation for *arbitrary* and includes short and long vowels, schwa, **v-e, C-le,** letter combinations, and phonograms.

dents must be secure with the difference between long and short vowel sounds, at least, and understand the concept and difference between closed and open syllables.

In a closed syllable, the vowel is followed by, or *closed* by, at least one consonant (**m** in ham and ham/mer, and **v** in sev/en); and in an open syllable, the vowel is at the end of the syllable or word (**o** as in n**o**), and thus the syllable is left *open*. In accented open syllables (no/ble), the vowel sound is long (nō' ble). In unaccented open syllables the vowel sound is usually half long and half short, or schwa, as the **a** is in **cadet** (/cə det'/). Thus, decoding Rule II words requires more complex decoding techniques and skills than decoding Rule I and III words. Teach Rule II decoding after Rule III decoding.

> ## *Learn: Word Division*
>
> Rule II: The second most common way to divide a word is *before* a single consonant (or consonant digraph, blend, or **C-le**) in a medial position. **(/C)**
>
> Rule III: The third most common way to divide a word is *after* a single consonant (or consonant digraph or blend) in a medial position. **(C/)**
>
> **Teach Rule III before Rule II.**
>
> Rule IV: The least common way to divide a word is *between* two vowels (often recognized as unstable diphthongs.[20] **(V/V)**

Teaching syllabification before a single consonant in a medial position (consonant digraph, blend, or **C-le** syllable) requires additional teaching so that your students understand the concept of an open syllable. Accenting is more important, too. Teach accented open syllables first. Introducing unaccented open syllables causes confusion at this early stage.

In *LessonPlanner,* words for /C syllabification can be retrieved by selecting from the second of the Decoding 2-Syllable menus. There are two categories of words:

♦ long vowel or /ə/ in either syllable and "arb" in the other

♦ phonogram in the first syllable and "arb" in the second

---

[20] An *unstable diphthong* is a pair of vowels that appears to be a diphthong but which is actually syllabified or divided between its two vowels (cre/**a**te, archa/**i**c). Recall that *diphthongs* are speech sounds made by gliding one vowel phoneme to another in one syllable (b**oi**l, cr**ou**ch). Another way to define a diphthong is to say that a diphthong is comprised of two consecutive vowels, each of which contributes to its sound.

Table 3–44. /C Syl-labification

Divide *before* a single consonant in a medial position; the vowel is long.	me/ter, baby
or *before* a consonant digraph; the vowel is long	se/quel, either
or *before* a consonant blend; the vowel is long	se/cret, cypress
or *before* a C-le syllable; the vowel is long	ti/tle, cycle, bicycle (more challenging), tricycle (adding the two new prefixes **bi** and **tri**)
Divide *before* a single consonant in a medial position; the vowel has its unaccented sound.	pa/rade, cadet, sedan
or *before* a consonant digraph; the vowel is unaccented	a/scend, re/quire
or *before* a consonant blend; the vowel is unaccented	re/fresh, degrade

Review: Begin your review with one-syllable decoding, but include two-syllable decoding with Rule I, II, and III words. Continue to weave into your word lists short vowels, digraphs, trigraphs, phonograms, letter combinations, words where spelling generalizations apply, homonyms, word families, confusables, the two new prefixes **bi** and **tri**, and suffixes. Include accent hints 1 and 2 words, too.

Initially, be careful to select only words where the vowel at the end of the open syllable is long and accented. Students can begin to decode such words once they understand the difference between closed and open syllables and are secure with card review of short vowels (in closed syllables) and long vowels (at the end of accented syllables). Teaching students to decode open syllable (/C) words where the vowel is in an unaccented syllable is taught later (Refer to the grapheme card sequence). It is discussed here because students come across such words in their reading and may ask about them, or you might mistakenly include several in your decoding lists. It's easy to do because hearing accents and the difference between short and unaccented vowel sounds is difficult for teachers as well as students.

Since all the words in *LessonPlanner* have been provided with their corresponding dictionary notations for pronunciation, it is easy to select only words where the open syllable is accented.

Table 3–45 shows Rule IV syllabification. In *LessonPlanner,* Rule IV words can be retrieved by selecting from the last of the Decoding 2-Syllable menus. There is only one category from which selections can be made, "arb" in either syllable. Begin by selecting from the options only words where the vowel at the end of the open syllable is long.

Table 3–45. V/V Syllabification

Divide *between* two vowels.	po/et, cha/os, stray/ing (reminder: in **ay** the **y**, **i**'s twin, is a vowel and not a consonant) thaw/ing (reminder: in **aw** the **w**, **u**'s twin, is a vowel and not a consonant)
Review: Beginning with one-syllable decoding and continuing to two-syllable decoding with Rule I, II, III, and IV words, weave into your review lists short and long vowels (at the end of accented syllables), digraphs, trigraphs, phonograms, letter combinations, words where spelling generalizations apply, homonyms, word families, confusables and affixes. Include hint 1 and 2 words for accenting review.	

Words With More Than Two Syllables

Once two syllable decoding begins, then syllabification with words of more than two syllables can be introduced providing that the syllabification does not include rules, hints, and generalizations that have not been taught. First are two-syllable words to which affixes are added, as shown in table 3–46. The "count back three" accenting hint (hint 3, table 3–47) should be taught.

Table 3–46. Decoding Words With More Than Two Syllables	**(C/C)**	
	with 2-syllable words with affixes, dividing *between* 2 consonants	dis/mis/sable, admittedly
	***between* two consonants with a C-le second syllable**	(un)gar/bled, candlelight
	***between* two consonants with a letter combination in one syllable**	in/ven/tion, suspension
	***between* two consonants with a phonogram and C-le**	re/mar/bling, turtledove
	(/C)	
	***before* a single consonant**	re/lo/ca/ted, demon<u>ize</u>
	***before* a consonant digraph**	ci/pher/able (re)sequenc<u>ing</u>
	***before* a consonant blend**	re/trace/able, cyclotron
	***before* a C-le syllable**	no/ble/ness, recabled
	(C/)	
	***after* a single consonant**	pol/ish/ing, venomously
	***after* a consonant digraph**	fath/om/ing, (re)graphable
	***after* a consonant blend**	stand/ee, unroastable
	(V/V)	
	between 2 vowels	li/on/ize, triumphantly

Table 3–47. Accenting hint 3	**Accenting hint 3**	**in**/cu/bate or **inc**/u/bate
	If the other accent hints do not apply, count back three syllables from the end of a word to accent, even if the accent falls on a prefix. This often applies to words ending in **v-e**.	**sob**bingly (un)**roast**able("able" is a 2-syllable suffix) **can**dleless **de**monize, **ci**phering (re)**graph**able **li**onize tri**umph**antly **ven**omous(ly)
	If you now accent the preceding three and four-syllable words, you will see that the majority are accented on the third syllable from the end of the word.	

Decoding Mixed Multisyllabic Words with Affixes

Your students should be ready now to decode multisyllabic words not only with a variety of affixes but also where more than one of the four syllabification rules apply with one of the first three accenting hints.

In *LessonPlanner*, a good way to retrieve multisyllabic words of this type is from the Blending "Phonemes Spelled As" menu. The selections can then be brought over to Decoding from Other Sources. The word list in table 3–48 was compiled by scrolling the Blending "Phonemes Spelled As" menu from the top downward, stopping to do word searches, and then selecting words to review.

Another way to obtain lists of multisyllabic words for decoding is to select them from the last two Decoding menus. The first of these contains words with advanced suffixes and endings and is shown as "suf'x/end's." It is a good plan to review the prompt lists that contain the more common suffixes and prefixes before selecting words from this menu. The last list contains Latin and Greek roots with accompanying word lists. It is shown as word roots. They are presented after suffixes and endings. The affix prompt lists are also available for use in Decoding.

Not yet available in *LessonPlanner* are Greek combining forms that are not the same as Latin and Anglo-Saxon roots and affixes. Connecting Greek combining forms is somewhat similar to connecting smaller words to form compound words. Most Greek combining forms are found at the beginning of words: telegram, biography, hydrometer, psychology, to name just a few.[21]

Example lists of affix and root words from *LessonPlanner* can be found in the running sidebars on the last several pages of this chapter. These lists were compiled by scrolling from the top downward and adding a base to each affix (in bold) in the suffix and prefix prompt lists. The words selected are those that students should have sufficient skills and techniques to decode successfully.

Additional suffixes are planned for the next version of *LessonPlanner* including those contained in the following words: hand**some**, knight**hood**, brace**let**, as well as others. Among Greek prefixes or combining forms are: **hyper**active, **macro**file, **phono**gram, **photo**graph, **astro**labe, and **tele**vise, plus others. The Lexia Institute welcomes suggestions for what to add to *LessonPlanner* from users and others.

---

[21] Both Jane Fell Greene (Green, 1997) and Marcia Henry (Henry, 1990) have produced excellent materials for teachers and students to learn and use Greek combining forms.

*Table 3–48.
Decoding
Mixed Multi-
syllabic Words
with Affixes*

Selected Words	Hints	Notes
smoke/stacks	1	**ck** at the end of a compound word
mech/an/ize	3	**ch** as /k/ hint 3, or count back 3, particularly from **v-e**
or/phan/age	3	
chlor/o/phyll	2, 3	Greek-based with **ch** as /k/, **ph** as /f/, **y** as /ĭ/, and the common Greek connective **o**
sledge/ham/mer	3	with **dge** seemingly in the middle, but actually at the end of the first half of a compound word
nos/**tal**/gic nos/**talg**/ic	4	**c** at the end of a multisyllabic word, not **ck**. You should help accent since hint 4 has not been introduced yet—accent the syllable preceding **ic**.
gym/**na**/si/um	3	Rule I, II, and IV. Help with the pronunciation of **i** as /ē/ when syllabification occurs in a reversed (or transposed) diphthong, **iu**, not **ui**.
cam/**paign**	1	Note **gn** as /n/ and that the accent falls on the second syllable infrequently.
re/de/signed	3	Two prefixes and the **ign** family where "never rely on **i**" is evident
script/wri/ter	3	twisty **wr** in twisty writing
trans/**lu**/cen/cy	2, 3	
hop/scotch	1	**tch** at the end of a compound word
strength/en **streng'**then	1	infrequent **eng**
ex/**tinc**/tion	2, 4	**inc** as a letter combination like **ink** hint 2: accent the root hint 4: accent the syllable before one that begins with /sh/ or /zh/
con/**clu**/sion	2, 4	
ex/**clu**/sion/ist	2, 3, 4	**ist**, meaning a person; not **est**, the superlative
bam/**boo**/zle	2	an inexplicable accent—it happens
tur/tle/dove	3	
pro/**nounce**	1, 2	
par/en/tage	3	
thread/bare	1	
in/ter/lude	3	hint 3 especially when counting back from **v-e**

Decoding Words with Three or More Syllables

If you and your students have followed the progression provided in this book, you should both now be able to decode words with three or more syllables that contain a variety of roots and affixes. To assist with accenting, it is beneficial to teach two more accent hints as shown in table 3–49.[22] Words with four or more syllables can be retrieved from *LessonPlanner's* Blending "Phonemes Spelled As" menu. Selections can then be brought over to Decoding from Other Sources.

Table 3–49. Accenting hints 4 and 5

Accenting hint 4

Accent the syllable immediately *before* suffixes beginning with **i** (ity, ic), including those where **i** is pronounced /y/ (ian, iel, ier, ial), *before* connective **i** (flexibility), and *before* any suffix beginning with a /sh/ or /zh/ sound (tial, cious, tious, cian, cial, tion, and sion with both phonemes).

In **ep**/i/sode, the connective **i** *connects* two syllables; it helps to make words easier to pronounce.

flex'/i/**bil**/i/ty (hints 3, 5)
prag/**mat**/ic
ci/**vil**/ian
span/iel
fa/**mil**/ial or fa/**mil**/i/al
ep/i/sode (hints 3, 4)
spa/tial
ca/**pa**/cious
nu/**tri**/tious
e'/lec/**tri**/cian
com/**mer**/cial
de/ter'/mi/**na**/tion
vi/sion/<u>ary</u>
con'/ver/**sa**/tion/al

Accenting hint 5

In words of five or more syllables, secondary accents often occur on every other syllable away from the primary accent. The words to the right with more than four syllables were accented by first finding the primary accent (in bold) using hint 4, and then applying hint 5. Affixes and **C-le** syllables are usually not accented; Latin and Greek roots frequently are.

flex'/i/**bil**/i/ty'
e'/lec/**tri**/cian
deter'mi**na**tion
visionar'y
con'ver**sa**tional

Yet another way to retrieve words to which the third, fourth, and fifth accenting

---

[22] Eight accenting hints are presented in *30 Roots to Grow On—A Teacher's Guide for the Development of Vocabulary* (Murray and Munro, 1989). Only the first five, most important accenting hints are presented in this book.

hints apply, is to select them from the Decoding "word roots" menu.

Last Gigantic Review

For all intents and purposes, you and your students will now have developed excellent decoding skills. To secure and maintain them, it is important to review frequently, beginning with the smallest **cvc** words and gradually progressing to ever larger and more complex words. Over a period of several weeks the following word types should all be reviewed—those with each of the short vowels and all the digraphs, trigraphs, letter combinations, and phonograms (including **v-e**).

Additionally, words to which various spelling generalizations and rules apply should be included, beginning with the first generalizations learned (the double **f, l, s, z** and **ck, tch,** or **dge** generalizations) as well as the generalization governing soft and hard **c** and **g** in words.

All the suffixes and prefixes that have been introduced must be included as well as all phonetic homonyms that have been taught. **Scribal-o** should not be omitted.

Continuing to two-syllable decoding, review will include **C-le** words, more advanced letter combinations (sion, ture), phonograms, affixes, homonyms, word families. There should be an increase in focus on vocabulary development.

Be sure not to neglect words that require difficult or more advanced decoding techniques: for example, double-duty **g** or **k** words (jungle, tinkle); those containing **w** or **qu** followed by **a** (watch, quad), **ar** (war, quarter), or **or** (world); and words with the seemingly myriad of phonemes for **i**.

Include a variety of words to which the four Syllabification

Common Affixes from LessonPlanner

play**able**
haunt**ed**
snow**ing**
hit**s**
box**es**
slash**er**
great**er**
smart**est**
thank**ful**
yellow**ish**
smoke**less**
swift**ly**
agree**ment**
frank**ness**
foam**y**
around
abstract
advice
allow
antechamber
antibiotic
bequeath
beneficial
complete
connect
collect
co-author
correct
contraindicate
decide
demigod
discharge
engulf
exit
eject
eccentric
effective
extracurricular
forbidden
forefront
injection

Rules and the first five accenting hints apply. If you are reviewing Rule I, C/C words, then be sure to have words with a short vowel in each syllable and like consonants (muf/fin), words where the second syllable ends in **er** (ham/mer), those with a short vowel in each syllable and unlike consonants (cac/tus), words with a short vowel and **C-le**-syllable (bat/tle), words with a variety of phonograms in the first syllable and ending with **C-le** (mar/ble), those with a short vowel and **v-e** syllable (stam/pede), and finally, words with a phonogram and short vowel (seam/stress). The same applies to each of the four Syllabification Rule types. Rule II words are particularly important because of the inclusion of accented and unaccented open syllables.

Of equal importance in review are any and all of the prefixes, advanced suffixes and endings that have been taught, as well as Latin and Greek roots, and "confusables." Always be as comprehensive as possible in your reviews.

Preparation for Reading

In the published document written by the California Reading Program Advisory and California Education Commission on Teacher Credentialing, *Teaching Reading, A Balanced, Comprehensive Approach to Teaching Reading in Prekindergarten Through Grade Three* (California Department of Education, 1996b), the following statement is made:

> Research shows that children are naturally inclined to view words as holistic patterns, rather than pictures. The drawback to this approach is that learning to recognize one word as a picture offers no advantage toward learning to recognize the next. Toward developing children's word recognition abilities, it follows that among the first and most critical challenges is that of persuading children to go beyond

Common Affixes from LessonPlanner, continued

intercede
intramural
malpractice
misapply
outside
overcast
perceptive
postscript
prescribe
protest
recreate
secede
self-service
semicircle
subway
superscript
translation
undecided
underscore
nonfunctional

Advanced Suffixes and Endings from LessonPlanner

voy**age**
dress**age**
extern**al**
appli**ance**
tru**ancy**
serv**ant**
burg**lar**
moment**ary**
dict**ate**
priv**ate**
fa**cial**
absorbefa**cient**
fero**cious**
employ**ee**

this tendency. . . . Research shows that it is important for children to practice the phonics they have learned. It is therefore essential that the initial books that children read on their own be composed of decodable text.

The genuine and legitimate concern of whole language and other literacy and meaning-based proponents with the above statement is twofold. First, there is the question of whether it is advisable or even possible for teachers to "persuade" their students to go beyond their tendency to view words as pictures and instead apply and practice supposedly "boring" code-emphasis techniques and strategies. Second, there is the concern that phonics instruction with its initial use of controlled or decodable text diminishes the opportunity to develop an appreciation of "true" quality literature. Slingerland had the same concern for she, too, recognized the benefits of exposing children to rich literature that reflects the sound, rhythm, and flow of natural language as it is spoken, heard in speech, and written. Slingerland therefore developed techniques and strategies for teachers and students that combine the best of literacy-based reading instruction with phonics-based (code-emphasis) reading instruction. With appropriate preparation in *Preparation for Reading* and *Reading from the Book*, Slingerland teachers enjoy the freedom to use literacy-based texts, controlled (phonics) readers, or almost any text, to their best advantage. Slingerland's *Preparation for Reading* and *Reading from the Book* constitute the most significant adaptations of the original Orton-Gillingham approach.

Preparation for Reading follows *Decoding* in the Daily Lesson Plan Format. Recall that the smallest units of sight, sound, and feel—single letters—are presented first (in *Learning to Write*), while slightly larger units or graphemes—digraphs, trigraphs, phonograms, etc.—are presented next (in Visual Cards). In *Decoding*,

---

Advanced Sufffixes and Endings from LessonPlanner, continued

tun**nel**
confe**rence**
consist**ency**
respond**ent**
gas**eous**
vari**ety**
magni**fy**
con**fine**
quarant**ine**
erm**ine**
glor**ious**
spa**cious**
barbar**ism**
ign**ite**
favor**ite**
captiv**ity**
surv**ive**
nonexplos**ive**
reflect**or**
fact**ory**
poison**ous**
essen**tial**
Mar**tian**
quo**tient**
cau**tious**
seven**ty**
inconspic**uous**

Latin and Greek Roots from LessonPlanner

pro**ject**or
de**ject**ed
portage
de**port**ee
in**flex**ible
genu**flect**ion

are yet larger visual units—individual words. Within *Decoding* there is also a sequence that begins with the smallest word units—one-syllable **cvc** words—that gradually progresses to one-syllable words with affixes, two-syllable words, two-syllable words with affixes, and ultimately to decoding the most complex multisyllabic words.

In *Preparation for Reading*, the next larger visual units, phrases, are selected by the teacher from the students' required reading. This is an instructional time when students learn to read phrases to acquire meaning, where they have the opportunity to practice effective eye-span and initial, preparatory, oral reading skills, and where words from *Decoding*, within the phrases, are presented for recognition, comprehension, and for integrated practice to further strengthen recall. This is also a time to teach and learn concepts or expected meaning from the phrases. These may include the concepts of singular and plural, possession, the various uses of commas and other punctuation, tense, case, and so on. The purpose of *Preparation for Reading* is to prepare students to successfully read their daily reading assignments, the next and largest and most complex visual units, in *Reading from the Book.*

For the most comprehensive instruction in the Slingerland approach to reading, Slingerland teacher education is recommended. For background, techniques, and discussion of *Preparation for Reading* and *Reading from the Book*, Slingerland's *Books 2* and *3* are recommended.

Briefly, in *Preparation for Reading*, the teacher carefully selects six to eight phrases from the day's reading. The phrases are then printed on a blackboard, put on sentence strips and placed in a card chart, or printed on chart paper. After Visual Cards and *Decoding*, four steps are followed in *Preparation for Reading*, summarized and edited slightly from Slingerland's *For Uniformity in*

Latin and Greek Roots from LessonPlanner, continued

pre**dic**tion
ab**dic**ation
com**puls**ive
ex**pel**led
in**tract**able
at**trac**tive
insect**icide**
de**cis**ion
extro**vert**
ad**vers**ity
com**pend**ium
pendulous
in**spect**or
per**spic**acious
mono**gram**
autobio**graph**ical
per**fid**ious
federal
re**fer**ee
in**suffer**able
retro**grade**
pro**gress**ion
en**vis**ion
e**vid**ent
re**cede**
an**ces**tor
sub**mit**
missionary
tendency
con**curr**ently
dis**course**
souve**nir**
pre**vent**ative
e**voc**ative
vociferous
super**script**ion
scribble
de**cad**ent
casualty

Practices to be Followed by Staff Members of Summer School Sessions for the Introductory Courses[23] (Slingerland, 1977), as follows:

> *Latin and Greek Roots from LessonPlanner, continued*
>
> de**cid**uous
> con**duc**ive
> pro**duct**ive
> **capt**ivating
> ac**cept**able
> de**posit**ion
> im**pound**
> pro**gen**itor
> **gen**uine
> de**fect**ive
> putre**fact**ion
> ef**fic**acy

1. Keep pointer under the phrase and read aloud for child (children) to hear and see and then repeat . . . needed clarification for meaning should be given at this time; all phrases should be introduced in this way.

2. The teacher reads a phrase (at random) aloud for a designated child to find and read. Class repeats if correct. The teacher continues, giving many individual children the opportunity to participate in this important step.

3. The teacher gives the meaning only, a clue, and one child finds the phrase, underlines it with a pointer, and reads it aloud. The class repeats if correct. Who, what, when, where, why, how, how many, typify and guide the clues and questions used by the teacher to convey the meaning or concept of each phrase.

4. The children take turns reading phrases, with the class repeating.

The way Slingerland developed the four steps of *Preparation for Reading* was by observing how mothers enhance their children's language skills by using baby books. Corresponding to Step 1, a mother, or father, points to a picture in a book and names it (object, animal, person, place) such as "chair" or "cat." She/he then waits for the child to point and repeat the word named (chair or cat) before naming something else. As in Step 2, the parent goes back through the book, without pointing, and names the pictures on each page. The child then finds, points to, and names. Corresponding to Step 3, the parent gives a clue for what the child is instructed to find and name. He or she might say, "Find the one that says meow." Finally, as in Step 4, the child eagerly goes through the book naming each picture with the parent, aunt, big brother, or other capable reader as guide, teacher, and class, repeating the child's correct responses.

---

[23] Available only to Slingerland teacher-education staff teachers and directors. The Slingerland Institute, Bellevue, WA.

Reading from the Book

Reading from the Book comprises the largest and most complex visual units (phrases, sentences, paragraphs, pages, chapters, and more). It follows *Preparation for Reading*, and it is the portion of the visual lesson when students learn to perceive phrases and practice reading phrases and sentences with correct rhythm and understanding from new material. During *Reading from the Book*, students are reminded to read phrases to derive their meaning, i.e., for information that tells when, how, who, where, etc. Teachers, as in any effective reading program, help or guide their students not only with reading phrases and sentences, but also with techniques for reading and comprehending larger paragraph units. Anticipation of what specific paragraphs will convey is often based on the content of the first sentence that must first be carefully read, comprehended, reflected upon, and interpreted. As techniques for projection of thought are acquired, decoding and other skills are reinforced at the same time, as needed.

As students learn to read, meaning occurs in two key ways. In the first, text conveys a literal understanding of what the author has written, i.e., literal comprehension. In the second, reading involves what the reader brings to reading as an individual. It involves reflection for purposeful understanding related to why the reader is reading a specific text and determining, while reading, what the author intended to convey and whether the author's perspective is similar or dissimilar to the reader's. (For example: this selection is literary criticism.) This higher-order analysis and thinking process[24] is enhanced by reading fluency, which in turn, is enhanced by one's overall command of language, including vocabulary. In both *Preparation for Reading* and *Reading from the Book*, the ability of students to reflect, evaluate, synthesize, and analyze is improved with direct instruction in comprehension which is precisely what is so strongly recommended by educational researchers (California Department of Education, 1996b).

Briefly, *Reading from the Book*, like *Preparation for Reading*, has several steps that require teacher planning and guidance. In the first, the teacher structures oral reading for individual students to develop correct eye-span, phrasing, rhythm, etc. In the second step, students study and read aloud with the teacher providing guidance in decoding,

---

[24] For an interesting and enlightening discussion of thinking, analyzing, and asking questions beyond the level of merely finding facts, read Jane Healy's discussion, in *Endangered Minds: Why Our Children Don't Think*, chapter 13, on how to ask questions that require application, analysis, synthesis, and evaluation skills (Healy, 1991). You will be compelled to read the entire book!

phrasing, and comprehension. In the third and fourth steps, there is less teacher intervention and more independence on the part of the students. In each of the steps, it is important that students respond to carefully constructed questions that stimulate thought.

Preparation for Reading and *Reading from the Book* can be applied when teaching any subject that requires reading. This includes science, social studies, and word problems in arithmetic to name just a few. Other reading material may include student compositions, biographies, class anthologies, chapter books, poetry, reference materials, recipes, cartoons, emails and other correspondence, magazines, core works of non-fiction and fiction, technical documentation, household labels, environmental print, newspapers, read-alouds, trade books, and, yes, even comic books. In *Preparation for Reading* and *Reading from the Book*, grammar can be taught and reviewed easily, as suggested earlier. For example, students can be taught to identify parts of speech, figurative language, clauses, compound sentences, tense, number, the use of punctuation, and distinctions between sentences written in the passive and active voice. Students can also apply their decoding skills to improve reading fluency and overall reading comprehension, paraphrase what they read, develop stronger vocabularies through incidental and direct instruction, and identify the exposition, complications, conflict, climax, and denouement (resolution) in literature. In *Preparation for Reading* and *Reading from the Book*, students can be taught not only to answer questions but also to generate questions, which the *NRP Report* emphasizes as being of particular importance.

Quoting directly from *Teaching Reading, A Balanced, Comprehensive Approach to Teaching Reading in Prekindergarten Through Grade Three:*

> . . . the single most valuable activity for developing children's comprehension is reading itself. . . . Through reading, students encounter new words, new language, and new facts. Beyond that, however, they encounter thoughts and modes of thinking that might never arise in their face-to-face worlds. In the interest of their own greatest potential and fulfillment, all students should be encouraged to read as frequently, broadly, and thoughtfully as possible.

4
Auditory Presentations

What Are Auditory Presentations?

Auditory presentations begin with alphabet card practice and review and are followed by blending, spelling, and writing from dictation. Movement progresses from the smallest units of sound (phonemes), feel, and sight and progresses to the next slightly larger units, words for encoding or blending and words for spelling with the application of spelling generalizations and rules. The largest auditory or sound units include written phrases, sentences, and dictations that lead to the composition of paragraphs, essays, and so on, until the goal of independent writing mastery is achieved.

Phoneme Awareness

We now know from research that lack of phoneme awareness contributes to poor levels of literacy. In the IDA position paper entitled *Informed Instruction for Reading Success: Foundations for Teacher Preparation* (Brady and Moats, 1997), the following is stated:

> . . . a major problem for children with reading problems is that they have not yet attained adequate awareness of the sound structure of words. That is, they have insufficient phoneme awareness. . . . Complete awareness of speech sounds in words typically develops over a number of years. . . . This awareness gradually progresses to the individual speech sounds in words (i.e., phoneme awareness) (e.g., sheep has three phonemes).

Most Orton-based programs include considerable alphabetics instruction, including both phoneme awareness (PA) and phonics instruction. From recent research findings, however, PA is not taught as directly or extensively as it should be to be as effective as possible. It is thus recommended that literacy teachers carefully access whether and how they should or should not augment their teaching with more contemporary direct phonemic awareness skill instruction. One of the most comprehensive sources for such instruction can be found in the extensive work of Jane Fell Greene (Green, 1997) which includes textbooks, classroom instruction, compatible readers, teacher education, and teacher-trainer courses. Another educator who has adamantly taken to heart the importance of providing current research-based literacy instruction and is the developer of similar up-to-date teacher education and teacher-trainer courses is the author of *Teaching Our Children to Read: The Role of Skills in a Comprehensive Reading Program,* Bill Honig (Honig, 1996).

Phoneme awareness, usually defined as the understanding that spoken words and syllables are made up of sequences of speech elements, includes the ability to recognize the number of individual phonemes in words and syllables, the ability to distinguish the number of syllables within words, and the ability to hear and count the number of individual words in sentences. It also includes the ability to recognize rhymes, to create rhymes, to identify and substitute phonemes – graphemes at the beginning, end, and middle of words—and to blend words.

Auditory Cards

Auditory cards provide a time for students to practice with simultaneous auditory-kinesthetic-visual association phonemes that are put to functional use in acquiring skills of language (including encoding and writing). Auditory card introduction, review, and practice are essential in establishing the foundation for the sequential development of subsequent auditory presentations. It is also a time to lay the foundation for phonics instruction that focuses on phoneme – grapheme correspondences.

Once the name, key word, and sound of a grapheme have been introduced with visual cards in an Orton-based program, the same grapheme can be reviewed in auditory cards. The procedure for the presentation of auditory cards is essentially the reverse of how cards are presented visually. For example, with auditory cards the teacher asks, "What spells /h/ as in **house**?" The student's response is, "/h/ - **h**", while writing **h** on paper or, as in Slingerland, "**h**", while forming **h** in the air; then "house - /h/". The **h** card is then exposed visually to complete the simultaneous auditory, kinesthetic-motor, visual response. In most Orton-based programs, auditory card practice is done in oral and written review. Regarding the latter, the teacher instructs students to write, for example, what spells /k/ as in cat, /r/ as in wrench, or /b/, sometimes without naming a key word.

The purpose of auditory cards is to ensure automatic association from a given auditory stimulus for simultaneous auditory-visual-kinesthetic association. It is important to integrate your auditory card review with your blending, spelling, and written lesson. The difference between auditory and visual cards is primarily in the scope of what can be presented. Once decoding is introduced, the visual card pack will gradually become larger than the auditory card pack because students progress more quickly visually in decoding and reading than auditorily in spelling and writing. To see why this is the case, imagine a student decoding the word **beast**. He has three options for the pronunciation of **ea**, /ē/, /ĕ/, or /ā/. Now, imagine that same student attempting to spell **beast**. There are at least nine ways to spell /ē/—**e**, **e-e**, **ea**, **ee**, **ie**, **ei**, **i**, **y**, **ey**. The student must decide which would be the most logical from those he has learned. This narrows the choices somewhat, perhaps to **ee**, **ea**, **ie**, and even **ei**, but still the opportunity for error is greater than when trying to decode a word that is presented visually.

The visual task of decoding and reading is less difficult than the inner auditory task of spelling and writing, so expect to progress more slowly auditorily, while following fairly closely the same sequence for visual cards and decoding.

Refer to Appendix B for a comprehensive list of phonemes with corresponding key words and graphemes. This list, originally developed for *LessonPlanner*, should help teachers become more secure in the use of auditory cards.

Yellow Auditory Cards

Since the recommended scope and sequence for visual cards applies immediately to auditory cards, and we are not teaching precise techniques for use with either auditory or visual cards, we will move quickly to a discussion of what are referred to as Slingerland yellow cards.[1] Similar exercises are done in other Orton-based programs, but usually without visual yellow card reinforcement. Visual reinforcement is provided when students see their written responses on their papers. Slingerland developed the larger yellow cards for classroom use from Gillingham and Stillman techniques. In traditional Orton-based instruction, the smaller *Phonics Drill Cards* box includes yellow cards.[2]

---

[1] The Slingerland *Yellow Card Pack* for classroom use are comprised of either single 8" by 5" or 8" by 10" yellow cards. They are available from EPS.

[2] Gillingham Phonics Drill Cards are also available from EPS.

Yellow cards are introduced during instruction as soon as students learn that there is more than one way to spell a specific phoneme, especially for vowels, since vowels usually constitute the difficult part of spelling.[3] The purpose of the yellow card exercises is to help students make wise, educated, logical choices when trying to spell and apply correct graphemes for corresponding phonemes.

In using yellow cards, the teacher gives a phoneme, /k/ for example, without a key word, for students to name and/or write the different graphemes they have learned to spell that phoneme. In Slingerland, students name the corresponding graphemes, saying the key word for each, and giving the phoneme last (**c** - cake - /k/, **k** - kite - /k/, **ck** - jack - /k/). Then the teacher exposes the yellow card visually for the class to respond to in the order in which the graphemes are arranged on the card, for those that have been introduced or taught only. In other Orton-based programs, the teacher says, "What spells /k/?" The student echoes the sound and writes **c, k, ck, ch**, etc. while naming the letters as they are written.

Yellow Auditory Card Scope and Sequence

Usually, the first auditory yellow card exercise begins when students have learned the first three spellings for /k/ made with **c, k,** and **ck**. When the second phoneme for **ch** is introduced, /k/, then **ch** is added to the /k/ yellow card. Eventually, **que** and **qu** are also added, ordinarily one at a time. The same procedure is followed with all the yellow cards. In the following, they are grouped into phonemes spelled with consonants and consonant digraphs and trigraphs; short vowels and phonograms; long vowels, diphthongs, phonograms including **v-e**; **r-controlled** syllables or phonograms; and phonemes spelled with **C-le**.

Frequency and difficulty are determining factors in deciding how to sequence the multiple spellings (graphemes) for each phoneme. Adherence to the order for phoneme-graphemes should not be rigid for all the reasons explained throughout this book, including whether instruction is to a class, to a small group, or to an individual student in tutoring. Other important factors include the age, maturity, motivation, and intelligence of the

---

[3] The first yellow card exercises that students usually do is not for a vowel; it is for the /k/ phoneme. Vowel yellow card exercises cannot begin until students learn more than one spelling for a vowel phoneme.

students—their grade level, prior educational experience, and the degree and type of learning disabilities they might have—in particular their auditory modality strengths and weaknesses.

How many graphemes you include on each yellow card will depend on the Orton-based program you use. Some programs strongly recommend limiting the number of graphemes to only those that constitute the most common spellings for each of the various phonemes.

Phonemes Spelled with Consonants, Consonant Digraphs, and Trigraphs

/k/ First, teach your students to respond with **c** (the most common spelling for /k/), **k** (often before **e**, **i**, or **y** to maintain the hard /k/ sound), and **ck** (immediately after one short vowel in one-syllable words); next, include **ch** (in Greek-based medical and scientific terms), then **que** (in French-based words), and finally, **qu** (also in French words). Some teachers combine **qu** and **que** by teaching them together and adding them to the yellow /k/ card in the following way: **qu(e)**. Determining how much of the parenthetical information you should give to your students depends on your sound judgment, and whether such information will enhance or complicate learning.

/s/ Younger students should respond with **s**, **ce**, **ci**, and **cy**, learned with key words. (A /s/ card is included in the EPS yellow card deck.) Older, more advanced students should say, "**s** - sun - /s/ and **c** - followed by **e**, **i**, or **y** says /s/." You might also want your students to write: **s**, **ce**, **ci**, and **cy** or **s** and **c** (**e**, **i**, **y**). For the latter, you must make a new yellow card. Next, you can have your students add **sc** and eventually **ps** and perhaps even **z** (or **tz**) as in **waltz**. These you must gradually add to the /s/ yellow card.

/ch/ Teach **ch** first, and then **tch** (immediately after one short vowel at the end of a one-syllable word). Eventually more advanced students will learn that **ti**, especially after an **s**, is pronounced /ch/. The **ti** is usually part of the letter combination **tion** (question), **tial** (celestial), **tian** (Christian).

/z/ Teach your students to respond with **z** and **s**. (**z** will be learned first, but is not as common as **s** for spelling /z/.) Include **x** (xerox) later.

/j/ Younger students should respond with **j** and **dge**; next, include **ge**, **gi**, and **gy**. The latter must be added to the EPS yellow card.

Older, more advanced students learn to say, "**j** - jam - /j/; **dge** - bridge (fudge) - /j/, comes directly (or immediately) after one short vowel at the end of a one-syllable word; and **g** - followed by **e**, **i**, or **y** *sometimes* says /j/." When writing their responses they should write: **j**, **dge**, and **ge**, **gi**, and **gy** or **g** (**e**, **i**, **y**). Students should also learn that **j** is not even close to being the most common spelling for /j/; **ge** is by far the most common. Also, **j** precedes the vowels **a**, **o**, and **u** more frequently than **e**, **i**, and **y** where **g** is the more common spelling. A frequent exception is found in words that contain the Latin root **ject** (rejection, projector).

In some programs the ligatures **du** (educate) and **di** (soldier) are given to more advanced students as additional ways to spell /j/.

/n/ First teach your students to respond with **n** and **kn**; next add **gn**; and finally **pn** (for more advanced students). It is recommended that **gn** and **pn** be added to the yellow card, but not to the hand pack.

/f/ First have your students respond with **f** and **ph**; later with **gh** (often spelling the /f/ sound at the end of words) as well. The latter must be added to the EPS yellow card.

/r/ Teach your students to respond with **r** (the most common spelling for /r/) and **wr** (found in words that pertain to twisting); and later add **rh** (in Greek-based, often scientific terms).

/g/ Your students should respond with **g** and **gh** (often spelling the /g/ sound at the beginning of words), first; later with perhaps **gu** (guest) and/or **gue** (league), as well. There is no /g/ card in the EPS yellow card deck.

/sh/ Teach younger children only the first two spellings for /sh/, **sh** and **ch**. Teach older, more advanced students several spellings for /sh/ in the following order: **sh**, **ch** (in French-based words), **ti** (the most common spelling for /sh/ partially because of its frequency in the letter combination **tion** as in na**tion** and elsewhere), and somewhat less frequently, **ci** and **si** (in **sion** especially), and far less common, **xi**, **ce**, **sch**, and **su**.

/m/ You must make an /m/ yellow card. It can be used once two spellings for /m/ have been presented. They could be either **m** and **mb** or **m** and **mn**. Eventually all three spellings will be on the /m/ yellow card. One additional infrequent spelling for /m/ is **gm** (phlegm).

/shən/ Another hand-made card is that for the two spellings of /shən/, **tion** and **sion**. Later add the frequently used **cian** (electrician, musician).

/y/ There are two spellings for /y/. They are the more common consonant **y** and infrequent **i** (mill**i**on). You will want to make a /y/ yellow card, particularly if you have a group of students who competitively relish such detail.

/w/ There are two spellings for /w/. They are the common **w** and the far less common **u** (suave). Since you teach the second spelling for /w/ at quite an advanced level, you might choose not to make a yellow /w/ card if your students are already familiar with most of the /w/ - **u** words. Remember, your yellow card exercises should be useful to your students, so if they do not need a particular card, do not make one for them.

/ks/ Although you will likely not want to have a /ks/ yellow card in your yellow card pack, you might, for a change and a challenge, require more advanced students to think about all the different ways /ks/ can be spelled at the end of words. Their responses should include the following: **x** (box), **cks** (shocks), **ks** (books), **cs** (picnics), **kes** (likes), **ques** (techniques), **ches** (aches), and **cts** (facts).

Phonemes Spelled with Short Vowels and Phonograms

/ĕ/ There are two common spellings for /ĕ/. They are **e** and **ea**.

/ĭ/ Two common spellings for /ĭ/ are **i** (in accented and unaccented syllables—never rely on **i**) and **y** (especially in multisyllabic Greek-based words). Far less common is **ai** (usually in unaccented syllables if not taught as /ĭn/ or /ən/ with **ain**). The least frequent /ĭ/ spelling is **ie** (in the unaccented syllables of **mischief, mischievous**—pronounced /**mis**-chĭv-əs/ and *not* /mis-chē-vē-əs/, **handkerchief, kerchief,** and in the one-syllable word **sieve**). Finally /ĭ/ is spelled with an **e** in some unaccented syllables as designated in more modern dictionaries. Unaccented **e** is often pronounced /ə/ as in **regard**, too. You can make your own yellow card for /ĭ/ if it seems appropriate for your students.

/o͞o/ Two spellings for /o͞o/ are **oo**, taught first, and **u** (as in pull), taught as a phonetic spelling much later. You can make your own yellow card if you have a class that responds eagerly to this type of reinforcement and review with yellow cards. Some teachers also teach /o͞o/ spelled as **ou** as in **would, could,** and **should**.

/ə/ In some dictionaries the diacritical notation for **u** in unaccented syllables is the schwa, /ə/. Perhaps in earlier times people could distinguish the difference between /ŭ/ and /ə/ pronunciations in speech, but rarely today. Therefore, you will want to teach advanced students to include the diacritical /ə/ to designate the unaccented phoneme spelled by **a** (as in cadet), **o** (as in polite), and **e** (in some unaccented syllables pronounced /ə/, as in regard, and not /ĭ/, as in sedan). When the /ə/ sound is heard at the beginning of words, it is most frequently spelled with an **a** (around, about, alone). A schwa at the end of words is often spelled with an **a** as well (drama, banana, panda). **U**, as /ə/ at the end of the unaccented first syllable of **supreme**, should be taught last, if at all, because of its infrequency. By the time your students understand unaccented syllables, you might not want to make an /ə/ yellow card, but you will want to do /ə/ exercises.

Phonemes Spelled with Long Vowels, Diphthongs, and Phonograms

/ā/ Although there are eight spellings for /ā/ on the EPS yellow cards, and the first spelling listed is the letter **a** (at the end of an accented open syllable), you can use the /ā/ card once you have taught **ai, ay,** and **a-e**. Just cover the **a** at the top of the card with your hand or a Post-it when you expose the card half with **a**, **a-e**, **ai**, **ay**, in that order.

Since you will not introduce **eigh**, **ea**, **ei**, and **ey** in a strict order, you can either cover or not cover the graphemes that have not been taught when exposing both halves of the /ā/ card, or you can make your own interim /ā/ card.

If you are working with more advanced students, you will soon teach /ā/ spelled with **a**, and eventually **et** and **é**. You can add the last two easily to your /ā/ yellow card.

In some Orton-based programs only half the yellow card is presented: **a**, **a-e**, **ai**, and **ay**. The other /ā/ spellings are not considered common enough to teach to SLD students.

/ē/   Although there are six spellings for /ē/ on the EPS yellow card, and the first spelling listed is the letter **e** (at the end of an accented open syllable), you can use the /ē/ card as soon as you have taught **e-e** and **ee**. Cover the letter **e** when you expose the card half with **e**, **e-e**, and **ee**, in that order.

Again, since you will not introduce **ea**, **ie**, and **y** in a strict order, you will need to cover up the graphemes that have not been taught or make your own interim /ē/ card. You may soon teach **e** and also add **ey** as spellings for /ē/, then eventually **ei** (as in c<u>ei</u>ling) and **i** (as in man<u>i</u>ac).

/ī/   Although there are six spellings for /ī/ on the EPS yellow card, you can use the /ī/ card once you have taught any two /ī/ spellings. These would likely be **i-e**, **igh**, **ie**, and/or **y**. The sequence for /ī/ on the EPS card is **i**, **i-e**, **igh**, **ie**, **y**, **y-e**. Teach **y-e** last or **ei** (as in Einstein) that you must add yourself.

/ō/   Do the same with the /ō/ card as you did with the other vowels. You will note that there are only five spellings for /ō/ on the ESP yellow card: **o** (at the end of an accented open syllable), **o-e**, **oa**, **ow**, and **oe**. If you want, you can add **ough** (although) as the sixth /ō/ spelling.

Once students have learned the open syllable spellings for the vowels **a**,

e, **i**, and **o**, it is important to impress upon them that when they are trying to recall the spellings for long vowels, they should immediately list the two that are the most common—the vowel itself (**a**, **e**, **i**, and **o** at the end of accented open syllables) and **v-e** (**a-e**, **e-e**, **i-e**, and **o-e**). Then they should try to recall the first phonograms that they learned. For example, in trying to recall the spellings for /ō/, if they had written **o** and **o-e**, they would then try to recall an early /ō/ phonogram and hopefully remember **oa**, the first phonogram likely learned. Eventually students should use the same strategy with /ū/ and /ōō/, as well. Another way to recall the first true phonogram taught for each long vowel phoneme is to think of the name of the long vowel and add a letter. If they think **a**, then recall for **ai** or **ay** may be triggered. For **e**, it would be **ee** or **ea**; **i**, **igh** or **ie**; and for **o**, three phonograms, **oa**, **ow**, **oe**, and perhaps **ough**.

/ū/ In all other instances when using EPS yellow cards, additions must be made when working in a continuum. Only on the yellow /ū/ card, is a deletion warranted since **ui** is usually not, in American English, pronounced /ū/ today. Thus, there are only five spellings for /ū/ although they are not easy to learn because they are less frequently used than the spellings for the other long vowel phonemes, and they are often confused with the similar and more common /ōō/ spellings. You can begin using the /ū/ yellow card as soon as you teach **u-e** and **ew** or **u** (at the end of an accented open syllable). The **eu** spelling for /ū/ is easily confused with the slightly more common **ue**, found at the end of words only. Complicating **eu** further, is the fact that many dictionaries do not represent **eu** with the /ū/ pronunciation. For amusement, check several dictionaries yourself.

/ōō/ As soon as possible you should teach your students to respond to the ways to spell /ōō/ by saying or writing the following: **u**, **u-e**, **oo** (the first phonogram usually taught with the /ōō/ phoneme), first, and then **ew**, **ou**, and **ue** in any order. (Some of the earlier EPS yellow card packs do not include **ue**; therefore, it must be added.) Later you must also add **ui** and **eu** to your yellow card once they are introduced; **ui** can be taught at almost any point, but you should be very careful not to introduce difficult **eu** too soon. You might also want to add **ough** (through) as another spelling for /o͞o/ with more advanced students. The EPS /o͞o/ yellow card that you must revise includes the following: **oo**, **ew**, **ou**, **u**, and **u-e**.

/ou/ There are two common spellings for /ou/. They are **ou** (at the beginning or middle of a word) and **ow** (at the end of a word (cow), when followed by a single **l** (howl), a single **n** (town), **el** (vowel), or **er** (tower), usually. You may add **ough** (drought) as another spelling for /ou/.

/ô/ There are also two common spellings for /ô/. They are **au** at the beginning or middle of a word (auto, launch) and **aw** at the end of a word (saw), when followed by a single **l** (awl), a single **n** (pawn), or single **k** (hawk). Additionally, there are **augh** and **ough** that spell /ô/, depending on how you teach the latter to more advanced students.

/oi/ There are two common spellings for /oi/. They are **oi** (at the beginning or middle of a word) and **oy** (usually at the end of a word or syllable).

Phonemes Spelled with R-Controlled Phonograms or Syllables

/ur/ There are several common spellings for /ur/ in accented syllables. They include **er** (the most common), **ir** and **ur** (the next most common), **ear** and **our** (less common), and **yr** (the least common). You must add **ear**, **our**, and **yr** to the EPS yellow /ur/ card when working with more advanced students. Note, too, that **ar** and **or** are included. Strictly speaking, they should not be since their phoneme is really /ər/, in an unaccented syllable, like the suffix **er**. In earlier days people could distinguish the sound /ur/ from /ər/ in speech. Today, the most we can say is that /ər/ represents the unaccented phoneme and /ur/ the accented phoneme.

Some teachers require advanced students to include **w** followed by **or** as another spelling to be added to the /ur/ card as **(w)or** (world), or **wor** (work). A preferable way to learn the phonemes for **w** followed by **a**, **ar**, and **or** is described next.

/ôr/   Teachers sometimes require advanced students to include **w** followed by **ar** to be added to the /ôr/ yellow card as **(w)ar** (warm) or **war**; and **(qu)ar** (quart) or **quar**.

From experimenting with many ways to teach **w** or **qu** followed by **ar** and **or** (also **a**), this teacher has found that both of the "choices" discussed earlier (see table 3–17. choices for teaching **w** and **qu**) are easy for students to learn if taught carefully. Students do remember either.

Yellow Card Exercises for C-le or Silent-e Syllables

/k'l/   There are three spellings for /k'l/. The most common is actually an extended suffix, **al** with the **c** usually included from the preceding suffix or ending **ic**, as in **music** changed to **musical**. Not all teachers treat **cal** in this way. They prefer separating **ic** from **al**. For those who treat **cal** as an ending, teach students how to differentiate between **kle** (usually at the end of two syllable words) and **cle** (usually at the end of words of more than two syllables except for **uncle**, **circle**, **chicle**, and **cycle**—but not bicycle, unicycle, and tricycle). It is helpful to note that words ending in **cal** are adjectives while **kle** words are usually nouns or verbs. Words ending in **cle** are most frequently nouns.

/f'l/   Because at times we truly are mush-mouthed Americans, students hear no differences in the phonemes for the **silent-e** syllable **fle**, the suffix **ful**, and the word **full**. Especially when spoken in sentences rather than individually, all three can be pronounced and sound the same. In isolation it is easier to detect that **full** is pronounced /fo͞ol/, and **fle** and the suffix **ful** are pronounced /f'l/ or /fəl/, respectively.

/s'l/   There are two spellings for /s'l/. There is the more common **stle** (whistle) and the infrequent **sle** (hassle).

Yellow Card Exercises for the Past Tense Suffix "ed"

/d/, /t/   The suffix **ed** has three phonemes: /ĕd/, /d/, and /t/. You can ask your students, "What are two ways to spell /d/?" The answer is **d** and **ed**.

You can also ask for the ways to spell /t/, **t** and **ed**, and, if taught, perhaps with caution, **bt**, **ght** and/or **pt**. Memorizing the following sentence, or one that you and your students compose, helps some students avoid confusion caused by **ed**: I jump**ed** into my rent**ed** boat and sail**ed** away.

A Yellow Card Exercise for the Suffix "ous" and the Noun Ending "us"

/əs/ The ending **ous** in the word **dangerous** and **us** in the word **campus** have the same /əs/ phoneme. The trick in knowing which to use when spelling is to remember that **ous** words are adjectives and that **us** words are nouns, usually. Therefore, when the adjective ending **ous** is removed, the base word should be readily detected as when **ous** is removed from **dangerous**, leaving **danger**. With words such as **famous** the task is a bit more difficult because the **e** in the base word **fame** was dropped (Silent-E Spelling Rule) when the **ous** suffix beginning with a vowel was added. The **e** must be replaced when the suffix is removed. Similarly, the **y** was changed to an **i** (Consonant-**Y** Rule) when the suffix **ous** was added to the word **victory** to form **victorious**.

Before teaching students to spell /əs/ words, it is beneficial to not only ask them to identify the two spellings for /əs/, but also to identify whether the words you want them to spell are adjectives or nouns. Of course, this implies that you have taught or reviewed parts of speech, at least. A list of **ous** words can be retrieved from the *LessonPlanner* Decoding panel in the "suf'x/end's" menu and brought over to either Blending or Spelling from Other Sources.

Here are some relatively common nouns ending in **us**: **bonus**, **cactus**, **circus**, **focus**, **minus**, **genius**, **census**, **sinus**, **octopus**, **stimulus**, **hippopotamus**.

Vowel Perception and Discrimination

In Orton-based programs, auditory card review prepares students for the more difficult tasks of encoding and spelling. As an interim step, some Orton-based programs also include excellent perception and discrimination exercises. The vowel perception exercise can be introduced as soon as several consonants and the first vowel have been taught; the vowel discrimination exercise can begin after two vowels have been introduced.

In an example of an early Slingerland vowel perception exercise, the teacher names a word with short-**a** (**shack**); the student repeats the word (**shack**), gives the vowel sound or phoneme, /ă/, and then names the **a**, while writing **a** in the air. This exercise typically includes several short-**a** words.

In *LessonPlanner*, words for perception can be retrieved from the "Phoneme Spelled As" menus in Blending or from the "1 Syllable" short vowel menus in Decoding that can be brought over to Blending from Other Sources.

In an example of a Slingerland vowel discrimination exercise, the teacher includes words with the next vowel taught, **i**, as well as **a** for students to discriminate between /ă/ - **a** and /ĭ/ - **i**. What is particularly appealing about sound discrimination is that it focuses on the most difficult part of spelling, the vowel sound and the spelling of that sound.

Later, other sound discrimination exercises are equally beneficial for reinforcing spelling generalizations and rules. For example, you can have your students identify only the final sound /j/ in words, and then the corresponding correct spelling, either **dge** or **ge**, to reinforce the generalization that **dge** comes directly after one short vowel at the end of a one-syllable word (**bridge/fudge**) while **ge** comes after a consonant (**large**), after more than one vowel (**gouge**), after a long vowel sound (**huge**), or after one short vowel in a multisyllabic word (**refrigerator**). If the teacher names **bridge**, the student says, "**bridge** - /j/ - directly (or immediately) after one short vowel - **dge**."

If the teacher then says **large**, the response should be, "**large**, /j/ - after a consonant or the phonogram **ar** (or **r-controlled** syllable) - **ge**."

In *LessonPlanner*, words for perception and discrimination can be retrieved from the "Phoneme Spelled As" menus in Blending. The first phoneme listed in *LessonPlanner* is /b/ as in **[b]all** and is useful if you want a list of words with /b/ spelled with **b**. The second or next phoneme is /k/ with six corresponding graphemes: **[c]ake, [k]ite, ja[ck], [Ch]ristmas, uni[que]**, and **[qu]iche**. One of the first discrimination exercises with /k/ might be with **c, k**, and **ck** words to reinforce the following spelling generalizations: **ck** comes directly after one short vowel at the end of a one-syllable word; **k** is often used before **e, i**, and **y** to maintain the hard /k/ sound (**kettle, kitchen, frolicky**); and **c** is the most common spelling for /k/, particularly as part of a blend (**clap, crush, fact**). Later you might wish to add /k/-**ch** words and the generalization that they are typically Greek-based and scientific (**chemistry, chemotherapy**) or artful French **que** words (**unique, boutique**). Later, you could compile a list of multisyllabic words that end in **ic** (**historic, arithmetic**), and a list of one-syllable words that end in vowel-**ck** (**heck, struck**).

Usually much work with vowel discrimination, including that with phonograms and **v-e**, is done before the exercises described above are included. Work with phoneme-grapheme discrimination helps bring sense to the ambiguities of spelling; therefore, the auditory yellow cards that focus on ambiguous spellings are invaluable as a resource for creating limitless discrimination exercises.

The Auditory Card Tables

If you are introducing letters in *Learning to Write*, you may prefer to use the manuscript or auditory sequences provided in the text and tables of Chapter 2, *Handwriting*. Otherwise, use the following tables, beginning with table 4–1 and continuing through table 4–7, which were derived and adapted from the manuscript and cursive grapheme tables in Chapter 3, *Visual Presentations*, for first, second, and third grade and above, for the introduction of visual cards.

The following auditory card sequence can be adapted for instruction to non-SLD and SLD students in the second grade and above, except where noted otherwise. The tables provide a slightly different sequence to emphasize the importance of being flexible about how and when to introduce new phoneme – graphemes as preparation for encoding and spelling. Your best guide for what to do auditorily is determined initially by the progress your students are making visually. Soon your students' visually presented work will outpace what they are doing auditorily because of the increase in the number of choices they must make in spelling.

A Quick Review of Auditory Card, Perception, Discrimination, and Yellow Card Techniques

Referring to table 4–1 for individual phoneme – grapheme auditory cards, imagine yourself beginning by asking your students, "What spells /l/ (as in lamp)?" The response will vary slightly depending on which Orton-based program is being used. After teaching the phoneme – graphemes on the left side of the table, include the exercises on the right side, as needed.

Table 4–1. First Pho-neme-Graphemes

/l/-**l**, /h/-**h**, /k/-**k**, /b/-**b** or /f/-**f**	
/ă/-**a**	As soon as **a** is introduced, include an /ă/-**a** (consonant) perception exercise.
/b/-**b** or /f/-**f**	
/k/-**c** and /g/-**g**	Include a /k/ - /g/ discrimination exercise, especially if students have difficulty distinguishing between the similar phonemes /k/ and /g/.
/d/-**d**, /t/-**t**, /ĭ/-**i**, /s/-**s**, /r/-**r**, /j/-**j**	Include an /ĭ/-**i** perception exercise first and then an /ă/-**a** (consonant) with /ĭ/-**i** (consonant) discrimination exercise.
/d/-/b/, /t/-/d/, /g/-/k/, etc.	Include several other discrimination exercises to prevent confusions.
/k/-**ck**	First yellow card exercise with /k/- **c**, **k**, **ck**.
/w/-**w**, /p/-**p**, /ŭ/-**u**	Remember to include /ŭ/-**u** perception on the day /ŭ/-**u** is introduced.
	Include a variety of discrimination exercises, such as:
	/ă/-**a** (consonant) with /ŭ/-**u** (consonant)
	/ĭ/-**i** (consonant) with /ă/-**a** (consonant)
	/ŭ/-**u** (consonant) with /ĭ/-**i** (consonant)
	/ă/-**a** (consonant) with /ŭ/-**u** (consonant) and with /ĭ/-**i** (consonant)
/sh/-**sh**, /ch/-**ch**	Possible /sh/-/ch/ discrimination.
/hw/-**wh**, /~~th~~/-**th** or /th/-**th**, /z/-**s**	/hw/-**wh**, /~~th~~/-**th** and/or /th/-**th** discrimination
/ŏ/-**o**	/ŏ/-**o** perception and then discrimination with other vowels
/kw/-**qu**	
/th/-**th** or /~~th~~/-**th**	/f/-/th/ discrimination
/ch/-**tch**	/ch/-**ch** and **tch** yellow card to aid students in learning when to choose **ch** versus **tch**
/f/-**ph**	/f/-**f** and **ph** yellow card
/n/-**n**, /m/-**m**, /v/-**v**, /y/-**y**, /z/-**z**, /ĕ/-**e**	/ĕ/-**e** perception and then discrimination with previously taught vowels

Table 4–1. First Pho-neme-Graphemes, continued		a /z/-**z** and **s** yellow card and perhaps /s/-/z/ discrimination
		perhaps /f/-/v/ discrimination
	/n/-**kn**	a /n/-**n** and **kn** yellow card
	/ō/-**oa**, /ē/-**ee**	
	/ā/-**ai** and **ay**	an /ā/-**ai** and **ay** yellow card
		a /d/-**d** and **ed** yellow card especially before spelling regular and irregular past tense words
		a similar /t/-**t** and **ed** yellow card exercise
	/iŋ/-**ing**, /aŋ/-**ang**, /uŋ/-**ung**, /oŋ/-**ong**, /aŋk/-**ank**, /iŋk/-**ink**, /uŋk/-**unk**, /oŋk/-**onk**, and /eŋ/-**eng** possibly or later	

For the first vowel discrimination exercise, once the second vowel has been introduced, name words that contain /ă/ and /ĭ/, and have your students follow the same steps as described in the previous paragraph for perception. Remember, discrimination exercises for phonemes include only those for which specific sounds have been introduced individually first. For example, you cannot discriminate between /ă/ and /ĭ/ until both /ă/ and /ĭ/ have been introduced individually.

For the first yellow card exercise, give the sound /k/ for a student to tell you about and/or write all the ways introduced to date for spelling /k/. It is advisable to include a yellow card exercise whenever a new option for how to spell a specific phoneme is added. In brief, as your students are taught new "options" for spelling, the burden for how to make the correct choice increases. Thus, as a responsible teacher you must provide considerable yellow card practice and review for success to ensue.

The auditory card tables show when individual phoneme – graphemes can be reviewed and where perception, discrimination, and yellow card exercises can best be applied. Auditory card tables also provide a nice review of the sequence for the introduction of visual-auditory and auditory-visual cards.

Although perception, discrimination, and yellow card exercises provide excellent preparation for encoding and spelling, they should not be done every day. Perception practice is particularly important as new phoneme-graphemes are introduced. Discrimination practice prevents difficulty in encoding and spelling when new phoneme-graphemes are introduced that can be easily confused with one (or more) that were introduced earlier.

Yellow card exercises are beneficial as new phoneme-graphemes are introduced and before encoding and spelling that require students to focus on one phoneme and the correct grapheme spelling in different word types. Again, do not overdo perception, discrimination, and yellow card practice and review.

Toward the end of the first month and beginning of the second, additional discrimination exercises may include:

/ŏ/-**o** (consonant) with /ă/-**a** (consonant) and /ŭ/-**u** (consonant);

/ĭ/-**i** (consonant) with /ŏ/-**o** (consonant) and /ă/-**a** (consonant);

/ŭ/-**u** (consonant) with /ŏ/-**o** (consonant), /ĭ/-**i** (consonant) and
/ă/-**a** (consonant).

Continuing on table 4–2, note that the auditory card review becomes increasingly difficult. In subsequent tables the word **consonant** will not follow the short vowels, but it should be understood that short vowels are usually followed by at least one consonant to form closed syllables. In some Orton-based programs, when responding to auditory or visual cards for the first vowels that are introduced, students include the word **consonant**. In visual cards they respond to an exposed card by saying, for example, the vowel name (**a**) plus **consonant**, the key word (apple), and then the phoneme (/ă/). With auditory cards they respond to the phoneme pronounced by their teacher, (/ă/), with: "**a-consonant** - apple - /ă/.

Use the procedures described immediately before table 4–1, for the use of individual auditory cards, for perception and discrimination, and for yellow card exercises.

At this point, as shown in table 4–3, you will do fewer perception exercises but more yellow card exercises as the number of spelling choices increases and becomes more complex and burdensome. How many discrimination exercises you include depends on how much difficulty your students have discriminating between and among phonemes. Include the exercises on the right side of the table after the phoneme-graphemes have been introduced from the left of the table, as needed.

Table 4–2. Phoneme-Graphemes for First Trimester	/r/-**wr**	possible /r/-**r** and **wr** yellow card now that students have two choices for spelling /r/
		possible /s/-**s** and /z/-**s** discrimination for plurals and third person singular
		discrimination for /s/ and/or /z/-**s** at the end of words versus /ĕz/-**es** after sibilants /s/, /z/, /x/, /ch/, and /sh/ to determine whether to use **s** or **es** for plurals or third person singulars
	/n/-**gn**	a /n/-**n**, **kn**, **gn** yellow card
	/g/-**gh** or /f/-**gh**	a /f/-**f**, **ph**, **gh** or /g/-**g** and **gh** yellow card exercise
	/j/-**dge**	a /j/-**j** and **dge** yellow card
		/ch/-/sh/ or /j/ discrimination if these are difficult phonemes for your students
	/m/-**mb**	perhaps an /m/-**m** and **mb** yellow card
	/m/-**mn**	and/or /m/-/n/ discrimination
		an /m/-**m**, **mb**, **mn** yellow card
	/f/-**gh** or /g/-**gh**	
	/k/-**ch**	/k/-**c**, **k**, **ck**, **ch** yellow card exercise
	/ā/- **a-e**	/ā/-**ai**, **ay**, **a-e** yellow card in preparation for spelling
	/ē/- **e-e**	/ē/-**ee** and **e-e** yellow card (plus **y** if taught as a suffix)
	/ī/- **i-e**, /ō/- **o-e**	/ō/-**oa** and **o-e** yellow card to aid with spelling **oa** and **o-e** words
	/ū/- **u-e** or /o͞o/- **u-e**, /shən/-**tion**, /shən/-**sion** or /zhən/-**sion**	possible /shən/-**tion** and **sion** yellow card and /shən/-/zhən/ discrimination and/or /ū/-/o͞o/ discrimination
	chər/-**ture**, /o͞o/-**oo** or /o͝o/-**oo**, /ou/-**ou**, /o͞o/-**u-e** or /ū/-**u-e**, /zhən/-**sion** or /shən/-**sion**	an /o͞o/-**oo** and **u-e** yellow card
	/är/-**ar**, /ŭ/-**scribal-o**	/ŭ/-**u** and **scribal-o** yellow card

Table 4–3. Phoneme-Graphemes for the Second Trimester or Beyond

/sh/-**ch**	/sh/-**sh** and **ch** yellow card (with **su** if students have learned that **su** spells /sh/ as in sugar and sure) Include exercises for discrimination between long and short vowel phonemes. Examples: between /ă/ versus /ā/ or /ŏ/ and /ō/
/t'l/-**tle** and /p'l/-**ple** (with auditory cards)	
/b'l/-**ble**, /d'l/-**dle**, /g'l/-**gle**, /ɪ'l/ -**zle** (usually not with cards)	many discrimination exercises with **C-le** syllables
/k'l/-**kle** (usually at the end of two-syllable words) and /f'l/-**fle** (not to be confused with the word **full** or the suffix **ful**)	/f'l/-**fle**, **ful**, and **full** discrimination and yellow card exercise although the phonemes are not exactly the same
/ī/- **y-e**	possible /ī/- **i-e** and **y-e** yellow card exercise with more advanced students (including **y** when students learn that **y** spells /ī/ in small words such as my, shy, and try)
/oi/-**oi** and **oy**	an /oi/-**oi** and **oy** yellow card exercise in preparation for blending now that your students have two spellings for /oi/
/ī/-**igh**	/ī/- **i-e**, **igh**, **y-e**, **y** yellow card
/ou/-**ow** or /ō/-**ow**	/ō/-**oa**, **o-e**, **ow** yellow card
/ī/-**ie** or /ē/-**ie**	/ī/- **i-e**, **igh**, **y-e**, **ie**, **y** yellow card
/ē/ or /ī/-**ie**	/ē/- **e-e**, **ee**, **y**, and **ie** yellow card
/ō/ or /ou/-**ow**	/ou/-**ou** and **ow** yellow card
/ā/-**ey** or /ē/-**ey**	possible /ā/-**ai**, **ay**, **a-e**, and **ey** or /ē/-**ee**, **e-e**, **y**, **ie**, and **ey** yellow card exercises
/s/-**c** (e, i, y)	/s/-**s** and **c** followed by **e**, **i**, and **y** yellow card (With less capable students, teach **ce**, **ci**, **cy** separately.)

Table 4–3. Phoneme-Graphemes for the Second Trimester or Beyond, continued	/j/-**g** (e, i, and y-sometimes)	/j/-**j**, **dge**, and **g** followed by **e**, **i**, **y** yellow card (With less capable students, teach **ge**, **gi**, **gy** separately.)
	/ā/-**a**, /ē/-**e**, /ī/-**i**, /ō/-**o** (Each vowel phoneme is at the end of an accented syllable.)	
	/ā/-**a**, **a-e**, **ai**, **ay**, **ey**; /ē/-**e**, **e-e**, **ee**, **y**, **ey**, **ie**; /ī/-**i**, **i-e**, **y**, **y-e**, **igh**, **ie**; /ō/-**o**, **o-e**, **oa**, **ow**	Note that the yellow card graphemes representing long vowel phonemes are now given a more consistent and logical order.

As you present phoneme-graphemes to a third grade continuum SLD class, it is especially important that you present the more logical sequence for long vowel graphemes noted at the end of the foregoing table, depending, of course, on the recommendations in your own program.

As you move along from level to level, pacing is crucial. When students learn the first spelling for /ʉr/ (table 4–4), spelling dictated /ʉr/ words in phrases and sentences should be relatively simple. When one or more additional spellings for /ʉr/ are introduced, then the task is more difficult and requires more practice, review, and horizontal learning than new, vertical learning. Proceed cautiously and review constantly. Include the exercises on the right side of the table after the phoneme-graphemes have been introduced from the left of the table, as needed.

Table 4–4 ends with the /ū/-/o͞o/ phonemes and table 4–5 begins with /o͞o/-/ū/. By far, the /o͞o/-**eu** or /ū/-**eu** spellings are the most difficult. Because they *are* difficult, teachers sometimes avoid them. One reason is that students and teachers alike often find that discriminating between /ū/ and /o͞o/ is just plain hard. Another reason is that their spellings are similar visually; **ew** and **eu** are similar in printing and in cursive. Adding to the confusion, **eu** and **ue** are the reverse of each other, and the dictionary often does not recognize the pronunciation of **eu** as /ū/. What is a poor distraught teacher to do? Be patient, introduce new /ū/-/o͞o/ spellings slowly, and review frequently. Include the exercises on the right, as needed.

In table 4–1 through table 4–5, you will note additional yellow card and discrimination exercises that were not described in the text preceding the tables. It is easy and fun to include a variety of such exercises. Certainly, you will devise discrimination and yellow card exercises of your own once you and your students begin to recognize, enjoy, and reap the benefits. Include the exercises on the right, as needed.

Table 4–4. Phoneme-Graphemes for Third Grade and Above	/ôr/-**or**, /ā/-**eigh**	an /ā/-**a, a-e, ai, ay, ey, eigh** yellow card
	/ur/-**er**, /ur/-**ur**, /ur/-**ir**	an /ur/ yellow card
	/ē/-**ea**, /ā/-**ea**, or /ĕ/-**ea**	/ē/-**e, e-e, ee, ea, y, ie, ey** and /ā/-**a, a-e, ai, ay, ey, eigh, ea** yellow card; or /ĕ/-**e** and **ea** yellow card
	/ô/-**au** or /ô/-**aw**	
	/ā/-**ea**, /ĕ/-**ea**, or /ē/-**ea**	an /ē/, /ā/, or /ĕ/ yellow card exercise that includes **ea**
	/ô/-**aw** or /ô/-**au**	an /ô/-**au** and **aw** yellow card
	/ū/-**ew** or /o͞o/-**ew**, /ū/-**ue** or o͞o-**ue**	a /ū/-**u-e** and **ue** yellow card or /o͞o/-**u-e**, **oo, ew** yellow card exercise
		a /s/-**s** and **c** followed by **e, i** and **y** yellow card
		a /j/-**j, dge**, and **g** followed by **e, i** and **y** yellow card exercise
	/o͞o/-**ew** or /ū/-**ew**	/o͞o/ or /ū/ yellow card that now includes **ew** and **ue**
	/ū/-**u** or /o͞o/-**u**	/ū/ or /o͞o/ yellow card to which **u, ew**, and **ue** are added
	/ĭ/-**y**	an /ĭ/-**i** and **y** yellow card
	/ī/-**y** (at the end of an accented open syllable)	an /ī/-**i, i-e, y** at the end of an accented open syllable, **y-e, igh, ie** yellow card
	/ū/-**eu** or /o͞o/-**eu**	

Table 4–5. Advanced Phoneme-Graphemes for Third Grade and Beyond	/o͞o/-**eu** or /ū/-**eu**	an /o͞o/-**u, u-e, oo, ew, ue, eu** yellow card exercise and/or a /ū/-**u, u-e, ew, ue, eu** yellow card
		many /o͞o/-/ū/ discrimination exercises since they are so difficult
	/ər/-**or** or /ər/-**ar**	
	/ĭ/-**ai** and/or /ə/-**ai**	/ĭ/-**i, y**, and **ai** yellow card exercise

Table 4–5. Advanced Phoneme-Graphemes for Third Grade and Beyond, continued	/ər/-**ar** or /ər/-**or**	an /ʉʀ/-**er**, **ur**, and **ir** yellow card Discuss schwa /ər/ and /ʉʀ/ differences. Add /ər/-**ar** and /ər/-**or** to the /ʉʀ/ yellow card.
	/s/-**sc**	a /s/-**s**, **sc**, and **c** followed by **e**, **i**, and **y** yellow card
	/r/-**rh**	a /r/-**r**, **wr**, **rh** yellow card
	/k/-**que**	a /k/-**c**, **k**, **ck**, **ch**, **que** yellow card
	/g/-**gu** and/or **gue**	a /g/-**g**, **gh**, **gu**, **gue** yellow card
	/ā/-**ei**	an /ā/-**a**, **a-e**, **ai**, **ay**, **ey**, **eigh**, **ei** yellow card
	/ʉʀ/-**ear** and /ʉʀ/-**our**	/r/-/ʉʀ/ discrimination, and a yellow card exercise with /ʉʀ/ or /ər/-**er**, **ur**, **ir**, **ear**, **our**, and **or** and **ar** (in unaccented syllables) Review /ər/ versus /ʉʀ/.
	/ō/-**oe** and maybe /ōō/-**oe**	an /ō/-**o**, **o-e**, **oa**, **ow**, **oe** yellow card exercise possible /ōō/-**u**, **u-e**, **oo**, **ew**, **ue**, **eu**, **oe** yellow card
	/ōō/-**ou**, /ŭ/ or /ə/-**ou**	an /ōō/-**u**, **u-e**, **oo**, **ew**, **ue**, **eu**, (**oe**), **ou** yellow card perhaps an /ŭ/-**u** and **ou** yellow card
	/ōō/-**ui** perhaps /ĭ/-**ui**	an /ōō/-**u**, **u-e**, **oo**, **ew**, **ue**, **eu**, **ou**, **ui**, **oe** yellow card
	/s'l/-**stle**, /s'l/-**sle**	a /s'l/-**stle** and **sle** yellow card, and an /əst/-**est** and **ist** suffix yellow card
	/k'l/-**cle**	a /k'l/-**kle**, **cle** yellow card (including the ending **cal** if introduced)
	/jōō/-**du**, /chōō/-**tu**, /zh/-**su**, /ô/-**augh**, /ô/-**ough**	discrimination possible /ô/-**au**, **aw**, **augh**, and **ough** yellow card
	/ō/-**ough**, /ōō/-**ough**	an /ōō/-**u**, **u-e**, **oo**, **ew**, **ue**, **eu**, **ui**, **ou**, **oe**, **ough** yellow card

Table 4–6. Advanced Phoneme-Graphemes for Fourth Grade and Beyond	/ôl/-**al**, /sh/-**ti**, /sh/-**si**, /sh/-**ci**, /sh/-**xi**, /sh/-**su**, /sh/-**ce**, /sh/-**sch**	See foregoing discussion to decide the number of phonemes to teach for **ough** and **augh**. Another option is to use the /ôt/-**aught** and **ought** spellings. a /sh/-**sh**, **ch**, **ti** yellow card exercise first As the other spellings for /sh/ are gradually added, expand the /sh/ yellow card exercise with **si**, **ci**, **xi**, **su**, **ce**, and **sch**.
	/s/-**sc** and /s/-**ps**	a /s/-**s**; **c** followed by **e**, **i**, and **y**; **sc**; **ps** yellow card
	/n/-**pn**	a /n/-**n**, **kn**, **gn**, **pn** yellow card
	/ʉʀ/-**yr**	a possible /ʉʀ/ or /ər/-**er**, **ur**, **ir**, **ear**, **our**, **or**, **ar**, **yr** yellow card
	/ā/-**et** and **é**	an /ā/-**a**, **a-e**, **ai**, **ay**, **ey**, **eigh**, **ei**, **et**, **é** yellow card
	/ĭr/-**ir**, /ĕr/-**er**, /ē/-**ei**	an /ē/-**e**, **e-e**, **ee**, **ea**, **y**, **ey**, **ie**, **ei** yellow card
	/s/-**z**	a /s/-**s**, **c** (**e**, **i**, **y**), **sc**, **ps**, **z** yellow card
	/gz/-**x** and perhaps /z/-**x**	discrimination as needed
	/o͞o/-**u** and /w/-**u**	/o͞o/-**oo** and **u** yellow cards, a /w/-**w** and **u** exercise, and /o͞o/-/w/ discrimination
	/zho͞o/-**su** as a ligature (usual)	
	/ī/-**ei**	an /ī/-**i**, **i-e**, **y**, **y-e**, **igh**, **ie**, **ei** yellow card
	/ăr/-**ar**, /ĭ/-**ie**	an /ĭ/-**i**, **y**, **ai**, **ie** yellow card exercise an /ē/-**e**, **e-e**, **ee**, **ea**, **y**, **ie**, **ei**, **ey** yellow card
	/wŏ/-**w(a)** and /kwŏ/-**qu(a)**, /wôr/-**w(ar)** and /kwôr/-**qu(ar)**, /wʉʀ/-**w(or)**	Perhaps have students write 2 spellings for /wʉʀ/-**w(or)** and **were**. an /əs/-**ous** and **us** yellow card exercise
	/k/-**qu** (if not yet introduced)	a /k/-**c**, **k**, **ck**, **ch**, **que**, **qu** yellow card

Table 4–6. Advanced Phoneme-Graphemes for Fourth Grade and Beyond, continued	/ə/-**a** and /ə/-**o** at the end of unaccented, open syllables	an /ŭ/-**u**, **scribal-o**, **a** and **o** at the end of unaccented, open syllables—yellow card exercise
	/ĭ/-**e** and /ĭ/-**i** at the end of unaccented, open syllables	an /ĭ/-**i**, **y**, **ai**, (**ie**), **e** and **i** at the end of unaccented, open syllables—yellow card
	/ē/-**i** and /y/-**i**	another /ē/-**e**, **e-e**, **ee**, **ea**, **y**, **ie**, **ey**, **ei**, **i**, and /y/-**y** and **i** yellow card exercises

Be sure to constantly review by providing lots of yellow card and discrimination practice as noted in the earlier tables, beginning with table 4–1, as well as the later ones. Whenever you spot an area of difficulty in pre-spelling or spelling, check to see if additional work with perception or discrimination is required, or if additional focus on how to choose specific correct spellings, with yellow card practice, would be of benefit. Examples are shown in table 4–7. Include the exercises on the right side of the table after the phoneme-graphemes have been introduced from the left of the table.

Table 4–7. Phoneme-Grapheme Oddities for Advanced Students in Fifth Grade and Beyond	/ĭ/-**ui** and/or **ui**-/ə/	If not taught previously. Include yellow card exercises for /ĭ/-**i**, **y**, **ai**, (**ie**), (**ui**), **e** and **i** at the end of unaccented, open syllables, and/or /ŭ/-**u**, **scribal-o**, (**ui**), **a** and **o** at the end of unaccented, open syllable.
	/zhə/-**sia**	
	/th/-**th(e)** (where **e** changes **th** to /th/)	a /th/-**th**, **th(e)** yellow card exercise
	/ĭj/-**age**, /äzh/-**age**	possible /əb'l/-**able** and /əb'l/-**ible** suffix exercise or /ĭj/-**age** and /äzh/-**age** discrimination
	/g/-**gu** (guilt, guest)	a /g/-**g**, **gh**, **gu**, **gue** yellow card
	/j/-**di** (soldier) and /jōō/-**du** (educate)	a /j/-**j**, **dge**, **g** followed by **e**, **i**, **y** yellow card; and perhaps ligatures **di** and **du**
	/ē/-**eo** (people), /ĕ/-**eo** (leopard) and/or /ə/-**eo** (luncheon), and perhaps /jə/-**geo** (pigeon)	an /əl/-**al** and /əl/-**el** suffix/ending exercise
	/ēn/-**ine** (machine)	

Other phoneme-graphemes that you might want to include for discrimination with cards are: /ī/-**uy** (buy); /ē/-**ae** (algae) and /ĕ/-**ae** (aesthetic).

Additional suffixes or endings that provide excellent discrimination or yellow card work include: /ĭj/, /äıh/, /āj/- all spelled **age**; /əns/-**ance**, **ence**, and **ense**; /ənt/-**ant** and **ent**; /ē/-**ee** and **y**; /ĭtē/-**ity** and **ety**; and /āt/-**ate** and /ət/-**ate**. Locate additional advanced suffixes and endings for similar exercises in *LessonPlanner's* Decoding.

In *LessonPlanner*, words for perception, discrimination, and yellow card practice and review can be retrieved from the "Phoneme Spelled As" menus in Blending, and in Spelling from the "Rules/Gen's" menus (1-1-1; sil-e; cons-y; ext1-1-1; f,l,s,z; add-s; s,x,z,ch,sh-es; y->i; (v)o, add s; (c)o, see dict'y; f,fe -> ves; and irreg. plural) and from the Spelling panel "Special Words" menus (Sight Words, Homonyms, Confusables, Word Families, and Silent Letters). Words for perception, discrimination, and yellow card exercises can also be retrieved in Decoding from the "1 Syllable" short vowel menus or from several other Decoding "1 or >2 Syllable" word menus (di/tri, phono, l.comb, not 1-1-1, soft c;g, suf'x/end's, and word roots). Similarly, in the two Syllable, Rules I, II, III, and IV word menus, a variety of word types can be retrieved. Words from Decoding must then be brought over to Blending from the Other Sources menu.

Scope and Sequence for Encoding and Spelling

Throughout this book I have mentioned both encoding and spelling—two terms that are often confused. Strictly speaking, "encoding" is a subcategory of "spelling" that involves a process of combining sounds or phonemes together to spell phonetic words. If words are irregularly spelled, or in other words, cannot be sounded out by combining their phonetic elements, as with **laugh** and **yacht**, then the words must be learned as sight or learned words, using a different process, to *spell* them.

In English there are far fewer non-phonetic or sight words than we are led to believe. The way we have been misled is by not usually being taught the phonetic structure, morphology, spelling generalizations, and other rules that govern language and enable us to identify the etiology of words and determine whether they are phonetic or not.

Further confusion arises when we discuss *ambiguous* spellings. Ambiguous words, referred to as yellow flags in Slingerland, are phonetic but require making at least one spelling choice between or among their phonetic elements. For example, in the strictly phonetic word **had**, referred to as a green flag word in Slingerland, no choices are necessary when spelling it, for there is only one grapheme possible for each phoneme: /h/-**h**, /ă/-**a**, /d/-**d**. The word **has**, on the other hand, requires making a spelling choice between **s** and **z** for spelling the final /ı/ sound. **Has** may initially be presented as a sight word. Later it becomes a phonetic, albeit ambiguous spelling word, when the second phoneme for **s** - /ı/, is taught. The fact that a choice must be made is what makes **has** an ambiguously spelled (yellow flag) word.

Encoding Phonetic Words

Encoding begins when the first introduced consonants and the vowel **a** can be encoded to form phonetic, one-syllable words. When encoding begins, referring to the auditory card, phoneme sequence, beginning with table 4–1, is helpful. The first words used in encoding are the same or similar to those that are decoded first. When using *LessonPlanner*, it is best to initially select words from the one-syllable, short vowel pull-down menus in Decoding. Next bring your selections over to Blending—referred to as *encoding* in the textbook—from the Decoding "Other Sources." Only one-syllable short **a** words should be encoded until the techniques for encoding become automatic. The first words selected from the numerous short **a** options should follow the same specific sequence designated as those for decoding, beginning with the easiest type or pattern and continuing with more difficult patterns. See table 3–24 for decoding. The easiest are **cvc** words wherein the vowel sound /ă/ is spelled with **a** or **a-consonant** (a-) in a closed syllable. Further distinction can be made regarding the difficulty of the first consonant in **cvc** words.

As discussed previously, some educators feel that a phoneme spelled with a stop sound consonant is more difficult than one with a continuous consonant sound. A continuous sound can be pronounced and maintained for several seconds without distorting its sound; whereas, a stop sound can be pronounced or enunciated only for an instant. Initially, you might want to avoid stop sounds in encoding with very young children or those who are language disabled. (Refer to page 79.)

Most of the following tables in this chapter were derived and adapted from the decoding tables in Chapter 3, *Visual Presentations*, intended for students in the third grade and above, and from selecting sample words from the Blending menus in *Lesson-*

Planner. The following encoding sequence can be used before the third grade with non-SLD students and classes.

Differences in Encoding Techniques

It is important that the letters your students use in encoding have been taught in handwriting. With regard to the techniques used for encoding, in most Orton-based programs, at the beginning, a student repeats the word to be encoded that the teacher dictates and then encodes the word sound by sound. If the word is **ham**, the student says, "**ham**" and then "/h/-**h**, /ă/-**a**, /m/-**m**" before writing it. In some programs the sound of each letter is not given first, and in other programs, letter cards or tiles are used at the beginning. In the Slingerland approach, a chart holder with small alphabet cards is used initially. After a student repeats a word to be encoded (**ham**), he or she gives the vowel sound (/ă/) before naming the vowel (**a**) while simultaneously forming the letter (**a**) in the air with an arm swing. Then the student returns to the beginning of the word and sounds out the word from left to right using the same techniques described first for encoding **ham**.

Slingerland recommends focusing on the vowel unit immediately to emphasize and tackle the most difficult part of a word in encoding or spelling. In most Orton-based programs, steps are gradually dropped so that when students encode they simply name their word "**slant**" and say "**s-l-a-n-t**" before and/or while writing it. In Slingerland, the student still, first, gives the vowel sound (/ă/) before naming the vowel (**a**) while simultaneously forming it in the air. See Slingerland's *Books I, II, and III* for the precise recommended steps for encoding and eliminating prompts.

In the sequenced lists in the tables that follow, sample words are included for most types of words. How and where to retrieve them (options) in *LessonPlanner* are noted. As with decoding, encoding resembles weaving, for one must constantly review words and concepts while carefully intertwining new concepts and word types for added texture, color, and enrichment.

In the tables that follow, when a second or third spelling for a particular phoneme is introduced, view it as a recommendation to guide your students carefully so that they will make informed choices independently when spelling ambiguous words. Other similar, but more obvious recommendations, visible from the tables or in the text immediately surrounding the tables, help you decide when to introduce suffixes and non-phonetic words, and when to teach spelling generalizations and rules. Incorporating new concepts should always be viewed in the context of putting them to functional use in phrase and sentence writing.

Table 4–8 shows the sequence for beginning encoding with cvc (- a -) one-syllable words, beginning with - a - words. In *LessonPlanner*, these may be initially selected from the one-syllable, short **a** pull-down menu in Decoding and brought over to Blending (encoding) from "Other Sources" and later from the "Phoneme (/ă/) Spelled As (**a-consonant**)" menu in Blending.

Table 4–8. Beginning Encoding with cvc (- a -) One-Syllable Words		
	- **a** - words	hat, fat, etc.
	- **a** - - words	cast (after **s** is introduced) and hand (after **n** is introduced)
	- **a** — words (with digraphs)	lash, hack (after the **ck** generalization has been taught)
	- - **a** — words	slap, flag
	— **a** - words (with digraphs)	shag, that
	- - **a** - - words (with digraphs)	clasp, grant, whack (when **wh** has been introduced)
	- - - **a** - or - - - **a** — words	sprat, scrap, splash
	Include words that begin with the recently introduced vowel **a**.	am, ant
	Include words with **x** having two consonant sounds—/k/ and /s/, /ks/, and **s** with two phonemes—/s/ and /z/.	tax, has, claps

Teach the **ck** spelling generalization early. (See Chapter 3 for a **ck** discussion and sidebar.) For a list of one-syllable words ending in **ck**, or containing **sh**, **ch**, or **th**, select from *LessonPlanner*'s one-syllable, di/tri pull-down menu in Decoding and bring them over to "Blending" from "Other Sources." Otherwise such words can be retrieved from the "Phoneme Spelled As" menus in Blending (back, deck, kick, lock, luck).

At about this time, the first suffix, **ing**, should be taught for spelling with concept.

Conceivably teach the first non-phonetic (red flag, sight, or learned) word. See techniques described in *Spelling Phonetic, Ambiguous, and Non-Phonetic Words* beginning on page 166. Choose one from the following, based on need, for phrase and sentence writing: **a**, **was**, **want**, **what**, perhaps **any**, with caution, and **have** or **been** if **e** has been taught for writing. Non-phonetic words in *LessonPlanner* are located in Spelling in the Sight Word menus. They include Basic I, II, III and Red Flag words.

Write phrases and perhaps a sentence to put to use words that were previously encoded and spelled. This may require prior instruction of capital letters and punctuation.

Discriminating Between the Phonemes /ă/ and /ĭ/

As explained earlier, discriminating between the phonemes /ă/ and /ĭ/ is the easiest among the short vowels because there is more difference between their two sounds than between any other pair of vowels. (Short /ĕ/ and /ĭ/ are the closest in sound, and therefore taught as far apart as possible.) Also, there is a greater difference in how /ă/ and /ĭ/ are formed and feel when enunciated that make them easier to differentiate, also.

Table 4–9 shows the sequence for encoding with cvc (- i -) one syllable words, beginning with **- i -** words. In *LessonPlanner*, these may be initially selected from the one-syllable, short **i** pull-down menu in Decoding and brought over to Blending (for encoding) from "Other Sources" and later from the "Phoneme (/ĭ/) Spelled As (**i-**)" menu in Blending.

The double **f**, **l**, **s**, and **z** spelling generalization should be taught in *Spelling* around this time, and included in encoding as reinforcement. Use one-syllable short **i** words ending in **ff**, **ll**, **ss**, and **zz** initially. In *LessonPlanner*, words of this type can be retrieved in Spelling quickly under Rules and Generalizations, designated as "f, l, s, z" and brought over to Blending from "Other Sources," or kept in Spelling.

The **tch** spelling generalization should be taught around this time, too. (See Chapter 3 for a discussion of **tch** and sidebar.) For a list of one-syllable words ending in **tch**, select from *LessonPlanner's* one-syllable, di/tri pull-down menu in Decoding and bring them over to Blending from "Other Sources." Otherwise **tch** words can be retrieved from the "Phoneme Spelled As" menus in Blending (match, fetch, itch, scotch, clutch).

After covering the material in table 4–9, continue teaching the first non-phonetic (red flag or sight) words per the subsequent discussion on "simultaneous oral spelling"

(S.O.S.) techniques. Choose one from the previous table, based on need, for phrase and sentence writing. Now that **i** has been taught, **said**, **give**, and **again** may be added. Write phrases and a sentence to put to use the words that have been encoded and spelled. This requires prior instruction of needed capital letters and punctuation.

Table 4–9. Encoding with cvc (- i -) One-Syllable Words	- **i** – words	big, lid, kid
	- **i** - - words	hint, silk
	- **i** — words (with digraphs)	fish, tick
	- - **i** – words	slip, brim
	— **i** - words (with digraphs)	chip, shin
	- - **i** - - words (with digraphs)	twist, chick
	- - - **i** - or - - - **i** - - words (with a digraph)	sprig, script, thrift
	with **i** at the beginning and with **s** - /z/	is
	with **x**	mix
	double **f**, **l**, **s**, and **z** words	sniff, grill, miss, frizz
	- **i** - — , - - **i** - — , or - - - **i** - - - words	finch, clinch, twitch, sprints
	Now mix one-syllable short **a** words with one-syllable short **i** words for discrimination. Adherence to the - **v** -, - **v** - - sequence need not be as strict.	raft, rift, brass, sixth, thick, scratch, snitch

Encoding Ambiguous and Phonetic Words

Words are not considered ambiguous until students have been given more than one choice for spelling each phoneme in the words they encode. For example, in table 4–8, the word **flag** is considered purely phonetic or green flag because **ph** had not been introduced. Once **ph** is taught, then the word **flag**, strictly speaking, becomes ambiguous. If a student has doubts about the spelling of a particular phoneme, the student should check with his or her teacher rather than guess. For example, with the word **kid** in table 4–9, the student should ask if the spelling for /k/ is **c** or **k**, at least. He might even ask if it is **ck** if he is not secure with the **ck** spelling generalization: **ck** comes directly after one short vowel at the end of a one-syllable word. You can see how important it is to include a /k/ yellow card exercise in preparation for encoding and spelling.

Be Careful About Nonsense Words in Encoding

In many Orton-based programs, it is adamantly recommended that nonsense or pseudowords *not* be included in students' encoding or spelling as they are in decoding and as discussed in Chapter 3. My personal recommendation is to select true syllables, instead of nonsense words, to encode and spell. While encoding basic **cvc** words, for example, include affix and root syllables that follow the **cvc** pattern (**dis**, **sub**) or **cvcc** pattern (**self**, **trans**), and so forth. These appear within real words (**dismay**, **subtract**, **myself**, and **transport**). Use your own favorite resources or create your own nonsense lists, if you use them at all.

Table 4–10 shows the sequence for encoding with **cvc (- u -)** one-syllable words, beginning with **- u -** words. In *LessonPlanner*, these may be selected from the one-syllable, short **u** pull-down menu in Decoding and brought over to Blending from "Other Sources" and later from the "Phoneme (/ŭ/) Spelled As (**u-**)" menu in Blending.

Table 4–10. Encoding with cvc (- u -) One-Syllable Words		
	- u - words	fun, tux
	- u - - words	bunt, duct
	- u — words (with digraphs)	rush, tuck
	- - u - words	smug, spun
	— u - words (with digraphs)	chug, thud
	-- u - - words (with digraphs)	chump, truck
	- - - u - or **- - - u - -** (with digraph)	crutch, thrust, thrush, struck
	- u - - -, **- - u - - -**, or **- - - u - - -**	dutch, brunch, scrunch
	with **u** at the beginning	us
	with **x**	flux
	with **s** - /z/	hugs
	mixed double **f, l, s,** and **z**	gruff, thrill, brass, frizz
	mixed **short a, i,** and **u**	jam, film, stuff, splash, scrimp, branch
	words with **suffixes**	bumps, drills, pumping, drilling
	Include digraphs and review continually.	**ck** - muck, brick, shack **sh** - ship, shack, lush **ch** - champ, lunch, chinch **th** - thus, width, than, thin

The plural and third person singular **s** ending should be introduced around this time, if not earlier.

Introduce the "doing" suffix **ing** in *Spelling* if not already introduced. Words with additional suffixes may be included for encoding. Use the pull-down suffix prompt menus in Blending (encoding), Spelling, or Decoding to help recall which suffixes have been introduced and can now be added to base words. Then type the new word into the User Entry window and add it to the Selections Blending list.

After covering the material in table 4–10, continue teaching non-phonetic words. Choose from the previous two tables or the *LessonPlanner* lists. Perhaps include **sure** and **says**. Write phrases and a sentence to put to use the day's encoded and spelled words. This requires prior instruction of needed capital letters and punctuation.

Encoding and Spelling Non-Phonetic and Phonetic Words

Non-phonetic or sight words, called red flag words in Slingerland, must gradually be woven into your word lists. They are usually introduced and reviewed in *Spelling*, and are included in the text following the blending (encoding) tables. They are mentioned here as a reminder that non-phonetic words must be woven into your plans just as phrases and sentences must be integrated into your written lessons.

Table 4–11 shows the sequence for encoding with **cvc (- o -)** one-syllable words, beginning with **- o -** words. In *LessonPlanner*, these may be selected from the one-syllable, short **o** pull-down menu in Decoding and brought over to Blending from "Other Sources" and later from the "Phoneme (/ŏ/) Spelled As (**o -**)" menu in Blending.

Teach the use of the apostrophe in contractions—first in *Decoding* and then in *Spelling*, and include additional non-phonetic words for spelling.

In *LessonPlanner*, non-phonetic words can be retrieved in Spelling from the Special Words menus. These include Sight Words, Homonyms, Confusables, Word Families, and Silent Letters. From the Sight Words, Basic 1, 2, 3, and Red Flag words can be retrieved.

The suffix **ed** requires special instruction because there are three phonemes for **ed**: /d/, /t/, and /ĕd/. In *LessonPlanner*, words with the suffix **ed**, pronounced /d/, and /t/, can be retrieved from the "Phoneme Spelled As" panel in Blending. The suffix **ed**, pronounced /ĕd/, can be retrieved by searching a variety of lists.

Table 4–11. Encoding with cvc (- o -) One-Syllable Words **- o -** words	hop, box
- o - - words	lost, romp
- o - - words (with digraphs and trigraphs)	jock, notch
- - o - words	smog, clot
— o - words (digraphs)	shot, chop
- - o — words (digraphs)	frock
- - - o - or **— - o - -** words (with a digraph)	phlox
- o — , **- - o —**, or	botch, blotch, off,
- - - o - - words, etc.	ox, throbs
1-syllable homonyms	in, inn
mixed double **f, l, s,** and **z** words for review	stuff, drill, grass, jazz, toss
mixed **short a, i, u,** and **o** words	jam, mist, stun, tromp
words with **suffixes** taught to date	tromp tromps tromping tromped (with care)

After covering the material in table 4–11, continue teaching non-phonetic words. Select from the previous tables or, when **o** has been taught, choose from the following as well: **of, who, one, once, only, does, come, some, gone,** and **move.** Require students to write phrases and sentences to put to use words that have been encoded and spelled. Do not overlook instruction of necessary capital letters and punctuation.

Table 4–12 shows the sequence for encoding with cvc (- e -) one syllable words, beginning with **- e -** words. In *LessonPlanner*, these may be selected from the one-syllable, short **e** pull-down menu in Decoding and brought over to Blending from "Other Sources" or from the "Phoneme (/ĕ/) Spelled As (**e -**)" menu in Blending.

The plural and third person singular **es** should be introduced around this time in *Spelling*, if not earlier, as well as the comparative and doer suffix **er**, the suffix **less,** meaning without, and the suffix **able,** meaning capable of.

Soft **c** and soft **g** words may be included soon after the vowel **e** has been taught to second grade continuum students or beginning third or fourth grade students. In *Lesson-*

Planner, use the pull-down "soft c; g" prompt menus in Decoding to obtain separate lists for **ce**, **ci**, **cy**, **ge**, **gi**, **gy** words. Then bring them over to Blending from "Other Sources." Perhaps begin only with **ce** and then **ge** as shown in table 4–12.

Table 4–12. Encoding with cvc (- e -) One-Syllable Words		
	- **e** – words	get, hex
	- **e** - - words	belt, kept
	- **e** - - words	heck, nest
	- - **e** – words	sled, stem
	— **e** – words	then, shed
	- - **e** - - words	crest, dwelt
	- - - **e** - or - - - **e** - - words	stress
	- **e** - —, — **e** - - -, or **e**— — **e** - - words, etc.	depth, wrench, elm, hex, sheds, drench
	review double **f**, **l**, **s**, and **z** words	staff, spell, moss, fuzz, kiss
	mixed **short a**, **i**, **u**, **o**, and **e** words	ham, list, wrap, quest (with care), splotch
	words with **suffixes**	stretch stretching stretches stretcher stretchless stretchable (advanced students) stretched (careful with **ed**)
	ce and **ge**	cent, cell, fence, thence, gent, gem, fringe, lunge

More sophisticated students might be told that **c** is the most common spelling for /k/, and that less frequently (25% of the time in words in which **c** appears) **c** has the /s/ pronunciation because it is followed by **e**, **i**, or, **y**. Here are three exceptions to **c** pronounced /s/ when followed by an **e** or **i** (**soccer**, **scena**, and **scinkadae**). Can you find more? On the other hand, **g** represents the /j/ sound with greater frequency than **c** as /s/.

Teach red flag words selected from the previous tables or from your own resources. After covering the material in table 4–12, continue writing integrated phrases and sentences.

Encoding One-Syllable Phonogram and Letter Combination Words

Once encoding is secure and several vowels have been taught, then encoding one-syllable letter combination and phonogram words can begin. Referring to the Manuscript Level I, Group II category in Chapter 3, for the introduction of graphemes with visual cards, note that the following graphemes are usually taught by the end of the first grade and included for encoding: all vowels except perhaps **e** and all consonants except perhaps **qu**; the phonograms **oa**, **ee**, and maybe **ai**, **ay**, **oo**, and **ou**; letter combinations **ing**, **ang**, **ung**, **ong**, **ink**, **ank**, **unk**, and **onk**; digraphs **ck**, **ch**, **sh**, **th**, and perhaps **wh**. In Cursive Level I, in the first trimester of a third or fourth grade, additional graphemes are usually taught that can be incorporated into encoding. These may include **wh**, **tch**, **kn**, **eng**, **ar**, **er**, **eigh**, **ey**, **a-e**, **e-e**, **i-e**, **o-e**, and **u-e**. More graphemes can be added for decoding one-syllable words than for encoding. The following are usually appropriate for either encoding or decoding: **wr**, and maybe **dge**, but **ph**, **gn**, **gh**, **mb**, **mn**, and **eng** should not be incorporated into encoding quite as quickly.

The techniques used for encoding words with phonograms and letter combinations are the same as that for encoding closed syllable, short vowel words. In most Orton-based programs, the student repeats and encodes the word from left to right. If the word is **soap**, the student says, "**soap**" and then "/s/-**s**, /ō/-**oa**, /p/-**p**" before or while writing it. In Slingerland, the student repeats the word to be encoded (**soap**), gives the vowel sound (/ō/) before naming the phonogram (**oa**) and forming the letters (**oa**) in the air. Then the student returns to the beginning of the word and encodes from left to right. Steps or prompts are gradually eliminated so that when students blend they may only name their word "**grain**" and say "**g-r-ai-n**" before and/or while writing. (Again, Slingerland students focus first on the vowel sound (/ā/) before naming the phonogram (**ai**) and simultaneously forming **ai** in the air. Then they encode across the word from left to right.)

At an early stage of encoding, when trying to decide which letter combination or phonogram to introduce next, ask yourself whether the phoneme-grapheme you have in mind is used frequently, if it has only one, easy grapheme possibility, if it occurs often in one-syllable base words, and whether it will not be too difficult for your students to learn. You should use the same type of questioning when deciding which digraphs and trigraphs to include.

Table 4–13 shows the sequence for beginning encoding with phonograms (**oa**). In *LessonPlanner*, these may be selected from the "Phoneme (/ō/) Spelled As (**oa**)" menu in Blending or from the one-syllable, phonogram pull-down menu in Decoding and brought over to Blending from "Other Sources."

Table 4–13. Beginning Encoding with Phonograms (oa)	**oa** phonogram words	soap (- **oa** -) toast (- **oa** - -) roach (- **oa** —) (with digraph) gloat (- - **oa** -) throat (— - **oa** -) (digraph) oats (**oa** at the beginning) coax (with an **x**)
	with **suffixes**	moans, coaches, boasting, toaster, soaped, soapy (if suffix **y** has been introduced), coatless, floatable (perhaps)
	Review: mixed **short a**, **i**, **u**, **o**, and **e** words, **digraphs**, **trigraphs**, **letter combinations**, and **oa** with new and review **suffixes**	graphs, trenches, twisted, cussing, splotchy, shifty, trumping, slackness (if suffix **ness** has been introduced), stringing, roachless

The suffix **ness** changes a word into a noun and should be introduced around this time in *Spelling*, if not earlier.

Teaching the **dge** spelling generalization requires greater care than teaching the **ck** or **tch** spelling generalization because it can be easily confused with **ge**. You must carefully reinforce that **dge** comes immediately after one short vowel at the end of a one-syllable word (**badge**) while **ge** comes after a consonant (**lunge**), after more than one vowel (**gouge**), after a long vowel sound (**stage**), or after one short vowel in a multisyllabic word (**refrigerator**). The difficulty arises particularly when students confuse the meaning or identification of short and long vowels (**badge** versus **stage**) which is not an issue with the **ck** and **tch** generalizations.

For a list of one-syllable words ending in **dge**, select them from *LessonPlanner's* one-syllable, di/tri pull-down menu in Decoding and bring them over to Blending from

"Other Sources." Otherwise **dge** words can be retrieved from the "Phoneme Spelled As" menus in Blending (fudge, ledge, fridge).

After covering the material in table 4–13, continue teaching red flag words and writing phrases and sentences. Also, include phonetic nonsense words and syllables.

Table 4–14 shows the sequence for beginning encoding with letter combinations. In *LessonPlanner*, these may be selected from the "Phoneme Spelled As" menus in Blending or the one-syllable, letter combination pull-down menus in Decoding and brought over to Blending from "Other Sources."

	letter combination words	
Table 4–14. Beginning Encoding with Letter Combinations	**ang**	fang, slang
	ing	ping, sting
	ung	lung, swung
	ong	song, throng
	with **suffixes**	gangs, wronging, stronger, stringless, swingable, twangy, and longed

To encode letter combination words in Orton-based programs, students repeat the word to be encoded and then sound out the word letter by letter. If the word is **string**, the student says, "**string**" and then "/s/-**s**, /t/-**t**, /r/-**r**, /iŋ/-**i-n-g**" before or while writing it. Steps are gradually eliminated so that when a letter combination word is encoded, the student names the word "**trunk**" and says each letter "**t-r-unk**" before or while writing each. If a student says /tr/ as the first sound of the word, it is obvious that he/she recognizes the blend **tr** and should be allowed to continue encoding the word without isolating the /t/–**t** and /r/–**r** individually. Slingerland students focus on the letter combination, the difficult part of the word, first, before encoding across the word from left to right.

Introduce the "describing" suffix **y** around this time if not earlier.

After covering the material in table 4–14, continue teaching red flag words. Select from the previous tables or, in *LessonPlanner*, locate them in Spelling in the Sight Word menus for selection. They include Basic I, II, III words and Red Flag words. Continue writing and integrating phrases and sentences.

A Note About the Inclusion of Suffixes in Encoding

When including words in encoding with suffixes, be sure that it is not necessary to apply any one of the four major spelling rules before spelling the word. The four rules include the **1-1-1** Vowel (Suffix), the Consonant-**Y**, the Extended **1-1-1** Rule, and the Silent-**E** Rule.[4] They are dealt with more fully in *Spelling* following this discussion of encoding.

In *LessonPlanner*, words ending in a consonant to which the **1-1-1** Vowel (Suffix) Rule does not apply, can be retrieved from the one or two syllable Decoding menus and brought over to Blending from "Other Sources" for encoding.

Before naming a word for a student to encode that has a suffix (**singable**), Slingerland teachers must be sure that the suffix has already been introduced in *Spelling*, with concept. Ask your student to say the whole word first, and then only the base word (**sing**) before encoding or spelling the base word with the suffix. When students are provided sufficient practice applying suffixes, and especially if they do so using a chart holder with alphabet and affix cards, they will be able to encode words with suffixes easily.

Table 4–15 shows the sequence for continuing encoding with phonograms (**ee**). In *LessonPlanner*, these may be selected from the "Phoneme (/ē/) Spelled As (**ee**)" menu in Blending or selected from the one-syllable, phonogram pull-down menu in Decoding and brought over to Blending from "Other Sources."

The suffix **ful**, meaning full of, the adverb suffix **ly** that tells how, and **ish**, meaning sort of, should be introduced around this time, if not earlier.

After covering the material in table 4–15, continue teaching non-phonetic words. Select from the previous tables, your own resource materials, or from *LessonPlanner*'s Sight Word menus in Spelling. Continue writing phrases and sentences for integration.

---

[4] The labels of the four spelling rules differ. The **1-1-1 Vowel Rule** is often referred to as the Doubling Rule or simply the 1-1-1 Rule. By including the word Vowel in the label, students are helped to remember that not only must the word be 1 syllable and end in 1 consonant, following 1 vowel, but the suffix to be added to the base word must begin with a vowel as well. The Consonant-**Y** Rule is frequently referrred to as the Y-Rule or Change Y to I Rule. Again, the purpose of including the word Consonant in the label is to remind students that there must be a consonant before the **y** of the base word if **y** is to be changed to **i** before the suffix is added. Finally, the Silent-**E** Rule is called more simply the **E**-Rule or the Drop-**e** Rule.

It is important that teachers advance more slowly auditorily than visually. Learning to encode, spell, and write is far more difficult than learning to decode and read, so the pace of instruction cannot be as swift.

Table 4–15. Continuing Encoding with Phonograms (ee)	**ee** words	feed (- ee -) seeds (- ee - -) teeth (- ee —) green (- - ee -) speech (- - ee —) screech (- - - ee —)
	with **suffixes**	peeps, queens, speeches, screening, seeded, sleeper, greenest (if suffix **est** has been introduced), cheerful (if suffix **ful** has been introduced), heedless, speedy, sweepable, sweetly (if suffix **ly** has been introduced), sheepish (if suffix **ish** has been introduced), deepness
	short vowels, **digraphs**, **trigraphs**, **letter combinations**, with **double f, l, s,** and **z**; also **oa** and **ee** with **suffixes**	tricks, branches, quickly, glossing, scratchy, French, brushing, slimness, graphable, stuffing, knocks, strongest, sweeter, coaches

Table 4–16 shows the sequence for continuing encoding with phonograms (**ai** and **ay**). In *LessonPlanner*, these may be selected from the "Phoneme (/ā/) Spelled As (**ai**)" menu in Blending or from the one-syllable, phonogram pull-down menu in Decoding and brought over to Blending from "Other Sources."

Phonogram **ay** words are often introduced at the same time as **ai**. Note that **ay** occurs most frequently at the end of one-syllable base words whereas **ai** is usually found at the beginning or middle of one-syllable words, often followed by **n** or **l**. To assist students to encode **ai** and **ay** words, instruct them to identify whether the /ā/ sound is at the end of the word (st<u>ay</u>) or syllable (pl<u>ay</u>able), thus spelled with **ay**, or whether the /ā/ sound is at the beginning (<u>ai</u>m) or middle (gr<u>ai</u>n) of the word, thus spelled with **ai**.

After covering the material in table 4–16, continue teaching non-phonetic words and writing integrated phrases and sentences with correct usage of punctuation.

Table 4–16. Continuing Encoding with Phonograms (ai and ay)	
ai words	gain (- **ai** -) paint (- **ai** - -) faith (- **ai** —) (with a digraph) drain (- - **ai** -) sprain (- - - **ai** -) (also with a digraph) ail (**ai** at the beginning)
ay words	may, sway, stray
ai and **ay** words with **suffixes** Prefixes would have been introduced by this time. Explaining the meaning of the prefixes, as with suffixes, is beneficial.	hails, drains, straining, painted, gainful, hairless, grainy, waistless, trainable, faintly (if suffix **ly** has been introduced) plays player playing playable
As a challenge to more advanced students, **ai/ay** words with **prefixes** and two **suffixes** added to the base may also be included.	replay misplayed unplayable underplayed displayed dismayed dismayingly
Review with **short vowels**, **digraphs**, **trigraphs**, **letter combinations**, **double f, l, s**, and **z**; **oa**; **ee**; **ai** and **ay**; and with **suffixes** and **prefixes**, perhaps.	wrist, mess, elm, gruff, pitched, hedge, crunchable, batches, knockless, scripts, crushes, hinge, chanced, swayable, hairy, gems, centless, chunky, bringing, binge, soapy, greeted, ailments, shrunken, trinket, wimpish, wishfully, thickest, gladness
homonyms	be and bee

Choices for What to Introduce Next

With all students, you can continue to introduce new phonograms gradually. These include any listed previously (**oo**, **oi**, **oy**, **ou**, **ow**, **igh**, etc.). A few additional digraphs should also be introduced, particularly at the third grade level or above for non-SLD or faster paced SLD students. The same applies for the introduction of soft **c** and soft **g** words for use in encoding. Introduce **v-e** words around this time, too, and words that end in **y** with the corresponding grapheme, long /ī/, to prevent confusion. There is a handful of common, one-syllable **y** - /ī/ words. The pace at which you can move your students along will be determined by the many factors discussed throughout this book.

Techniques for Encoding v-e Words

The techniques used for encoding **v-e** words is similar to that for encoding closed syllable short vowel, phonogram, and letter combination words. In most Orton-based programs, students say the word to be encoded and then sound out the word letter by letter. If the word is **safe**, the student says, "**safe**" and then "/s/-**s**, /ā/-**a-consonant-e**, **a-f-e**" before or while writing. In Slingerland, students repeat the word to be encoded (**safe**), give the vowel sound (/ā/) before naming the spelling for /ā/ (**a-consonant-e**) while forming the letters in the air. Then the word is encoded from left to right.

Table 4–17 shows the sequence for encoding with **y** - /ī/ and **v-e** words. In *LessonPlanner*, these may be selected from the "Phoneme (/ī/) Spelled As (**y**)" menu in Blending or from the one-syllable, long vowel, pull-down menu in Decoding and brought over to Blending from "Other Sources."

Table 4–17. Encoding with y - /ī/ and v-e Words	**y** - /ī/	pry, shy
	with **suffixes** that do not require a change in the application of the **Consonant-Y** Rule	shyness, crying
	vce or **v-e** words	pave, brace (soft **c**), crane (hard **c**), stage (soft **g**), grave (hard **g**), write (twisty **wr**), tribe, chrome (with the /k/ phoneme for **ch**), smoke, chore
	A word about **e-e** words: Although **e-e** appears less frequently in one-syllable base words than the other **v-e**'s, "here" and "these" are particularly common and important.	here, these, mere, eve, theme, breve, scene, sphere
	with **suffixes**	smokeless, merely, hateful, stoked

Constantly review words with the already taught short vowels, di- trigraphs, letter combinations, phonograms, the double **f**, **l**, **s**, and **z** spelling generalization, soft and hard **c** and **g**, and words with a variety of affixes, as well as homonyms.

In *LessonPlanner*, **vce** or **v-e** words may be selected from the "Phoneme Spelled As" menus in Blending, or selected from the one-syllable, phonogram pull-down menus in Decoding, with only **a-e**, **i-e**, **o-e**, and **e-e**, at first, and brought over to Blending from "Other Sources."

After covering the material in table 4–17, continue teaching non-phonetic words. Select from the previous and following tables depending on need in phrase and sentence writing: **lose** and any of the non-phonetic numerals, such as **two** and **four** (also homonyms). Continue writing phrases and sentences for integration.

Continue with phonogram words, as shown in table 4–18. In *LessonPlanner*, phonogram words may be selected from the "Phoneme Spelled As" menus in Blending for one and more-than-one-syllable words or selected from the one-syllable, phonogram pull-down menus in Decoding and brought over to Blending from "Other Sources."

Teach **ow** and **ou** at the same time with only the /ou/ phoneme and noting, perhaps, that **ou** is usually found at the beginning or middle of words; **ow** is often at the end of syllables, at the end of base words, or when followed by a single **l** or **n**, or by **el**, or **er**.

For **oi** and **oy** words, use an exercise similar to that for **ai** and **ay**: Students identify whether the /oi/ sound is at the end of the word (b<u>oy</u>) or syllable (flamb<u>oy</u>ant), thus spelled with **oy**, or whether the /oi/ sound is at the beginning (<u>oi</u>l) or middle (c<u>oi</u>l) of the word, thus spelled with **oi**.

Recall that **au** is usually found at the beginning or middle of words; **aw** is at the end of syllables and base words or when followed by a single **l**, **n**, or **k**. There are always exceptions, of course. For **aw** and **au**, a variation of the **oi** and **oy** exercise in this table or the earlier **ai** and **ay** exercise is helpful in solidifying skills.

Around this time the first of the three major spelling rules should be introduced (in *Spelling*), such as the Silent-**E** Rule. See Learning and Incorporating Spelling Rules on page 184.

Table 4–18. Continuing Encoding with More Phonograms

ou words	proud, ground
oo words with the long /o͞o/ phoneme	stoop, tooth
oo words with the short /o͝o/ phoneme	book, brook
ow words with one or both corresponding phonemes, /ou/ and long /ō/	how, scow<u>l</u>, tow<u>n</u>, vow<u>el</u>, cow<u>er,</u> grow, thrown
oi and **oy** words	boil, moist, toy, Roy
igh words	fight, fright
ar words	stark, parch
or words	born, forth
er words	verge, swerve
ir words	skirt, twirl
ur words	burn, church
ea with the long /ē/ phoneme	heat, cheat
ea with short /ĕ/	tread, thread
ea with its long /ā/ phoneme, the least common	steak, wear
mixed **ea** words with **affixes**	peals, unreal, weakness, dreamer, wearable, treatments, retreated, steady, unsteady, deafen, breaker
ie with the long /ī/ phoneme	tie, tries
ie with long /ē/	chief, grieve
eigh	weigh, sleighs
aw and **au**	jaw, braw<u>l</u>, draw<u>n</u>, squaw<u>k</u>, vault
ew words with the long /ū/ phoneme	pew, hew
ew words with the long /o͞o/ phoneme	brew, shrewd

Continuing Mixed Encoding

Options for what to encode next should include words containing some or all of the preceding phonogram word types and/or **u-e** and **eng** words, as well as words with newly introduced digraphs, trigraphs, and soft **c** and soft **g**, as shown in table 4–19, Continuing Mixed Encoding. You can also encode words with something new, such as **scribal-o**. In *LessonPlanner*, all are selectable from the Blending or Decoding menus.

Table 4–19. Continuing Mixed Encoding	with **ph**	graph, phone
	u-e words with the long /ū/ phoneme	pule, spume
	u-e words with /o͞o/	rude, spruce
	eng words	length, strength
	soft **c** and soft **g** words	cinch, gin, fancy, stingy
	scribal-o words	son, month, glove

In addition, continue review of encoding words. Include those with short vowels, digraphs, trigraphs, letter combinations, phonograms, with double **f**, **l**, **s**, and **z**, also **ck**, **tch**, **dge**, soft and hard **c** and **g**, **scribal-o**, homonyms, and words with a variety of affixes. Also include Silent-**E** Rule words for spelling.

Continue teaching non-phonetic (learned, sight, or red flag) words. Select from *LessonPlanner,* the previous tables, from your own favorite lists of non-phonetic words, or from the following depending on need in phrase, sentence, and paragraph writing: **could**, **would**, **should**, **young**, and **laugh**. Writing should be integrated with all relevant sections of the daily lesson plan.

Scope and Sequence for Spelling

As we continue with the encoding scope and sequence, we will include words that fall in the category of true spelling whereby students learn to spell words that are non-phonetic (red flag, learned, or sight), and they learn to make spelling choices necessary to spell ambiguous words (yellow flag) correctly. Particularly in the Slingerland daily lesson plan format, *Spelling* is where affixes are taught with concept and put to functional use, and where the three main spelling rules are learned and applied. As the first step in written expression, phrases—and soon short sentences—are written using words containing the first vowel taught (short **a**) and words with the first suffixes. Gradually phrase and sentence writing become more sophisticated as new affixes, vowels, phonograms, spelling generalizations, punctuation, and rules are learned.

Review the previous tables in this chapter and take note of the accompanying recommendations for how and when to teach ambiguous spellings, when to introduce affixes and non-phonetic words, and when to teach spelling generalizations and rules. Always be sure to think of them in the context of putting new concepts to functional use in phrase and sentence writing. This occurs in *Spelling* in a Slingerland program. In a traditional Orton-Gillingham program this constitutes the fifth section of a typical one-hour daily lesson plan. Immediately following the various patterns for visual-auditory-kinesthetic learning and simultaneous oral spelling, single-word dictation is expanded to phrases and sentences.

Over the next several pages, some attention is given to the techniques for teaching spelling with concept.

Introducing Suffixes with Concept

Recall that the first suffix usually taught is **ing** with short **a-consonant** words. The suffixes or endings that follow are **ed**, **er**, **s-es**, added to verbs, and **less**, **able**, **y**, **ness**, **ly**, **ish**, **ful**, **ment**, **est**, **en**, **et**, and **ling**. Teaching suffixes with concept enables students to put to functional use the words with suffixes in order to write short dictated phrases, first, and then sentences. This type of dictation leads to the development of myriad skills necessary for independent written expression.

Techniques vary as to how suffixes are added to base words, beginning with the **ing** "doing" suffix. Most Orton-based programs require that a student name and then encode a base word to which one of the key spelling rules does not apply. If the teacher dictates the word **mash**, the student encodes **mash** in a chart holder with alphabet cards or encodes it in the air and/or writes it. Next, the teacher traditionally asks how **mash** can be made into a "doing" word or to show present tense—what someone is doing now. After explaining how this is done, the student repeats the base word with the suffix added (mashing) before adding the suffix **ing** to **mash** in the chart or writing **mashing** directly beneath **mash**. The new extended word is then spelled before moving on.

Similar words are practiced to prompt students to apply different suffixes. For instance, the teacher may ask how a base word can be changed to show what someone *does* (by adding **s** or **es**), or to make a word tell about something that happened before now, to show past time, or, with more advanced students, to show past tense (by adding **ed**). Concept is important, as is guiding students to understand that suffixes, in the words of Slingerland, "lend shades of meaning" to words. To reinforce the importance of starting with a base word (root) to build new words, students write the words with suffixes directly beneath the base:

> mash
>
> mashing
>
> mashed
>
> mashes

Encoding/Spelling Non-Phonetic, Word Family, and Homonym Words

Non-phonetic words in *LessonPlanner* are located in Spelling in the Sight Word menus. They include Basic I, II, III, and Red Flag words from *LessonPlanner's* approximately 15,000 word bank. These words are non-phonetic unless there are spelling generalizations or rules that remove them from their non-phonetic status once the specific rules or generalizations that govern them are learned. Then the words that were once categorized as non-phonetic become either phonetic or ambiguous. To use the examples given previously, to spell the purely phonetic word **had**, no spelling choices are required, for there is only one grapheme possible for each phoneme: /h/–**h**, /ă/–**a**, /d/–**d**. To spell the word **has**, however, a choice between using **s** or **z** for spelling the final /z/ sound is required. **Has** may initially be presented as a sight word, but becomes an ambiguous spelling word once the second phoneme for **s**, /z/, is taught. The fact that a choice was required is what makes **has** an ambiguous (yellow flag) spelling word.

Using a new example, the word **want** is usually presented first as non-phonetic (sight, learned, or red flag) because, phonetically, **want** sounds as if it should be spelled with a short **o**, /ŏ/, instead of with an **a**, that is, until students learn that **a** preceded by a **w** is frequently pronounced /ŏ/ or /ô/. Refer to the discussion on the effect of **a**, **ar**, and **or** on **w**; and **a** and **ar** on **qu** in the section on *Advanced Group II Graphemes* on page 66; and table 3–17, *Choices for Teaching w and qu* on page 69.

Whenever students are in doubt about the correct spelling of particular phonemes, they should not guess. It is important that the correct pattern be established rather than an incorrect pattern. With the word **want**, if the student is not sure of which vowel to use, he/she should ask if the spelling for /ŏ/ is **o, a,** or **au**.

Words such as **has** and **want** are found in the Basic I, II, III word lists of *Lesson-Planner* as well as in other lists. The Basic I, II, III lists include several Word Family words that some teachers have their students blend while others teach as non-phonetic. Consider the **ign** word family. It can be taught as non-phonetic or as ambiguous after students learn that **gn** is a spelling for /n/ and that **i** can never be relied upon, as in the instance when **i** spells /ī/ instead of /ĭ/ in **ign**. In either case, students write the base word first and beneath the base, they write the base again with a variety of affixes added:

> sign
> assign
> assigned
> assigner
> assignee

Homonyms must also be analyzed to determine whether they are ambiguously spelled (yellow flag) or non-phonetic (red flag). For example, the homonyms **ail** and **ale** are clearly ambiguous spellings; whereas, the second of the homonym pairs **air** and **heir** must be taught as a true non-phonetic spelling since the **h** is silent. See the procedure for teaching non-phonetic words in the next section.

Words that are always considered non-phonetic rather than ambiguous are designated as Red Flag in *LessonPlanner* in the Sight Word menus of the Spelling panel. They include words such as **yacht, eye, mustache, boycott,** and **built. Built** becomes ambiguous when or if the second phoneme for **ui**, /ĭ/ is taught. The same occurs with **mustache** if **che** is taught as a French spelling for /sh/. No two teachers concur that all the designated red flag words in *LessonPlanner* are truly non-phonetic.

Spelling Phonetic, Ambiguous, and Non-Phonetic Words

Gillingham coined the term "simultaneous oral spelling" (S.O.S.) to describe the techniques that are incorporated in teaching and learning to orally spell and write phonetic, ambiguous, and non-phonetic words using kinesthetic-auditory-visual associations to create linkages of sound with letter formations that impress and solidify recall of letter sequences in words. With any type of word, the key is for students to simultaneously name aloud the letters as each letter is written. In the early Green Manual, Gillingham states:

> The sequence is echo speech, oral spelling, written spelling. The child hears the teacher's voice—auditory. He hears his own voice—auditory. He feels his own speech organs—kinesthetic. He hears the name of the letters—auditory. He sees the letters— visual. He feels his hand form the letters—kinesthetic.

Exceptionally good spellers usually use their excellent visual recall of word letter sequences to spell correctly. Average spellers often use a combination of visual and auditory recall to spell. For example, young students frequently say aloud, or at least to themselves, /dŏk-tôr/ (for doctor), with the second syllable overenunciated using the most common phoneme for **or**, /ôr/, for better recall of the **or** ending, rather than the more common **er**. Spellers with dyslexia and weak visual recall must use all three modalities simultaneously—auditory, visual, and kinesthetic-motor—to become adequate spellers. S.O.S. was developed for SLD students; yet, because not many of us have perfect visual recall, S.O.S. is an excellent spelling strategy for many students. SLD students must study more diligently than their peers and review far more frequently.

Most of our troublesome, short, everyday, non-phonetic words (what, one, could) come to us from Anglo-Saxon. Anglo-Saxon is the language that early tribes developed over many years in the land that is now known as England. These tribes were comprised of the Angles, the Saxons, the Jutes, and others. As the new language, Old English, evolved, some of the Anglo-Saxon phonemes began to disappear until, in Modern English, many do not exist at all. Thus, although the pronunciation of these words changed, their spellings often remained unchanged.

To teach non-phonetic words in most Orton-based programs, the teacher first writes the new non-phonetic word to be learned (**trouble**) with large, neat letters, and then points out the non-phonetic element or elements of the word. (Until **ou** as /ŭ/ is taught, **ou** is non-phonetic and the difficult phonogram or letters to remember when spelling **trouble**.) The teacher might then discuss **ou** further, and perhaps explain the etymology of **trouble**—that it comes from Old French—or that it will not always be considered non-phonetic, to whet students' appetites. The students then pronounce the word and copy while naming each letter while copying, in the S.O.S. manner.

To study non-phonetic words using S.O.S. techniques, students pronounce the word again and trace over the copied word while naming each letter. They do this as many times as necessary, or that time allows, to be able to write the word from memory. To check if they have overlearned the word sufficiently, they then write the word on a separate paper from memory. If their hand hesitates in the least, they are alerted that the word has not been fully committed to memory and that more practice tracing while naming each letter is required.

> ### *Note on Encoding and Spelling*
>
> Subsequent tables reflect the inclusion of non-phonetic and ambiguous words. Words to which spelling rules apply are included too.
>
> As used in this book, **encoding** refers to the process of spelling phonetic (green flag) words by sounding them out. In *LessonPlanner* the older term *blending* is used.
>
> **Spelling** includes ambiguous and non-phonetic words as well as phonetic words to which affixes are added or generalizations and rules applied. These require attention to concept or cannot be sounded out without thought.

Continuing with the options you have for what to weave into encoding and spelling, new phonetic and non-phonetic homonyms can be added, and phonetic and non-phonetic selections from Word Families can be made.

Table 4–20 shows the sequence for spelling homonyms, word family words, plurals, and words with rules. In *LessonPlanner*, use the pull-down Special Words menu to find Homonyms or Word Families, in Spelling. Select the homonyms you wish to teach from one lengthy list of 420 words and then return to Blending to retrieve them from "Other Sources."

Although /ôl/ spelled **al** is designated as a phonogram in *LessonPlanner*, it can just as easily be taught as a word family—**all** or **al**—especially after the common one-syllable **all** words are introduced. When treating **al** as a phonogram, do not introduce it too soon for spelling. In this book, it is included in the most Advanced Oddities list. Small, easy **al/all** words should be taught much earlier. Remember that **al** words are more sophisticated and frequently multisyllabic (paltry, saltine, alternative, Guatemala).

Teachers find that middle and junior high students enjoy and have no difficulty with the /ŭ/ - blood/flood - **oo** words. They can be taught as phonogram or **oo** word family words. They are retrievable from the Spelling Word Family pull-down menu.

Table 4–20. Spelling Homonyms, Word Family Words, Plurals, and Words with Rules	**homonyms**	sons (with **scribal-o**) and suns
	ind word family	find, grind
	al phonogram or **word family**	gall, stall, ball, call, fall, halls, tall
	oo word family (or **phonogram**)	blood, bloody, floods, floodable
	/s/-**plural s** or **third person singular**	toys, brings, shoves
	/ĕz/-**es**, used after the phonemes made by **s**, **x**, **z**, **ch**, and **sh** (sibilants)	misses, boxes, frizzes, matches, fishes
	irregular plurals	mice, geese, women (non-phonetic)

Teaching and reviewing plurals are appropriate options to weave into encoding and spelling now. Plurals are found in Spelling in the pull-down Rules/Gen's menu. **S**, **es**, and **irregular** plurals are entitled "add -s", "s,x,z,ch,sh -s" and "irreg. plural," respectively.

Review newer teachings from the above options (plurals, perhaps the **al** word family, and **ind**). Also include words with short vowels, some digraphs, trigraphs, letter combinations, phonograms, double **f**, **l**, **s**, or **z**; **ck**, **tch**, and **dge**; soft **c** and soft **g**; **scribal-o**, phonetic and non-phonetic homonyms, and words with a variety of affixes. In *Spelling*, review the first spelling rule that has been taught, likely the Silent-**E** Rule. And, encode nonsense words or syllables that sound and look like real words and syllables, but are not.

After covering the material in table 4–20, continue teaching sight words. Select from your own resources, *LessonPlanner,* or from the previous tables as needed for phrase and sentence writing. The second spelling rule, perhaps the **1-1-1** Vowel Rule, should now be taught. In *LessonPlanner*, 1-1-1 words are retrievable from the Spelling Rules/Gen's 1-1-1 menu. Continue writing phrases and sentences for integration. Incorporate new and old learnings into dictations.

Encoding and Spelling Closed Two-Syllable Words with Two or More Consonants in the Medial Position

The techniques used for encoding two-syllable words with short vowels, phonograms, and letter combinations are similar to encoding one-syllable words with an additional step. Among Orton-based programs there are slight variations in how students are taught to encode two-syllable words, but, essentially, they are required to do the following:

1. Repeat the whole word dictated by the teacher to be encoded (**campus**).

2. Say each syllable distinctly (**cam•pus**).

3. Repeat the first syllable (**cam**) and encode or sound it out letter by letter (**c-a-m**) while, optionally, simultaneously writing the letters as they are named (in the air or on paper).

4. Repeat the next syllable (**pus**) and sound it out letter by letter (**p-u-s**) while, sometimes, simultaneously writing the letters as they are named.

5. Then the student repeats the whole word (**campus**) and spells it again (**c-a-m-p-u-s**) letter by letter.

Slingerland students are required, as an additional step between 3 and 4 above, to give the vowel sound (/ă/) and the name of that vowel (**a**) after repeating the first syllable to be encoded (**cam**) and before encoding it (**c-a-m**). They do the same with the second syllable, saying, "**pus** - /ŭ/ - **u, p-u-s**."

Refer to table 4–21, Encoding and Spelling Closed Two-Syllable Words with Two or More Consonants in the Medial Position. Some instructors prefer to begin two-syllable word encoding with words that contain like consonants. When this is done, it is important that they pronounce the word as they do in normal speech first (**tennis**) and then overenunciate the word so that the two syllables are distinct and the two like consonants (**nn**) are clearly heard (**ten•nis**). Beginning two-syllable encoding with words containing "unlike" consonants is easier.

After covering the material in table 4–21, continue teaching non-phonetic words. Select from *LessonPlanner,* the previous tables, or from the following useful words with two consonants in medial positions: **Tuesday** (non-phonetic only until **ue** is taught) and

Wednesday (3-syllable). Continue writing phrases and sentences for integration.

Table 4–21. Encoding and Spelling Closed Two-Syllable Words with Two or More Consonants in the Medial Position	**two-syllable words with a short vowel in each closed syllable and two unlike consonants in the medial position**	vel/vet, cam/pus; im/pinge and con/demn for more challenge
	with a short vowel in each syllable and like consonants	tennis, gossip, pollen
	with a short vowel in the first syllable and C-le second syllable	giggle, ramble
	with a short vowel in the first syllable and a letter combination in the second	friction, culture
	with a phonogram in the first syllable and a C-le second syllable	garble, curdle
	with a short vowel in either the first or second syllable and a letter combination in the other syllable	chipmunk, thankless, rapture, and sanction with two letter combinations (anc and tion)
	with a short vowel in either the first or second syllable and a phonogram in the other	Sunday, Monday, nourish
	with a short vowel in the first syllable and v-e in the second	stampede, and more challenging, exchange (v—e)
	with a phonogram in one syllable and one short vowel, letter combination, another phonogram, v-e, or C-le in the other	blackbird, yearling, perfume, whirlpool, foible, earshot

Encoding and Spelling Review

Refer to table 4–22, One and Two-Syllable Word Encoding and Spelling Review. Daily encoding review should include one-syllable words with several short vowels, a variety of digraphs, trigraphs, phonograms, double **f**, **l**, **s**, and **z**, as well as **ck**, **tch**, and **dge**, spellings for soft **c** and soft **g**, **contractions**, **scribal-o**, **homonyms**, and with a variety of **affixes**. Additionally, two-syllable words with short vowels, soft **c** and soft **g**, **scribal-o**, **v-e**, **C-le**, **letter combinations**, **phonograms**, **affixes**, as well as **homonyms**, and **word family** words, should be included. Be sure not to forget nonsense words and syllables, grammar, and vocabulary development.

Table 4–22. One and Two-Syllable Word Encoding and Spelling Review

beginning with **cvc** words	bat (- **v** -) best, can't (- **v**- -) with (- **v** —)(digraph) grim (- - **v**-) than (— **v** -) (a digraph) slump (- - **v** - -) splash (- - - **v** —) or (- - - **v** - -) filth, brunch, scratch (- **v**- —) and (- - -**v** —)
ce and **ge**	cent, fringe
homonyms	seem and seam
letter combinations with **suffixes**	clang, slink branchless, thrillingly, drunkenness
phonograms and more **suffixes**	rings, swinging, honked, toasted, soapy, thickness, stringing, greenest, sweepable, sweaty, sweetly, meanish, knocks, straining, pained, replayed, smoothness, spoiled, eastern, verged, thirsty, hurling, preached, tears, cries, eighty
y - /ī/ words	sly, sky
more **phonogram** words with **affixes**	trawlers, faulted, brewed, pews
v-e (phonogram) words	brace (soft **c**), page (soft **g**), flameless, merely, spiteful, smoked, ruled, muted
scribal-o	hovers
alk family **al** or **all**	talk, walk fall, hall
irregular plural	man – men
two-syllable encoding	
mixed review	bandit, funnel, little, simple, fraction, lecture, gurgle
singular possessive	Betty's, player's
contraction	hadn't
plural possessive	players'
mixed	success, gypsum, texture, factoring
double-duty g	jingle, tangle
homonyms	sealing and ceiling
word family words	bloodhound, floodgate
confusables	oyster, ouster

Confusables, easily confused words, are retrieved from the *LessonPlanner's* Special Words menus in Spelling, as are Homonyms and Word Families.

Encoding and Spelling Closed Two-Syllable Words with a Single Medial Consonant

The techniques used for encoding two-syllable words with one consonant in the medial position is only slightly different from encoding two-syllable words with two consonants in the medial position. Among Orton-based programs there is some variation in how students are taught to encode these words, but essentially, they do the following:

1. Repeat the whole word as dictated by the teacher to be encoded (**seven**). To avoid difficulty caused because the **e** in the second syllable (**en**) is not pronounced /ĕ/, initially, the teacher and student should both say the word (**seven**), first, as it is pronounced naturally and, second, with the **e** overenunciated so that it sounds like an /ĕ/. This is a particularly important step to include before students learn about the different phonemes for vowels in unaccented syllables.

2. Say each syllable distinctly (**sev**) (**en**); overenunciate as recommended above.

3. Repeat the first syllable (**sev**) and sound it out letter by letter (**s-e-v**) while simultaneously writing the letters as they are named (in the air or on paper) in the S.O.S. fashion.

4. Repeat and perhaps overenunciate the second syllable (**en**) and sound it out letter by letter (**e-n**) while simultaneously writing the letters as they are named.

5. Then the student repeats the word (**seven**) and spells it again (**s-e-v-e-n**).

Again, Slingerland students are required, as an additional step, to give the vowel sound (/ĕ/) and the name of that vowel (**e**) after repeating the first syllable to be encoded (**sev**) and before encoding it (**s-e-v**). They do similarly with the second syllable.

Cover the material in table 4–23, Encoding and Spelling Closed Two-Syllable Words with a Single Consonant in the Medial Position, and then review encoding of one-syllable words as well as two-syllable words with a variety of closed syllable types or patterns. Constantly thread and intertwine, weaving in one- and two-syllable words with short vowels, digraphs, trigraphs, phonograms, letter combinations, doubled **f, l, s,** and **z**; **ck, tch,** and **dge**; hard and soft **c** and **g, scribal-o, homonyms, contractions, word families, confusables, idioms,** and affixes. Include both words with two consonants and only one consonant in the medial position. Also review the spelling rules that were introduced (**1-1-1 V**owel and Silent-**E**).

Continue teaching non-phonetic words. Select from *LessonPlanner,* the previous tables or from the following common words: **enough, women,** and **country** (until **ou** with its /ə/ phoneme is taught). Write phrases and sentences to put to functional use words that were encoded and spelled, and for integration.

Table 4–23. Encoding and Spelling Closed Two-Syllable Words with a Single Consonant in the Medial Position	**two-syllable words with a single consonant in the medial position and closed syllables**	sev/en, pol/ish, com/et
	with a consonant digraph	rath/er, plumber, weather
	with a consonant blend	front/age, sharpen

Encoding and Spelling Two-Syllable Words with One Open Syllable and a Single Consonant in the Medial Position

The techniques used for encoding two-syllable words with one consonant in the medial position is significantly different, and more difficult, than encoding two-syllable words with either two consonants or a single consonant in the medial position that constitute closed syllables. As stated several times before, Orton-based programs differ in how students are taught to encode open syllable words, but, essentially, they do the following:

1. Repeat the whole word as dictated by the teacher to be encoded (**tulip**).

2. Say each syllable distinctly (**tu**) (**lip**); overenunciate if necessary and particularly while learning the new techniques for open syllable encoding.

3. Repeat the first syllable (**tu**) and sound it out letter by letter (**t-u**) while simultaneously writing the letters as they are named (in the air or on paper).

4. Repeat and perhaps overenunciate the second syllable (**lip**) and sound it out letter by letter (**l-i-p**) while, sometimes, simultaneously writing the letters as they are named.

5. Then the student repeats the whole word (**tulip**) and spells it again (**t-u-l-i-p**).

Slingerland students, as an additional step, give the vowel sound (/ū/)[5], name the vowel (**u**) after repeating the first syllable to be encoded (**tu**), and say, "**u** at the end" (or at the end of an accented open syllable), before encoding it (**t-u**). For the second syllable, students follow the same procedure as taught previously for encoding closed syllables.

Table 4–24 shows the sequence for encoding and spelling two-syllable words with a single consonant in the medial position and one accented open syllable. After teaching this material, begin your review of one-syllable encoding, but also include two-syllable encoding with closed and open syllables. Continue to pull into your tapestry more from word lists: short vowels, digraphs, trigraphs, phonograms, letter combinations, long vowels in open syllables, words where spelling generalizations apply, homonyms, word families, confusables, contractions, colloquialisms, several new prefixes (**bi** and **tri**), suffixes, spelling rules, and if you have so chosen, a few pseudowords.

Continue teaching learned words. Select from your own resource materials, *LessonPlanner*, or the previous tables. Perhaps teach the Consonant-**Y** Spelling Rule. Words for this rule are retrieved from the "cons-y" menu in Rules/Gen's in Spelling. Write phrases and sentences, to put to functional use, words that were encoded and spelled in the day's lesson and for integration.

---

[5] The first syllable of the word **tulip** is pronounced either /tū/ or /tōō/.

Encoding and Spelling Words of Two or More Syllables

Once two syllable encoding is secure then multisyllabic encoding can begin by first adding suffixes to two-syllable words where spelling rules are not applicable, and then encoding words of three and more syllables. In *LessonPlanner*, a good way to retrieve multisyllabic words is from the Blending (encoding) "Phonemes Spelled As" menu.

Table 4–24. Encoding and Spelling Two-Syllable Words with a Single Consonant in the Medial Position and One Accented Open Syllable

two-syllable words with a single consonant in the medial position and a long vowel sound in the accented open syllable	ti/ger, tu/lip
with a consonant digraph	se/quel, ether
with a consonant blend	se/cret, cypress
with C-le syllables	Bi/ble, title, staple, scruple, cycle bi/cy/cle, tricycle
with open phonogram syllables and a C-le syllable	needle, steeple
with unstable or reversed diphthongs	di/et, li/on, ne/on, trying sawing (here **y** and **w** are vowels)
In the above, the vowel at the end of each open syllable is long. If you wish to encode open syllable words where the vowel has its unaccented phoneme, pronounce the word as you do in normal speech first and then, initially, say the word again and overenunciate the unaccented syllable with a long vowel sound. Refer to the phoneme card sequence for when to introduce words of this type.	re/fine, omit, begin, alone, and cadet
with a single consonant in the medial position; the vowel has its unaccented sound	pa/rade, po/lite, di/vine
with a consonant digraph; the vowel is unaccented	ma/chine, brochure
with a consonant blend; the vowel is unaccented	pa/trol, ablaze, oblige

Since the purpose of including a scope and sequence for encoding and spelling is not primarily to instruct teachers on encoding and spelling techniques, but rather to provide the sequence in which words should be presented, as well as to recommend the scope to be introduced and reviewed during daily lessons, it is recommended that you refer to Orton-Gillingham-Slingerland instructional texts for precise techniques.

With the techniques for encoding presented thus far, it is relatively easy to extrapolate and apply those that are applicable to encoding words of *three* or more syllables. The procedures for encoding with short vowels in one- and two-syllable words, and with vowels, letter combinations, and phonograms in both closed and open syllables provide the foundation for all encoding.

This is an appropriate time to reiterate that scope and sequence depends on whether instruction is to a class, to a small group, or to an individual student. The design of scope and sequence is also influenced by the age, maturity, motivation, and intelligence of the students—their grade level, previous spelling and writing instruction and practice—and the degree and type of learning disabilities they have, if any, including, in particular, kinesthetic-motor, auditory, and visual modality strengths and weaknesses. All these factors are important to the rationale upon which any scope and sequence for encoding and spelling can be recommended in order to ensure mastery.

Table 4–25 shows the sequence for encoding words of more than two syllables. After covering the material, continue teaching non-phonetic words. Select from *Lesson-Planner*, the previous tables, or from your own resources. Write phrases and sentences to put to functional use those words that were encoded and spelled in the day's lesson for integration. Again, some teachers will not want to forget short nonsense/pseudowords.

Encoding and Spelling Words with Common Suffixes and Prefixes

Note that there are prompt lists in *LessonPlanner* that contain the more common suffixes and prefixes that are usually introduced in *Spelling*, in Slingerland instruction. Similar common prefix and suffix prompt lists are also available in *Decoding*. The lists in table 4-26 were compiled by adding an affix (in bold) from the suffix and prefix prompt lists to base words. The words selected are those for which students should have sufficient skills and techniques in order to encode successfully.

Table 4–25. Encoding Words of More than Two Syllables	with **2 consonants in the medial position, plus an affix**	mis/spell/ings, in/ten/tion/al/ly, ex/pres/sion/less
	beginning with two-syllable words with short vowel or ə in each closed syllable	of/fen/ded, shel/lack<u>ing</u>, at/tach/ments
	with **a C-le second syllable**	gen/tle/man, smug/gler, puz/zle/ment, fee/ble/ness
	with **a letter combination in one syllable**	blank/et/ed, ex/tinc/tion
	with **a phonogram and C-le syllable or suffix**	re/mar/bling, tur/tle/dove
	with **a single consonant in the medial position**	whi/ten/ing, no/bil/i/ty
	and **at least 1 open syllable, plus affixes**	re/lo/ca/ted, de/mon<u>ize</u>
	with **a consonant digraph**	ci/pherable (re)se/quen/c<u>ing</u>,
	with **a consonant blend**	re/trace/able, cy/clo/tron
	with **a silent-e syllable**	no/ble/ness, re/ca/bled
	with **closed syllables**	pol/ish/ing, ven/om/ous/ly
	with **a consonant digraph**	fath/om/ing, (re)graph/a/ble
	with **a consonant blend**	stand/ee, un/roast/<u>able</u>
	with **no consonants in the medial position**	li/on/ize, tri/umph/ant/ly

Encoding Mixed Multisyllabic Words with Affixes

Your students should be ready now to encode a variety of multisyllabic word types that include an ever increasing variety of affixes. In *LessonPlanner*, you can retrieve multisyllabic words from the Blending "Phonemes Spelled As" menu. The list in table 4–27 was obtained from table 3–48 and was originally compiled for decoding. It works just as well for encoding at this stage. Additional similar words can be obtained by scrolling the Blending "Phonemes Spelled As" menu from the top downward and stopping to execute word searches and selections.

play**able**	**a**round	**demi**god	**out**side
haun**ted**	**ab**stract	**dis**charge	**over**cast
snow**ing**	**ad**vice	**en**gulf	**per**ceptive
hit**s** (plural & 3rd person sing.)	**al**low	**ex**it	**post**script
box**es**	**ante**chamber	**e**ject	**pre**scribe
slash**er** (doer)	**anti**biotic	**ec**centric	**pro**test
great**er** (comparative)	**be**queath	**ef**fective	**re**create
smart**est** (superlative)	**bene**ficial	**extra**curricular	**se**cede
thank**ful**	**com**plete	**for**bidden	**self**-service
yellow**ish**	**con**nect	**fore**front	**semi**circle
smoke**less**	**col**lect	**in**jection	**sub**way
swift**ly**	**co**-author	**inter**cede	**super**script
agree**ment**	**cor**rect	**intra**mural	**trans**lation
frank**ness**	**contra**indicate	**mal**practice	**un**decided
foam**y**	**de**cide	**mis**apply	**under**score
			nonfunctional

Table 4–26. Blending with Common Suffixes and Prefixes

After covering the material in table 4–27, continue teaching sight words. Select from *LessonPlanner* or the previous tables. Write phrases and sentences to put to functional use those words that were encoded and spelled, and for integration.

Table 4–27. Encoding Mixed Multisyllabic Words with Affixes and Endings	smoke/stacks	**ck** at the end of a compound word
	mech/an/ize	**ch** as /k/ and **v-e**
	or/phan/age	
	chlor/o/phyll	Greek-based with **ch** as /k/, **ph** as /f/, and **y** as /ĭ/
	sledge/ham/mer	with **dge** seemingly in the middle, but actually at the end of the first half of a compound word
	nos/tal/gic	soft **g**, and **c** at the end of a multisyllabic word, not **ck**
	gym/na/si/um	/ē/ spelled **i** before another vowel
	cam/paign/ing	**gn** as /n/
	re/de/signed	2 prefixes and the **ign** word family where "never rely on **i**" is evident
	script/wri/ter	twisty **wr**
	trans/lu/cen/cy	
	hop/scotch/es	**tch** at the end of a compound word
	strength/en/ing or streng/then/ing	infrequent **eng**
	ex/tinc/tion	**inc** as a letter combination like **ink**
	con/clu/sion	
	ex/clu/sion/ist	**ist** meaning a person, not **est**, the superlative
	bam/boo/zled	**C-le**
	tur/tle/dove	**C-le** and **scribal-o**
	pro/nounce/ments	soft **c**
	par/en/tage	**ar** as /ăr/
	thread/bare	
	in/ter/lude	

Encoding and Spelling Words with Advanced Suffixes and Endings

Another way to obtain lists of multisyllabic words for encoding is to select them from the last two Decoding menus and bring them over to Blending or Spelling from Other Sources. Table 4–28 contains words with advanced suffixes and endings and is shown as "suf'x/end's." Table 4–29 contains Latin and Greek roots with accompanying word lists.

It is shown as word roots. They are presented after suffixes and endings. The tables were derived from the lists in the sidebars at the end of Chapter 3.

Table 4–28. Encoding Words with Advanced Suffixes and Endings

voy**age**	tunn**el**	favor**ite**
dress**age**	confer**ence**	captiv**ity**
extern**al**	consist**ency**	surv**ive**
appli**ance**	respond**ent**	nonexplos**ive**
tru**ancy**	gas**eous**	reflect**or**
serv**ant**	vari**ety**	fact**ory**
burgl**ar**	magni**fy**	poison**ous**
moment**ary**	conf**ine**	essent**ial**
dict**ate**	quarant**ine**	Mart**ian**
priv**ate**	erm**ine**	quot**ient**
fac**ial**	glor**ious**	cau**tious**
absorbefa**cient**	spa**cious**	seven**ty**
fero**cious**	barbar**ism**	inconspi**cuous**
employ**ee**	ig**nite**	

The Ending /əs/ Spelled Ous or Us

As a reminder, **ous** in the word **poisonous** in the above table, and **us** in the word **bonus** have the same /əs/ phoneme. To know which to use in spelling you must recall that **ous** words are usually adjectives and that **us** words are nouns. Therefore, when the adjective ending **ous** is removed, the base word should be readily detected as when **ous** is removed from **poisonous**, leaving **poison**. With words such as **famous** the task is slightly more difficult because the **e** in the base word **fame** was dropped (Silent-**E** Spelling Rule) when the **ous** suffix, beginning with a vowel, was added. The **e** must be replaced when the suffix is removed. Similarly, the **y** was changed to an **i** (Consonant-**Y** Rule) when the suffix **ous** was added to the word **glory/glorious** (see above). More difficult still is the change in words such as the noun **caution** to the adjective **cautious** (above). Understanding that **cautious** is an adjective is helpful.

Do the /əs/ yellow card exercises that were recommended previously to prevent errors before they occur. The **ous** words can be retrieved from the *LessonPlanner* Decoding panel in the "suf'x/end's" menu and brought into either Blending or Spelling from Other Sources.

The following are some relatively common nouns ending in **us**: **bonus, cactus, circus, focus, minus, genius, census, sinus, octopus, stimulus,** and **hippopotamus**.

Encoding and Spelling Words with Latin and Greek Roots

The following words with Latin and Greek roots are retrievable from the Decoding "word roots" menu and then brought over to Blending or Spelling from Other Sources. One or two samples are provided for each underlined root.

Diana King[6], founder of Kildonan School—a college preparatory school for students with dyslexia—recommends that prefixes be taught with key words and meanings once students understand that Latin words consist of a prefix, a root, a connective, and a suffix. For example, she suggests that students learn and repeat **ex - exit - out, re - reverse - back** and **re - recopy - again**, and so on. She also recommends that practice be given decoding many words that contain the prefixes that are introduced. Next, she suggests that Latin roots be taught similarly. For example, students learn and say **ject - eject - throw, dict - predict - say,** and **mis/mit - transmit, transmission - send,** and so forth. After students learn several easier Latin prefixes and approximately ten Latin roots, King recommends that students begin to tackle the chameleon prefixes[7] before moving on to Greek based words, often comprised of two roots (Greek combining forms), frequently joined by connective **o,** such as **biography, monogram, photograph**. Students learn, for example, **mono - monogram - one, theo - theology - God,** and **ped/pod - pedal, podiatrist - foot**. King also suggests that some of the Greek roots may be taught as pairs (**telephone - distant sound** or **biology - life study**).

In an updated version of *LessonPlanner* there will be additional information and material for working with older, more advanced students.

---

[6] Diana Handbury King is not only the founder of Kildonan School in Amenia, New York, but she is also a long-time active member of the International Dyslexia Association, a recipient of their annual award, and charter member of the Orton-Gillingham Academy, as well as mentor teacher, consultant, and author.

[7] Chameleon prefixes are prefixes that change depending upon the spelling of the beginning of the root or base to which the prefix is affixed. For example the final letter of the prefix **sub** changes to a **c** before a base word or root that begins with a **c** (success), to an **f** before an **f** (suffer), and to **p** before **p** (support). Other common chameleon prefixes include **in, ex, dis, ad, ob,** plus several others.

Table 4–29. Encoding with Latin and Greek Roots

pro**ject**or	com**pend**ium	sub**mit**	de**cad**ent
de**ject**ed	**pend**ulous	**mis**sionary	**cas**ualty
portage	in**spect**or	**tend**ency	de**cid**uous
de**port**ee	per**spic**acious	con**tent**ion	con**duc**ive
in**flex**ible	mono**gram**	sub**sist**ence	pro**duct**ive
genu**flect**ion	autobio**graph**ical	de**sist**	**capt**ivating
pre**dict**ion	per**fid**ious	**cred**ulous	ac**cept**able
ab**dic**ation	**fed**eral	ac**cred**itation	de**pos**ition
com**puls**ive	re**fer**ee	con**curr**ently	im**pound**
ex**pell**ed	in**suffer**able	dis**course**	pro**gen**itor
in**tract**able	retro**grade**	sou**ven**ir	**gen**uine
at**tract**ive	pro**gress**ion	pre**vent**ative	de**fect**ive
insecti**cide**	en**vis**ion	e**voc**ative	putre**fact**ion
de**cis**ion	**evid**ent	**voc**iferous	**effic**acy
extro**vert**	re**cede**	super**script**ion	
adversity	an**cest**or	**scrib**ble	

Encoding Words with Three or More Syllables

If you and your students have followed the progression provided in this book, you should now be able to encode words and spell words with three or more syllables that contain a variety of roots and affixes.

In *LessonPlanner*, a good way to retrieve words of more than four syllables is from the Blending "Phonemes Spelled As" menu. Continue teaching non-phonetic words. Select from *LessonPlanner* or previous tables, or from your own resource materials. Write phrases and sentences to put to functional use those words that were encoded and spelled, and for integration. Refer to table 4–30 on page 185 for multisyllabic encoding of **i** pronounced /ĭ/ and **i** pronounced /y/.

Learning and Incorporating Spelling Rules

The three main spelling rules that govern spelling are:

1. the Silent-**E** Rule

2. the **1-1-1** Vowel Rule

3. the **C**onsonant-**Y** Rule

Additionally, there is an extension of the **1-1-1** Vowel Rule aptly referred to as the Extended **1-1-1** Rule.

The order in which the rules are taught is not as important as ensuring that they are taught using the structured steps for teaching any new learning and that they are reviewed often. In the Gillingham Manuals, in Slingerland's *Book 3*, the word list books for teachers (Slingerland and Murray, 1985), there are excellent, detailed descriptions of how to teach the spelling rules. In most Orton-based programs, they are referred to simply as the **1-1-1**, the Silent-**E**, and the **Y**-Rule. You will note wording variations for the rules that are not as important as using consistent wording with your students within programs. Some of the reasons for wording differences are given in the discussion of the rules individually, particularly for the **1-1-1** Vowel and **C**onsonant-**Y** rules.

The Silent-E Rule

The Silent-**E** Rule is stated first because it is the easiest of the three rules to teach and learn, and because it is often taught first, as follows:

If a word ends in a silent-e, (usually) *drop* the silent-e before adding a suffix that begins with a vowel (**like** + **ing** = **liking**). Do not drop the silent-e when adding a suffix that begins with a consonant (**like** + **ness** = **likeness**).

The word "usually" is inserted to accommodate words that end in **ce** or **ge** where the **e** is retained to maintain the soft /s/ and /j/ sounds, especially when adding the suffixes **able** and **ous** (noticeable, outrageous). To recall the most common exceptions to the second half of the Silent-E Rule—do *not* drop the silent-e when adding a suffix that begins with a consonant—the following is helpful: **Truly**, the **truth** of the **ninth argument** was **wholly** and **duly awful**. The base words in bold each end with an **e** that is dropped when a suffix beginning with a consonant (a consonant suffix) is added. At one time **judgment** and **acknowledgment** were also included in the list, but today **judgement** and **acknowledgement** are also acceptable spellings.

Table 4–30. Encoding Words of Three or More Syllables with Affixes	words with **i** pronounced /ĭ/	flex/i/bil/i/ty, episode, pragmatic, nutritious, electrician, determination visionary
	words with **i** pronounced /y/	civilian, spaniel, clothier, familial

There are words that retain the **e** when a consonant suffix is added to maintain the meaning of the base word and to avoid confusion with similar words. These include **dyeing** and **dyed** not to be confused with **dying** and **died**; **singeing** and **tingeing** not to be confused with **singing** and **tinging**; **hoeing** not to be confused with Santa's **ho-ho-hoing** and **toeing** versus **toing**, not quite a real word, but a plausible construction just the same. Similarly, we have **canoeing** and **shoeing**. For a slightly different reason, the **e** is retained in two forms of measurement, **mileage** and **acreage**.

Finally, the following similar exceptions must be memorized: **die - dying**, **tie - tying**, and **lie - lying**. Unfortunately there are a few other exceptions, too.

The 1-1-1 Vowel Rule

If a word is just one (1) syllable, and ends in just one (1) consonant, *directly* after just one (1) vowel, and if the suffix begins with a vowel (**V**) double the final consonant when adding a suffix that begins with a vowel (**hit** + **er** = **hitter**). Do not double the final consonant if the suffix begins with a consonant (**hit** + **less** = **hitless**).

The word "just" has been inserted into this rule three times because experience has shown that students frequently will say and look at a word such as **hunt** and think that it ends in one consonant and double the **t** when adding the suffix **ed** (**huntted**). Or, in the word **stoop**, they will see one vowel and double the final **p**. The word *just* emphasizes the fact that having one consonant at the end, with another consonant preceding it, means the word ends in two consonants.

The word **Vowel** has been added to the **1-1-1** Vowel Rule, again, because of the confusion caused when it is omitted. When the simpler title **1-1-1** Rule is used, students have nothing to prompt them when trying to remember the fourth important part to the rule. The word **Vowel** (or vowel suffix, as some teachers prefer) triggers this cognition—that the suffix must begin with a vowel.

The word *directly* has been inserted to emphasize that another letter cannot occur between the final consonant and the preceding single vowel for the **1-1-1** Vowel Rule to apply.

Exceptions exist only if students are not taught to never double **w**, **x**, and **y**. The reason **w** and **y** are not doubled is that at the end of one-syllable words after a vowel, they act as vowels. Perhaps many of you recall from your own early days at school that the vowels are **a**, **e**, **i**, **o**, **u**, and sometimes **y**. A few of you will also remember that **w** was included with **y** as a vowel. When **w** and **y** are pronounced /w/ and /y/, respectively, they are consonants, but in phonograms they are often vowels (**aw**, **ew**, **ay**, **ey**, etc.). The letter **x** does not double because it is already doubled in sound (/k/ + /s/ = /ks/).

Another case where additional instruction is required is with words such as **quiz** and **quizzes**. Although **quiz** appears to have two vowels, the **u** following **q** is acting as a consonant with the consonant **w** phoneme; the **z** is thus doubled. Again, you will find true exceptions, as well.

The Consonant-Y Rule

If a word ends in a *consonant*-**y**, change the **y** to **i** when adding *any* suffix (**cry** + **ed** = **cried** or **lovely** + **ness** = **loveliness**) except when the suffix begins with an **i**. Do not change **y** to **i** when the suffix begins with an **i** (**cry** + **ing** = **crying**, **copy** + **ist** = **copyist**), and do not change **y** to **i** if the base word ends in vowel-**y** (**play** + **ed** = **played**, **gray** + **er** = **grayer**).

Common exceptions include **daily**, **paid**, **said**, **laid**, **mislaid**, **lain**, **slain**, and less common, **gaily**, because of the currently popular meaning of **gay**.

Other Consonant-**y** Rule exceptions that can be grouped together for memorization are: **shyly** and **shyness**; **dryly** and **dryness**; **slyly** and **slyness**; **spryly** and **spryness**.

The Extended 1-1-1 Vowel Rule

If a word is more than **1** syllable, but ends in **1** consonant, after **1** vowel, and the suffix begins with a **vowel**, double the final consonant if the final syllable of the base word is accented (**occur'** + **ed** = **occurred**). Do not double the final consonant if the final syllable is unaccented (**o'pen** + **ing** = **opening**).

The words "just" and "directly" are usually not necessary with the Extended **1-1-1** Vowel Rule because the more advanced and older students who are learning the rule should already be secure with the simpler **1-1-1** Vowel Rule.

Some teachers feel that the extended **1-1-1** Vowel Rule is too time consuming and difficult to teach. They recommend instead that their students check the spellings of such words with a computer spell check, in the dictionary, or with one of the most useful tools ever produced for children and adults with dyslexia, the hand-held, *speaking* electronic dictionary.[8]

The most difficult aspect of teaching the Extended **1-1-1** Vowel Rule is its prerequisite accenting. That is just one of many reasons why the generalizations that govern accenting should be introduced early. The third grade level, or earlier, is not too soon to begin to work with accents.

The Letter "l" and the Extended 1-1-1 Vowel Rule

Another reason that some teachers avoid the Extended **1-1-1** Vowel Rule, is that it appears that more than one spelling is often acceptable for Extended **1-1-1** Rule words. This occurs because we see common Extended **1-1-1** Vowel Rule words ending in **l** doubled despite the placement of the accent. In the word **travel**, the accent is clearly on the first syllable; yet, often, the final **l** is doubled anyway (**travelled**, **travelling**, **traveller** or **traveled**, **traveling**, **traveler**). The British seem to have a spelling generalization that sometimes takes precedence over the Extended **1-1-1** Vowel Rule. The British generalization calls for doubling **l** frequently at the end of base words. Americans spell **woolen** and **jewelry** with one **l**; the British use two **l**'s, **woollen** and **jewellery** (plus an additional **e**). Yet, both Americans and British spell many words such as **cooler** and **toiling** with only one **l**.

---

[8] One of the best on the market today is the Bookman Merriam-Webster's Collegiate Dictionary, 1996. Published by Franklin Publishing, Inc. Burlington, NJ. Further information is available online at http://www.franklin.com.

There are other exceptions to be mastered when teaching the Extended **1-1-1 V**owel Rule. It is recommended that you refer to one of the Gillingham Manuals or to *How to Teach Spelling*, and the latter's accompanying fourth workbook, *How to Spell* (Rudginsky and Haskell, 1985), for exceptions to all four rules.

An Active Way to Look at Spelling Rules

If a word ends with an **e**, the big question is whether to ***drop*** the **e** or ***not drop*** the **e** when adding a suffix.

If a word ends with a **consonant**, the big question is whether to ***double*** the final consonant of the base word or ***not double*** when adding a suffix.

If a word ends in **consonant-y**, the big question is whether to ***change***, or ***not change*** the **y** to an **i** when adding a suffix.

Phrase and Sentence Writing to Reinforce Spelling Skills

Until students can spell, they cannot really express themselves in writing. When they write phrases that are dictated to them by their teacher, they are taking the first steps toward independent writing. For SLD students this is more difficult than it is for non-SLD students, for they must initially concentrate so carefully on how to spell the words within the phrases and sentences, even if the teacher has taught and reviewed the words extensively beforehand. This in turn distracts SLD students from the content of what they are writing.

Teachers are frequently dismayed and alarmed when the reverse occurs and they see how their SLD students' spelling deteriorates when asked to do creative, expository or other more independent writing. While writing "independently" students focus more on content at great cost to their spelling performance in the same way they focus more on spelling than on content when writing carefully planned and integrated, dictated phrases and sentences. That is why some educators feel so strongly that SLD students should be discouraged from independent writing until they become relatively secure spellers, for the pattern for every misspelling is carried to the brain where it stays. Spelling will become secure only after considerable practice with cards, encoding, spelling, and phrase and sentence writing of the type described.

Then students can move on to propositional writing which is more controlled than independent writing, but less controlled than writing teacher-dictated phrases and sentences. It also leads to fewer errors in spelling.

Traditional Orton-based instructors stress that the main purpose of their dictations, comparable to phrase and sentence writing in Slingerland *Spelling*, is not only for the students to apply what they have already learned, but also to stretch short-term auditory memory inherently requisite of dictations. Another Orton-based teacher's prime objective is to create a situation where students succeed at the task at hand, particularly one toward the end of the lesson.

When spelling is taught sequentially and as recommended in this book, students gradually begin to understand and appreciate the regularities of our English spelling system and become alert to its patterns, how words are constructed, and to conventions of correctness. The following quote from *Teaching Reading, A Balanced, Comprehensive Approach to Teaching Reading in Prekindergarten Through Grade Three* (California Department of Education, 1996b) lends further support for teaching spelling early as recommended, and outlined in this book:

> Good spelling is much more than a literary nicety. Poorly developed spelling knowledge is shown to hinder children's writing, to disrupt their reading fluency, and to obstruct their vocabulary development (Adams, Treiman, and Pressley, 1996; Read, 1986). Although it is appropriate to encourage beginners to use temporary or invented spellings to express their thoughts in print, programmatic instruction in correct spellings should begin in first grade and continue across the school years. In addition, and increasingly across the school years, children should be expected to attend to the correctness of their spelling in writing.

Dictations

In Chapter 4, we have followed an auditory progression that began with the smallest units of sound, sight, and feel (auditory cards) and progressed to the next larger units (words for encoding and spelling) and on to phrase, and then, sentence writing. Now we come to one of the last stages on the path to independent written expression, dictations. Dictations are excellent for teaching and reinforcing vocabulary and grammar, as discussed in the last section of this chapter.

In the Slingerland daily lesson plan format, *Dictation* is a time for students to study for output with careful teacher guidance. Initially, small paragraph dictations are presented visually for students to copy. The dictations provide guidance in review of previous learnings and as a place for new learnings. In the early elementary grades, dictations usually consist of one paragraph that conveys a single idea or thought. An introductory sentence introduces the topic; the sentence or perhaps more than one sentence of the body enriches the topic; and the final sentence concludes or summarizes the topic.

Eventually, in the upper elementary grades most often, skilled teachers elicit dictations from their students that have actually been carefully prepared and often written beforehand by the teacher. The purpose of dictations at this level is to teach students to verbalize and write good introductory paragraphs; to verbalize and write body paragraphs to support the introductory paragraph and/or lead smoothly into another paragraph; and to verbalize and write strong concluding paragraphs that tie the whole dictation together. Dictations also teach pre-writing skills, such as gathering facts, taking notes, organizing thoughts, and preparing progressively more precise outlines. Included, too, are other writing skills, such as, proofing, editing, and rewriting drafts so that the final drafts are ready to be submitted for grading.

Following the Orton-Gillingham sequence of instructional activities that comprise the one-hour daily lesson plan, the last stage of learning is usually dedicated to dictation of the kind described in *Spelling* in the Slingerland daily lesson plan format. Paragraph dictations were adapted by Slingerland from Orton-based tutorial or small group instruction for classroom use.

If you are desirous of learning to work with paragraph dictations, then it is recommended that you study the sections on dictations in Slingerland's *Books 2* and *3*.

Independent Writing

Independent writing or composition is the goal of instruction beginning with an auditory stimulus. It begins with auditory cards, and continues to the following: encoding; phonetic, non-phonetic, and ambiguous spelling practice and review, including the study of spelling generalizations, rules, and exceptions; phrase and sentence writing; and dictation composition and study. Once students learn these skills, they are freed to express their own thoughts in writing for a myriad of academic and personal purposes.

Integrating Grammar into Dictations and Composition

One of the best ways to integrate grammar skills and concepts that have been introduced visually is to put them to functional use in writing. This can be accomplished in the section of the lesson where dictated phrases and sentences are written, when composing dictations, and in propositional, narrative (storytelling) and expository (factual and informational) writing.

To cite just a few skills to reinforce in writing, the following are extrapolated from the vocabulary and grammar discussion and listed in Chapter 3: the capitalization of proper nouns, the indentation of paragraphs, the use of correct verb tense and number, the active voice, the writing of dialogue with correct punctuation, the variation of sentence patterns, the use of adjectives and adverbs to write more vividly, the use of appropriate informal writing, dictionary and thesaurus skills to enhance writing, the use of future tense, subject and predicate agreement, the correct punctuation of complex sentences, the application of hyphens, the correct usage of relative pronouns and clauses, combining sentences to vary sentence patterns, the ways to offset independent clauses including the em dash, the correct understanding and usage of similes and metaphors, the incorporation of figurative language, composition of different types of paragraphs (introductory, body and concluding), and the development of themes.

Written communication, like oral communication and other literacy skills, is a worthy goal to help your students achieve. Writing reflects good thinking; it is thinking on paper.

5
Conclusions

Three Lesson Plans

One of the primary purposes of this book is to help teachers improve their instruction of literacy skills by providing a scope and sequence that supports successful educational practices and research. The following three lessons show pictorially or more graphically how language units (cards, decoding, spelling, phrase writing, etc.) are integrated as a unified whole. The lessons are presented in three daily lesson plan formats: Slingerland, traditional Orton-Gillingham, and whole language augmented with phonics. As you view each plan, you will note differences, but those differences are not nearly as important as the similarities.

Overview of the Lesson's Content

This lesson is intended either for a beginning manuscript or cursive class—SLD or non-SLD—at an approximate second-third grade level. It is also appropriate for tutoring. No new letters are introduced in handwriting, but several are reviewed for integration.

Included in what we can now refer to as the visual lesson is the introduction of how to decode **v-e** words. The reading selection for the Slingerland and whole language lessons is taken from Clara McCulloch's *Selections for Teaching Reading* (McCulloch, 1990). The Orton-Gillingham reading selection was written by the instructor.

The same reading selection could not be used for the Orton-Gillingham lesson because, in Orton-based instruction, reading texts and materials are usually phonetic or controlled at this level of instruction. Since **v-e** was introduced in the lesson, the reading contains an abundance of **v-e** words to reinforce the new teaching in decoding and cards. In Slingerland instruction, the reading material, as in whole language, is usually not *controlled*, but techniques to prepare students to read literature-based texts successfully are presented in *Preparation for Reading* and in *Reading from the Book*. In the whole language lesson, comparable preparation was made before the students read the story.

For the spelling and written sections of the lesson, compiled from Slingerland's *Book 1,* the next new concept to be presented is for when to apply the plural (or third person singular) **es** ending. In the Slingerland lesson it is taught the same day as **v-e**, but on the auditory side of the daily format. In the Orton-Gillingham and whole language lessons, the teaching of **es** is postponed until a later lesson so as not to introduce two new concepts (**v-e** and **es**) visually in one lesson.

Another reason two new concepts would usually not be introduced in the Orton-Gillingham lesson is that Orton-based tutorials are usually slightly less than an hour; whereas, Slingerland daily lessons are usually slightly less than two hours. One hour is devoted to the visual side of the lesson and one hour is devoted to *Learning to Write* and the auditory side. Although the whole language lesson is also nearly two hours, it includes so many other required activities, the teacher felt that it would not be wise to introduce two new concepts, such as **v-e** and **es**, in the same lesson.

The Format of the Lesson Plans

Traditional Orton-Gillingham and whole language lesson plan formats are similar in that they are written from the top of a page downward and usually begin with what will be taught or reviewed first. Typically, a Slingerland lesson is written using a T-sheet format. *Learning to Write* is presented along the horizontal of the T while the *Visual Lesson* is placed to the right of the vertical of the T, and the *Auditory Lesson* is placed to the left. For consistency and readability, and to emphasize the similarities of Orton-Gillingham, whole language, and Slingerland, all three lessons are presented here using the same (linear) lesson plan format.

The described content of each lesson is briefer than the actual lessons in order to highlight similarities and explain differences.

The Slingerland Simultaneous Multisensory Lesson
Question of the Day

The *Question of the Day* is an integral part of Slingerland instruction. Its purpose is to help structure oral language skills. The question in this lesson is integrated into the reading of the day. It is:

In what way does a newborn baby differ from you?

Students are required to respond clearly in sentences using correct syntax[1] and grammar.

Learning to Write

The letters in *Learning to Write* are reviewed because they will be written later in blending, spelling, and in the phrases and sentences.

Review: **s**

Capital: **T**

Letter Groupings: **es**, **tch**, **zz**, **nd**, **tw**, **tr**, **ee**, **th**, **bl**, **uns**, **tches** and the word *a* spelled **a**

Visual Lesson
Cards

New: **a-e**, **e-e**, **i-e**, **o-e**

Review: **a, e, i, o, u, qu, y, ck, s**

Note how the graphemes in visual cards are integrated with the words that are included for decoding and also found in the reading selection.

Decoding

Decoding words include words that reinforce the newly introduced **v-e** decoding skills immediately after their introduction:[2] They also include review words selected from the story. Note the sequence of word patterns and concepts in the review list.

---

[1] Syntax refers to the way words are put together to form phrases, clauses, and sentences.

[2] Refer to Slingerland's *Book 1*, p.226 (Slingerland, 1971) to see how Slingerland teaches children to see the effect of the final **e** on the vowel in **v-e** words.

Decoding Words (printed in large letters on the blackboard)

New Words	Words from the Reading Selection	Words from Reading Requiring Teacher Assistance
lame	like	happy
lake	home	windows
raze	has	sister
babe	Mom	blanket
pale	bed	curtains
game	will	ready
wade	not	
haze	them	
shave	Then	
chase	black	
slave	with	
brake	rug	
flare	fast	
plane	my	
skate	bring	
shake	pink	
quake	good	
	for	
	short	
	girl	
	play	
	now	
	too	
	they	
	see	
	grow	

The Reading Selection

A New Baby

Mother is coming home
today. She will bring
the new baby with her.
I will be happy
to see them.

Mom has a room ready
for the new baby.
The bed is very small.
A small pink blanket
is in it. Pink curtains
are at the windows.
It is a good room
for a new baby.

The new baby is a girl.
She has short black hair.
Her eyes are blue.
My new baby sister
is pretty.

My baby sister is tiny
now, but she will grow
very fast. Then
we can play together
in my room.

My room is all blue.
A blue rug
is on the floor.
A new blue blanket
is on my bed.
My curtains are blue,
but they are not new.
My new baby sister
will like my room.

Today is a happy day.
My new baby sister
is coming home.
MY MOTHER
is coming home, too.

Preparation for Reading

Refer to *Books I and II* or this book for the *Preparation for Reading* techniques.

Phrases and Clues

The phrases are taken from the last three paragraphs of "A New Baby."

1. **for the new baby**

   ♦ Find and read the phrase that tells why Mom has a new room ready.

   ♦ Find and read the phrase that tells why or for whom someone might heat milk.

2. **very small**

    ◆ Read the phrase that tells about size.

    ◆ Read the phrase that tells how large or tiny something is.

    ◆ Read the phrase that denotes size but not color.

3. **short black hair**

    ◆ Find the phrase that tells about a part of the body.

    ◆ Find the phrase that is what (give the name of a child in the class with short black hair) has at the top (of his/her body/head).

4. **a small pink blanket**

    ◆ Find the phrase that describes what may be used to cover a baby.

    ◆ Find one of two phrases that tell about size.

5. **Pink curtains**

    ◆ Read the phrase that tells what may be at the windows.

    ◆ Read the phrase that begins a sentence.

6. **at the windows**

    ◆ Find the phrase that tells where curtains hang.

    ◆ Find the phrase that tells where you might look to find finger smudges.

In *LessonPlanner* in the third DEMO plan, you can find additional clues to apply to the above phrases, as well as an optional exercise to provide more practice reading the phrases. Questions and topics suggested by McCulloch to pose to the children are also included, such as, Why is there no mention of a father?

Reading from the Book

Before reading from the reader that contains the above phrases, the teacher usually reviews the previous day's reading, and asks review questions, such as, How did the person telling the story feel about the new baby? . . . How do you know?[3] The teacher also asks questions to help the children project forward from the reading se-

---

[3] The same lesson in *LessonPlanner* is more comprehensive than the one in this book and contains many more how, who, what, where, when, etc. questions.

lection. For example, she might ask, Where do you think the children might sleep? Will the baby be a brother or sister? Next, the teacher will apply the four steps of Reading from the Book as needed.

In Step One, structured reading, the teacher "structures" the reading, for instance, by asking a student to read the first two words that stay together (**Mom has**), then the next three words to the end of the line (**a room ready**), and the next line that tells us why the room is ready (**for the new baby**). After the student re-reads the sentence in its entirety, and other students read it also, the teacher will structure as many more sentences as are felt necessary before moving on to the next step.

In Step Two, studying aloud, a student is asked to do his own structuring by reading aloud with correct phrasing. In the third paragraph, a child might read **The new baby/ is a girl./ She has/ short black hair./**

In Step Three, studying silently, the children read and study silently applying the skills they applied in the previous steps and other skills, such as decoding, as needed. Then several children are called upon to read. They are guided and corrected supportively.

In Step Four, studying independently and then orally, the teacher asks the students to find out, for instance, as much as they can about the storyteller's room in the second to last paragraph of the story. Later the children will return to describe and read about the room.

Students may then work individually doing follow-up seatwork.

Auditory Lesson

Cards

New from the visual lesson: /ā/ as in s<u>afe</u> (**a-e**), /ē/ as in th<u>ese</u> (**e-e**), /ī/ as in d<u>ime</u> (**i-e**), and /ō/ as in h<u>ome</u> (**o-e**)

Review in preparation for words to be blended and spelled: /z/ as in **z**ebra, /ks/ (**x**), /s/ as in **s**un, /ă/, /ĕ/, /ĭ/, /ŭ/, /k/ as in bla**ck**, and /z/ as in ha**s** or wa**s**.

Yellow cards: /ch/ (**ch**air, ma**tch**) and /k/ (**c**ake, **k**ite, ja**ck**, **Ch**ristmas or **ch**emistry)

Note how the phonemes in auditory cards are integrated with words that are included for encoding and spelling.

Blending

Discrimination

With short vowels: **bland, flit, grunt, grant, as, grudge**

For /sh/ - /ch/ endings: **fish, crunch, branch, brush, fresh**

Blending words

and, **up**, **runs**, **black**, **twig**, and **tree** and **green** to review **ee** blending from the previous day (**v-e** words will not be blended until the following week for the auditory lesson is outpaced by the visual lesson).

Spelling

The teacher directs the children to listen to what happens to words that end in **s, x, z, ch,** and **sh** (or that end with the sounds /s/, /x/, /z/, /ch/, and /sh/) when someone tells about another person or thing. Words: **hitch - hitches, hush - hushes, smash - smashes, buzz - buzzes, frizz - frizzes, dash - dashes, catch - catches, dress - dresses, pass - passes, lunch - lunches, box - boxes**. The students then blend the **es** words with short-**a** and short-**u**, in or out of the chart, and write as many as time allows. Various previously taught suffixes are added to at least one base word:

> **dash**
> **dashing**
> **dashed**
> **dashes**

Phrases

After a phrase is dictated by the teacher, the children are often asked to identify the number of words in the phrase (phonemic awareness) before repeating the phrase and writing it.

> **runs and pants**
> **a dashing run**
> **dashes and runs**
> **catches a twig**

Sentences

Sentences are used to integrate phrases, spelling, blending, auditory cards, and *Learning to Write*. After reviewing the red flag word **the**, the teacher dictates the first sentence for the students to write phrase-by-phrase after repeating each phrase before writing. The second sentence is presented in the same way.

> **The black cat/ dashes and runs/ up a tree.**
> **The fat cat catches a twig.**

The Orton-Gillingham Simultaneous Multisensory Lesson

In a traditional Orton-Gillingham lesson, the introduction of vowel-consonant-**e** occurs at the end of Level I. Some concepts from Level II were already known by the student for whom this lesson is intended. (See tables 3.1 and 3.2.) Of the six syllable types—closed, v-e, open, r-controlled, diphthong, and consonant-le—only the identification and division (syllabification) of closed syllables (**cvc**) has been introduced previously. Generally, when **v-e** is introduced, its identification as the second syllable type (**v-e**) will not be introduced in the same lesson.

For this particular lesson, it is assumed that the student has learned one phoneme for each letter of the alphabet. The letter **y** was learned only as a consonant. Digraphs **th**, **ch**, **sh**, and **wh** were introduced as well as **ck** and **tch**. Gillingham's first spelling generalization, pertaining to words ending in **ff**, **ll**, and **ss**, has also been taught and mastered.

Within the past several weeks of tutoring the student learned definitions for the following: consonant, vowel, syllable, and digraph. These definitions were written into the student's notebook. It is assumed that the student needs extra review of the digraph **sh**. The Orton-Gillingham tutor addresses such individual needs by adding difficult elements throughout the lesson, even redesigning or adapting the lesson to fit the special needs of the student. A particularly difficult concept might altogether be re-introduced. For the purposes herein, it is also assumed that during the last tutoring session, the tutor noted that her student required additional review in the division of two-syllable **cvc** words.

The progression for the lesson follows:

I. Phonogram Review

Review phonogram cards (symbol-to-sound review): **a**, **b**, **c** as /k/, **f**, **h**, **i**, **j**, **k**, **m**, **p**, **t**, **g** as /g/, **o**, **r**, **l**, **n**, **th**, **u**, **ch** as /ch/, **e**, **s** as /s/, **sh**, **d**, **w**, **wh**, **y** as /y/, **v**, **x**, **z**, **ck**, and **qu**.

II. Presentation of a New Concept

The tutor places **a-e**, **e-e**, **i-e**, and **o-e** cards on the desk. An explanation of the cards is given as well as the key word and sound for each card. Information about **v-e** is written into the student's notebook with the help of the tutor. The tutor explains how the **e** at the end of many words is silent, i.e., cannot be sounded out as it can at the beginning of the word **elephant** or in the middle of the word **get**. The **e** at the end of the word, furthermore, makes the preceding vowel long, i.e., makes it say its name. Depending on the ability of the student, the definition for long and short vowel sounds may be added to the student's notebook. Syllable type **v-e** will be added to the notebook at a later date. Immediately following the introduction of the new concept, the tutor presents approximately ten words to be decoded that illustrate the **v-e** concept. The following, presented in large print on a separate sheet of paper, is typical.

Decoding

<u>cvc</u>	<u>v-e</u>
rat	rate
pal	pale
can	cane
hid	hide
win	wine
bit	bite
cop	cope
rob	robe
mop	mope

A paragraph for further exposure to **v-e** is read aloud by the student. Words such as <u>the</u>, <u>he</u>, and <u>a</u>, containing concepts that the student has not yet learned, are treated as learned (sight) words. They are underlined. The following story was written by the tutor who knows her student has a penchant for kites. The tutor could have used a phonetic reader.[4]

Mat's Kite

Mat will take a bike and ride it up <u>a</u> big hill. With <u>a</u> dime, <u>he</u> will get <u>a</u> kit and take it with him. <u>He</u> will take a thin rope and a bit <u>of</u> tape. <u>He</u> will make <u>a</u> fine red and white kite. Then <u>he</u> will sit on <u>the</u> site and hope that <u>the</u> kite will not rip.

---

[4] EPS has an excellent selection of phonetic stories, workbooks, and readers that are compatible with Orton-based instruction. A west coast resource is Academic Publications in Novato, CA 94949-6191. Academic Therapy Publications is well known for its *High Noon Books* series.

III. Words Read in Isolation

Decoding and syllabification of words from a prepared list is presented in order to review concepts that were either recently learned or that need additional review or re-introduction. A few **v-e** words are included in this exercise. The words can be presented in a variety of formats, such as in a game with cards or on sentence strips to be cut into syllables by the student. The following **cvc** word list and nonsense word list are presented separately.

First Word List

yell	zest	wish
whiff	lash	swish
loft	slash	raft
ship	splash	stuck
mass	thick	struck
less	dine	shone
gate	drive	yoke
crave	vote	trick
hitch	chum	notch

Second Word List

zesh	shass	plit
voth	sime	cruss
whid		

Third Word List

rustic	picnic	tablet
plastic	rabbit	bandit
spastic	dismiss	confess
metric	quintet	canyon
cutlet	fabric	campus

The third word list is intended for an exercise in syllable division. The students are asked to cut the words into syllables with scissors. This can be executed into a game format with dice, wagering, and bingo, etc. Later, when the Doubling (1-1-1) and Silent-E spelling rules have been taught, this simple game format involving the separation of syllables, including affixes, will become a powerful vehicle by which to reinforce when and when not to double the final consonant of a base word when adding a suffix or when and when not to drop the silent-**e** on a word when adding a suffix. Conversely, the game can be used to put various syllables together for further reinforcement of easily confused, often painful spelling concepts.

IV. "What says . . . ?"

The following is based on the Gillingham (yellow) Drill Cards for sound-to-symbol review. It is often referred to as "What says?" In this lesson there are the following: /ă/, /b/, /k/ (**c**, **k**, and **ck**), /f/, /h/, /ĭ/, /j/, /m/, /p/, /t/, /g/, /ŏ/, /r/, /l/, /n/, /th/, /ŭ/, /ch/, /ĕ/, /s/, /sh/, /d/, /hw/, /y/, /z/, /ā/ (**a-e**), /ē/ (**e-e**), /ō/ (**o-e**), and /ī/, (**i-e**).

V. S.O.S. and Dictated Phrases

Simultaneous Oral Spelling (S.O.S.) and dictated phrases are presented next. Words to be blended or spelled with S.O.S. include the following: **the, posh, chin, hiss, zip, whale, moss, shin, van, fluff, spell, dish, shine, vane, dine**.

Learned words are reviewed first. No dictated phrases will be given in this lesson; however, the following sentences will be dictated:

> <u>**The**</u> **white dog will run and hide.**
> **It will zig and zag up hill.**
> <u>**The**</u> **sun will shine.**

With a slightly more skilled student, the following little poem, composed by the tutor, would have been dictated for the student to write:

> <u>**The**</u> **haze and fog will swell and fade.**
> **It will zig and zag up hill.**
> <u>**A**</u> **plane not made to land will win.**
> **It will shine while in <u>the</u> sun.**

In the next lesson, the **v-e** syllable type will be introduced as a new concept, and definitions for both closed and **v-e** syllables will be compared and written into the student's notebook. Since many Orton-based tutorials are less than an hour, it is usually inadvisable to introduce two new concepts in one lesson. The plural **es** will be taught after plural **s** is reviewed.

VI. Oral Reading

At this point in the lesson, the student would read another phonetic story, such as the "The Whale" from the packet of *Little Stories* that accompany Gillingham and Stillman's remedial training program.

The Whale

This is a ship. It went to get fish. A big wave broke on the ship.

The ship had a bad time. The nets tore and let the fish swim off. A man fell from the mast. Then the mast broke.

"The men must help," said the mate. "Get ropes! Mend the mast and the nets!"

A big hulk swam up. "A whale!" said the mate.

The whale ate up the fish from the nets. The mate shot a gun. The shot had a line on it. It hit the whale. The whale did not bump the ship. It swam off with the rope and the fish.

At last the ship is home. The mate is glad the ship is safe. But he is sad that the whale ate the fish.

The Whole Language Lesson Augmented with Phonics

This whole language lesson was written for a heterogeneous class of third graders from approximately ten different cultural backgrounds. Integrating English instruction is particularly essential for students whose native tongue is not English as well as for students from disadvantaged environments. The academic skill levels range from primer to fourth grade.

I. Daily Oral Language

Every day starts with a daily oral language exercise. Today, the students are required to read and correct a sentence or two from the following paragraph that is projected on a screen from an overhead projector. Skills and corrections the teacher will focus upon include grammar, punctuation, capitalization, vocabulary, phonics, identification of learned phonograms, spelling, and comprehension.

Family Paragraph

> jim lives with his family in daly city he has a pesty younger
> sister named maria who is chubby and has wavy black hair
> his favorite pet is a frisky brown and black puppy named
> coco. jim and maria enjoy playing with there puppy in the
> bake yard

II. Vocabulary Development

Vocabulary instruction is preparatory to reading the story, "A New Baby." Students are asked to name *family* words. As they name each word, the teacher writes the word on a 4×6 index card. The cards are given to students to illustrate. They become a part of the class's permanent vocabulary board. The teacher adds additional words not named by the students that are part of the programmed vocabulary for the family theme. These words are also illustrated by the students and added to the vocabulary board. Later they will be clipped together on a large ring rather than displayed individually. When students need *family* words, they then know where to locate them.

Family Words

Some of the *family* words are contained in "A New Baby."

mother	father	sister	brother
aunt	uncle	cousin	girl
boy	man	woman	baby
sister	stepsister	stepfather	stepmother
stepbrother	grandmother	grandfather	

III. Reading

A New Baby

Mother is coming home
today. She will bring
the new baby with her.
I will be happy
to see them.

Mom has a room ready
for the new baby.
The bed is very small.
A small pink blanket
is in it. Pink curtains
are at the windows.
It is a good room
for a new baby.

The new baby is a girl.
She has short black hair.
Her eyes are blue.
My new baby sister
is pretty.

My baby sister is tiny
now, but she will grow
very fast. Then
we can play together
in my room.

My room is all blue.
A blue rug
is on the floor.
A new blue blanket
is on my bed.
My curtains are blue,
but they are not new.
My new baby sister
will like my room.

Today is a happy day.
My new baby sister
is coming home.
MY MOTHER
is coming home, too.

Prior to Reading

Before the story is read together the following types of questions will be asked of the students who are required to respond in complete sentences:

1. **What do you think is going to happen in the story now?**
2. **Who do you think the story is going to be about?**

Reading

As the students read, the teacher clarifies unfamiliar vocabulary, such as the word **curtains** for the ESL[5] children as well as those who might not have curtains in their homes or in the homes of friends and relatives. Every student is given the opportunity to read aloud daily.

The more difficult words that the children misread will be noted and included in the following day's vocabulary development.

After Reading

After reading, the teacher will ask **who, what, when, where, why, how,** and **how many** questions. When a student makes grammatical or other errors when responding, the teacher will repeat a corrected version of what the student said. Depending on how smoothly the students read, they might be required to write their responses to questions. When they are in doubt about the spelling of words they want to use, they can ask their teacher or refer to the vocabulary board. The writing assignment today or within the next few days is for each student to describe his or her own family and then to illustrate their written text. If time is limited, the teacher will have several students summarize the story up to the point where they stopped reading. They will also be asked **what** they think is going to happen next in the story, and **why**.

The following day, vocabulary development will include *house* words because they tie in nicely with "A New Baby" and the family theme.

IV. Handwriting

Cursive handwriting today will include writing **v-e** words.

---

[5] ESL is the abbreviation for <u>E</u>nglish as a <u>s</u>econd <u>l</u>anguage.

V. Phonics, Spelling and Writing

In today's lesson, the students will learn the silent-**e** generalization. First, the teacher will demonstrate in a chart with alphabet cards what happens to words like **pin** when an **e** is added: the vowel preceding the added **e** becomes long; the final **e** is silent. The students have already been taught the breve and macron diacriticals. Additionally, they have learned that an **x** above a letter indicates that it is silent. Several students come to the chart and add a silent-**e** to words while explaining how and why the pronunciation of the word changes.

Adding Silent-e

$$pin + e = pine$$
$$can + e = cane$$
$$rod + e = rode$$
$$cut + e = cute$$
$$pet + e = Pete$$

The next step for the students is to write and change a list of similar words provided by the teacher (**rip - ripe, not - note, us - use, cub - cube, fin - fine, tap - tape**). As they write the words they are required to place a breve above the short vowel of the words in the first list. In the second list, they must place a macron above the first vowel and an **x** over the silent-**e**. Students then use the words in oral sentences to ensure knowledge of their meanings.

On Thursday, the students will have a spelling test. Most of the words will be **v-e** words. Super spellers (challenge words) for the more advanced students include several of the family words (mother, father, grandmother, etc.). For either class or homework, the students might be asked to alphabetize the spelling words, to write definitions from the dictionary, and/or to write sentences using the **v-e** words. Another day, they will be asked to write a poem using **v-e** or *family* words. The poem is placed in a folder entitled *Family*. In this class, students are exposed to poetry early. A poem a day is presented after *Daily Oral Language* to introduce, reinforce, and extend vocabulary, grammar, and phonics.

Although nearly two hours daily are devoted to language arts instruction, the introduction of plural **es** must be postponed until the following day. With the introduction of **v-e** and all twenty-six children reading aloud daily in this class, the teacher will not have time to teach another new concept. Plural **s** will, however, be reviewed in preparation for the introduction of plural **es**. Words from the vocabulary board will be used to review the **s** plural and to introduce the **es** plural. Using the new *house* words, the students have the following **s** and **es** plurals.

Singular	**Plural s**
window	windows
chair	chairs
door	doors
rug	rugs
curtain	curtains
table	tables

Singular	**Plural es**
couch	couches
dish	dishes
glass	glasses
duplex	duplexes
mailbox	mailboxes
mattress	mattresses
latch	latches

VI. Seatwork

Students are given sentences with blanks that they are to fill in with nouns or adjectives. For example, carrying through with the family theme, the students will fill in the following:

My _____ is as _____, _____ as a _____.
      (noun)   (adjective)   (adjective)   (noun)

One little girl wrote the following poem about members of her family.

My Family is a Rainbow

My father is as beautiful blue as the sky.
My mother is as pretty pink as a rose.
My sister is as graceful green as springtime.
My dog is as pillowy white as a cloud.
My brother is as brilliant black as a panther.

Referencing the Research

Educational research is having a significant impact on literacy. Never again is it likely that teachers will teach literacy using either a strict phonics approach *or* a meaning-emphasis approach, such as whole language. This is because teachers are gradually and surely becoming better informed in not only how to teach literacy, but also in how to prepare themselves to do so effectively.

In this book, much that is compatible with literacy research is included, but obviously not all. As discussed in Chapter 4, a myriad of different types of direct, explicit phonemic awareness skills must be incorporated into early and later instruction, and written expression must be sequenced and extended. The instruction of vocabulary and grammar, as discussed and outlined in Chapter 3, must also be expanded and enhanced, and pseudowords and/or nonsense words should frequently be created and included for decoding and perhaps cautiously for spelling development and skill. There must be increased focus on fluency to improve reading, especially reading comprehension. Equally important, teachers must teach students how to read so that they can answer questions that pertain to the reading successfully. These skills may be taught in *Reading from the Book* and in *Question of the Day*. They are of especial importance because they help students learn how to generate their own questions.

As literacy teachers gradually change how they teach, they will be confronted with the task of deciding what kinds of reading materials to use. Their selections should not be either-or as in either meaning-based *or* phonics-based. Any recommended solution should involve informed, improved compromise: Students can, for instance, review, solidify, and practice recently acquired decoding skills by reading some controlled reading texts. Alternatively, or additionally, teachers can learn and apply the techniques developed by Slingerland to prepare and assist students to read rich meaning-based literature, as outlined in Chapter 3 in *Preparation for Reading* and *Reading from the Book*. Or, they can adapt their own program to satisfy other research findings. Whatever the choices are, they should be based on the results of newer, more appropriate, and accurate assessment of literacy skills and needs.

To be an informed educator is crucial; therefore, both review and study of research are necessary. Mentioned already, are the *National Research Panel Report* and the

International Dyslexia Association's position paper entitled *Informed Instruction for Reading Success: Foundations for Teacher Preparation* (Brady and Moats, 1997). Both provide clearly written, up-to-date, reviews of why changes in reading instruction and teacher preparation are necessary, what we have learned about reading from research, what the resources are for children who struggle with learning to read, what distinguishes them from good readers, what an informed approach to reading is, and what the significant requirements are to become expert reading instructors or professionals in related fields. Excellent references and resources for more in-depth study about literacy and literacy research are also provided in these works.

A Final Word

As you come to the conclusion of *Scope & Sequence for Literacy Instruction*, take a little time to reflect upon what you learned. I hope that *Scope & Sequence for Literacy Instruction* satisfies the requests of many dedicated teachers for ways to lighten and clarify the awesome task of literacy instruction. As an experienced or newer teacher you should now know a lot more about the subject you teach, understand the rationales for instruction better, and be able to instruct with deeper pleasure and expertise, and with improved results. You have taken the initial steps to be in the mainstream of this exciting time when research in education demands change. You can reap the benefits of contributing to a world where everyone is literate.

LessonPlanner Graphemes
with Keywords and Phonemes

b	[b]all	/b/		m	[m]ittens	/m/
c	[c]ake	/k/		mb	co[mb]	/m/
k	[k]ite	/k/		mn	colu[mn] (au-tumn)	/m/
ck	ja[ck]	/k/		n	[n]est	/n/
ch	[Ch]ristmas	/k/		kn	[kn]ife	/n/
que	uni[que] (an-tique)	/k/		gn	si[gn] (gnat)	/n/
qu	[qu]iche	/k/		pn	[pn]eumonia	/n/
d	[d]uck	/d/		p	[p]ig	/p/
ed	stay[ed]	/d/		qu	[qu]een	/kw/
f	[f]ish	/f/		qua	[qua]d	/kwǒ/
ph	[ph]one	/f/		quar	[quar]t	/kwôr/
gh	lau[gh]	/f/		r	[r]ug	/r/
g	[g]oat	/g/		wr	[wr]ench	/r/
gh	[gh]ost	/g/		rh	[rh]ubarb	/r/
gue	intri[gue]	/g/		s	[s]un	/s/
h	[h]ouse	/h/		z	walt[z]	/s/
j	[j]am	/j/		ce	[ce]nt	/s/
dge	bri[dge] (fudge)	/j/		ci	[ci]ty	/s/
ge	[ge]ntle	/j/		cy	fan[cy] (cycle)	/s/
gi	[gi]nger (gi-raffe)	/j/		ps	[ps]ychology	/s/
				sc	[sc]ience	/s/
gy	[gy]psy	/j/		t	[t]urtle	/t/
l	[l]amp	/l/		ed	wish[ed]	/t/

v	[v]ase	/v/	tu	mu[tu]al	/ch$\overline{oo}$/
w	[w]agon	/w/	sia	A[sia]	/zhə/
u	s[u]ave	/w/	ang	s[ang]	/aŋ/
wa	[wa]tch	/wŏ/	ing	s[ing]	/iŋ/
war	[war]m	/wôr/	ong	s[ong]	/oŋ/
wor	[wor]ld	/wur̵/	ung	s[ung]	/uŋ/
x	bo[x]	/ks/	eng	l[eng]th	/eŋ/
x	e[x]ist	/gz/	ank	s[ank]	/aŋk/
y	[y]ellow	/y/	ink	s[ink]	/iŋk/
i	mill[i]on	/y/	unk	s[unk]	/uŋk/
z	[z]ebra	/z/	onk	h[onk]	/oŋk/
s	wa[s] (rose)	/z/	tion	na[tion]	/shən/
sh	[sh]ip	/sh/	sion	mis[sion]	/shən/
ch	[Ch]icago (champagne)	/sh/	tion	ques[tion]	/chən/
			sion	vi[sion]	/zhən/
sch	[sch]wa	/sh/	tle	lit[tle]	/t'l/
ci	so[ci]al (musician)	/sh/	ple	pur[ple]	/p'l/
			kle	pic[kle]	/k'l/
ti	spa[ti]al (partial)	/sh/	cle	bicy[cle]	/k'l/
			stle	bri[stle] (whistle)	/s'l/
si	controver[si]al	/sh/			
xi	an[xi]ous	/sh/	ble	a[ble]	/b'l/
ce	o[ce]an	/sh/	dle	grid[dle]	/d'l/
su	[su]gar	/sh/	fle	waf[fle]	/f'l/
ch	[ch]air	/ch/	gle	bu[gle]	/g'l/
tch	ma[tch]	/ch/	sle	has[sle]	/s'l/
wh	[wh]eel	/hw/	zle	fiz[zle]	/z'l/
th	[th]imble	/th/	ture	pic[ture]	/chər/
th	[th]is	/t̵h̵/	a	[a]pple	/ă/
du	e[du]cate	/j$\overline{oo}$/	e	[e]lephant	/ĕ/
su	u[su]al	/zh/	ea	h[ea]d	/ĕ/

i	[i]nch	/ĭ/
y	m[y]th	/ĭ/
ie	misch[ie]f	/ĭ/
ai	mount[ai]n	/ĭ/
o	[o]lives	/ŏ/
u	[u]mbrella	/ŭ/
o	h[o]ney	/ŭ/
ou	d[ou]ble	/ŭ/
au	P[au]l (author)	/ô/
aw	s[aw]	/ô/
al	[al]most	/ôl/
augh	c[augh]t	/ô/
ough	f[ough]t	/ô/
oi	[oi]l	/oi/
oy	b[oy]	/oi/
ou	[ou]ch	/ou/
ow	c[ow]	/ou/
ough	dr[ough]t	/ou/
or	c[or]n	/ôr/
ar	st[ar]	/är/
age	sabot[age]	/äzh/
er	h[er]	/ʉɼ/
ir	b[ir]d	/ʉɼ/
ur	b[ur]n	/ʉɼ/
ear	[ear]n	/ʉɼ/
our	n[our]ish	/ʉɼ/
yr	mart[yr]	/ʉɼ/
er	hard[er]	/ər/
or	doct[or]	/ər/
ar	doll[ar]	/ər/
oo	b[oo]k	/o͝o/

u	f[u]ll	/o͝o/
ar	c[ar]ry	/ăr/
er	ch[er]ry	/ĕr/
ir	m[ir]ror	/ĭr/
a at the end of an accented syllable	b[a]by	/ā/
a-e	s[a- f -e]	/ā/
ai	r[ai]n	/ā/
ay	pl[ay]	/ā/
eigh	sl[eigh]	/ā/
ea	st[ea]k	/ā/
ei	v[ei]n	/ā/
ey	th[ey]	/ā/
é	souffl[é]	/ā/
et	val[et]	/ā/
e at the end of an accented syllable	m[e]ter	/ē/
e-e	th[e- s -e]	/ē/
ee	f[ee]t	/ē/
ea	[ea]t	/ē/
ie	ch[ie]f	/ē/
y	cand[y]	/ē/
ey	k[ey]	/ē/
ei	rec[ei]ve	/ē/
i	man[i]ac	/ē/
i-e	mach[i- n -e]	/ē/
i at the end of an accented syllable	t[i]ger	/ī/

i-e	p[i- n -e]	/ī/
igh	n[igh]t	/ī/
ie	p[ie]	/ī/
y at the end	m[y] (sky)	/ī/
y-e	t[y- p -e]	/ī/
ei	[Ei]nstein	/ī/
o-e	h[o- m -e]	/ō/
oa	b[oa]t	/ō/
ow	sn[ow]	/ō/
oe	t[oe]	/ō/
o at the end of an accented syllable	p[o]ny	/ō/
ough	alth[ough]	/ō/
u at the end of an accented syllable	m[u]sic	/ū/
u-e	m[u- l -e]	/ū/
ew	f[ew]	/ū/
eu	[Eu]rope (feud)	/ū/
ue	val[ue] (rescue)	/ū/
ou	s[ou]p	/o͞o/
u at the end of an accented syllable	l[u]nar	/o͞o/
eu	n[eu]tral	/o͞o/
u-e	fl[u- t -e]	/o͞o/
ue	tr[ue]	/o͞o/
oo	m[oo]n	/o͞o/
ui	fr[ui]t	/o͞o/
ough	thr[ough]	/o͞o/

ew	fl[ew] (grew)	/o͞o/
a at the end of an unaccented syllable	c[a]det	/ə/
e at the end of an unaccented syllable	s[e]dan	/ə/
o at the end of an unaccented syllable	p[o]lite	/ə/
u at the end of an unaccented syllable	s[u]perb	/ə/

Appendix B

LessonPlanner Phonemes with Keywords and Graphemes

/b/	[b]all	b		/n/	[n]est	n
/k/	[c]ake	c			[kn]ife	kn
	[k]ite	k			si[gn] (gnat)	gn
	ja[ck]	ck			[pn]eumonia	pn
	[Ch]ristmas	ch		/p/	[p]ig	p
	uni[que] (antique)	que		/kw/	[qu]een	qu
	[qu]iche	qu		/kwŏ/	[qua]d	qua
/d/	[d]uck	d		/kwôr/	[quar]t	quar
	stay[ed]	ed		/r/	[r]ug	r
/f/	[f]ish	f			[wr]ench	wr
	[ph]one	ph			[rh]ubarb	rh
	lau[gh]	gh		/s/	[s]un	s
/g/	[g]oat	g			walt[z]	z
	[gh]ost	gh			[ce]nt	ce
	intri[gue]	gue			[ci]ty	ci
/h/	[h]ouse	h			fan[cy] (cycle)	cy
/j/	[j]am	j			[ps]ychology	ps
	bri[dge] (fudge)	dge			[sc]ience	sc
	[ge]ntle	ge		/t/	[t]urtle	t
	[gi]nger (giraffe)	gi			wish[ed]	ed
	[gy]psy	gy		/v/	[v]ase	v
/l/	[l]amp	l		/w/	[w]agon	w
/m/	[m]ittens	m			s[u]ave	u
	co[mb]	mb		/wŏ/	[wa]tch	wa
	colu[mn] (autumn)	mn		/wôr/	[war]m	war

/wʉr/	[wor]ld	wor	/iŋk/	s[ink]	ink
/ks/	bo[x]	x	/uŋk/	s[unk]	unk
/gz/	e[x]ist	x	/oŋk/	h[onk]	onk
/y/	[y]ellow	y	/shən/	na[tion]	tion
	mill[i]on	i		mis[sion]	sion
/z/	[z]ebra	z	/chən/	ques[tion]	tion
	wa[s] (rose)	s	/zhən/	vi[sion]	sion
/sh/	[sh]ip	sh	/t'l/	lit[tle]	tle
	[Ch]icago (champagne)	ch	/p'l/	pur[ple]	ple
	[sch]wa	sch	/k'l/	pic[kle]	kle
	so[ci]al (musician)	ci		bicy[cle]	cle
	spa[ti]al (partial)	ti	/s'l/	bri[stle] (whistle)	stle
	controver[si]al	si	/b'l/	a[ble]	ble
	an[xi]ous	xi	/d'l/	grid[dle]	dle
	o[ce]an	ce	/f'l/	waf[fle]	fle
	[su]gar	su	/g'l/	bu[gle]	gle
/ch/	[ch]air	ch	/s'l/	has[sle]	sle
	ma[tch]	tch	/z'l/	fiz[zle]	zle
/hw/	[wh]eel	wh	/chər/	pic[ture]	ture
/th/	[th]imble	th	/ă/	[a]pple	a
/th̶/	[th]is	th	/ĕ/	[e]lephant	e
/jo͞o/	e[du]cate	du		h[ea]d	ea
/zh/	u[su]al	su	/ĭ/	[i]nch	i
/cho͞o/	mu[tu]al	tu		m[y]th	y
/zhə/	A[sia]	sia		misch[ie]f	ie
/aŋ/	s[ang]	ang		mount[ai]n	ai
/iŋ/	s[ing]	ing	/ŏ/	[o]lives	o
/oŋ/	s[ong]	ong	/ŭ/	[u]mbrella	u
/uŋ/	s[ung]	ung		h[o]ney	o
/eŋ/	l[eng]th	eng		d[ou]ble	ou
/aŋk/	s[ank]	ank	/ô/	P[au]l (author)	au

	s[aw]	aw
/ôl/	[al]most	al
/ô/	c[augh]t	augh
	f[ough]t	ough
/oi/	[oi]l	oi
	b[oy]	oy
/ou/	[ou]ch	ou
	c[ow]	ow
	dr[ough]t	ough
/ôr/	c[or]n	or
/är/	st[ar]	ar
/äzh/	sabot[age]	age
/ʉr/	h[er]	er
	b[ir]d	ir
	b[ur]n	ur
	[ear]n	ear
	n[our]ish	our
	mart[yr]	yr
/ər/	hard[er]	er
	doct[or]	or
	doll[ar]	ar
/o͝o/	b[oo]k	oo
	f[u]ll	u
/ăr/	c[ar]ry	ar
/ĕr/	ch[er]ry	er
/ĭr/	m[ir]ror	ir
/ā/	b[a]by	a
	s[a- f -e]	a-e
	r[ai]n	ai
	pl[ay]	ay
	sl[eigh]	eigh

	st[ea]k	ea
	v[ei]n	ei
	th[ey]	ey
	souffl[é]	é
	val[et]	et
/ē/	m[e]ter	e
	th[e- s -e]	e-e
	f[ee]t	ee
	[ea]t	ea
	ch[ie]f	ie
	cand[y]	y
	k[ey]	ey
	rec[ei]ve	ei
	man[i]ac	i
	mach[i- n -e]	ine
/ī/	t[i]ger	i
	p[i- n -e]	i-e
	n[igh]t	igh
	p[ie]	ie
	m[y] (sky)	y
	t[y- p -e]	y-e
	[Ei]nstein	ei
/ō/	h[o- m -e]	o-e
	b[oa]t	oa
	sn[ow]	ow
	t[oe]	oe
	p[o]ny	o
	alth[ough]	ough
/ū/	m[u]sic	u
	m[u- l -e]	u-e
	f[ew]	ew

	[Eu]rope (feud)	eu
	val[ue] (rescue)	ue
/o͞o/	s[ou]p	ou
	l[u]nar	u
	n[eu]tral	eu
	fl[u- t –e]	u-e
	tr[ue]	ue
	m[oo]n	oo
	fr[ui]t	ui
	thr[ough]	ough
	fl[ew] (grew)	ew
/ə/	c[a]det	a
	s[e]dan	e
	p[o]lite	o
	s[u]perb	u

Appendix C

Two Exercises for You

Just for fun, syllabify and accent the following words. See if you can identify the decoding Rules and accenting hints that apply. The list was compiled by scrolling *LessonPlanner's* Blending "Phonemes Spelled As" menu and stopping periodically to do searches here and there for options from which the words listed were selected.

Word	*Apply Syllabification Rules and Hints*
chronography	
parapsychologist	
chemotherapy	
amphitheater	
astrophysics	
philodendron	
fragility	
indigestible	
vegetation	
gesticulation	
quartermaster	
psychedelic	
condescension	
miscellaneous	
rubefacient	
sacrificial	
confidential	
expeditious	
controversial	
countermeasure	

euthana<u>si</u>a

premoni<u>ti</u>on

indivi<u>du</u>al

contrac<u>tu</u>al

retrogres<u>si</u>on

exclu<u>si</u>onists

thi<u>stle</u>down

irresponsi<u>ble</u>

horticul<u>ture</u>

unmeasur<u>able</u>

hi<u>er</u>oglyphic

stenograph<u>er</u>

hypothyr<u>oi</u>d

th<u>or</u>oughgoing

espion<u>age</u>

diversif<u>ie</u>d

propriet<u>or</u>

oblit<u>er</u>ate

communiqu<u>é</u>

Penns<u>y</u>lvania

amphetam<u>ine</u>

bilin<u>gu</u>al

philosoph<u>ize</u>

psychoanal<u>yze</u>

<u>ei</u>nst<u>ei</u>nium

c<u>oi</u>ncident

beatit<u>ude</u>

<u>eu</u>phemism

D<u>eu</u>teronomy

<u>re</u>productive

Here is another exercise. Syllabify and then accent the following words. See if you can identify the Rules and hints that apply. This list was obtained from *LessonPlanner* by selecting from the Decoding "suf'x/end's" menu and retrieving words to which the third, fourth, and fifth accenting hints apply.

Word	*Apply Syllabification Rules and Hints*
pilgrim<u>age</u>	
mechanic<u>al</u>	
precipit<u>ance</u>	
precipit<u>ancy</u>	
decolor<u>ant</u>	
caterpill<u>ar</u>	
contempor<u>ary</u>	
postgrad<u>uate</u>	
superfi<u>cial</u>	
insuffi<u>cient</u>	
perspica<u>cious</u>	
consig<u>nee</u>	
parall<u>el</u>	
correspond<u>ence</u>	
persist<u>ency</u>	
superintend<u>ent</u>	
contempora<u>neous</u>	
nondiscov<u>ery</u>	
notori<u>ety</u>	
electri<u>fy</u>	
reexamine	
illustri<u>ous</u>	
anachron<u>ism</u>	
indefi<u>nite</u>	
desirabil<u>ity</u>	

quantitat<u>ive</u>

illustrat<u>or</u>

introduct<u>ory</u>

monoton<u>ous</u>

equinoc<u>tial</u>

Lillipu<u>tian</u>

dissen<u>tient</u>

supersti<u>tious</u>

bloodthirs<u>ty</u>

inconspic<u>uous</u>

Glossary

accent

prominence or stress placed on a syllable or syllables in words. Accented syllables are pronounced louder or with higher pitch than unaccented syllables in words.

affix

a *prefix* added to the beginning of a base or root word that changes the word's meaning, or a *suffix* added to the end of a base word that gives a different shade of meaning to the word. Affixes produce derivative words or inflectional forms.

base word

the smallest, real or meaningful word to which prefixes and suffixes may be added to create derivative words.

blending

In Slingerland, *blending* was used synonymously with the term *encoding* and considered a subcategory of spelling on the auditory side of the daily lesson plan. Encoding/blending involves a process of combining (blending) sounds or phonemes together to spell phonetic words. Slingerland teachers are now going back to using the term *encoding* instead of *blending* since the latter means decoding more often today. (See decoding.) In encoding, each phoneme is represented by a corresponding grapheme. The techniques for encoding require the segmentation of phonemes with their corresponding graphemes. (See encoding.)

breve

the curved diacritical mark placed above a vowel to indicate that the vowel sound is short.

capitals or capital letters

uppercase manuscript or cursive letters.

closed syllable

In a closed syllable, the vowel in the syllable is followed by or *closed* by at least one consonant (**m** in ha<u>m</u> and ha<u>m</u>/mer and the **v** in se<u>v</u>/en). It is usually short, except when followed by **r**.

code-emphasis

is a term used by some educators to distinguish *phonics-based* reading programs from *meaning-emphasis* or *literacy-based* programs such as *whole language*.

confusables

words that are readily *confused*, particularly by students with learning disabilities, such as **compiled** and **complied**, or **specific** and **Pacific**.

connective i

connects two syllables often in Latin-based words and helps to make words easier to pronounce.

consonant blend

two or more consonants sequenced together within a syllable that flow together and are at the beginning or end of words (**br** as in **br**and, **scr** as in **scr**een, **nd** as in wi**nd**, **lk** as in si**lk**).

consonant-le syllable (C-le)

a final syllable in a word that begins with a consonant and ends with **le** (ble, cle, dle, fle, gle, kle, ple, sle, stle, tle). In Slingerland, consonant-le syllables are referred to as *silent-e syllables* whereas they are called *consonant-le syllables* in traditional Orton-based programs. In this book they are abbreviated as **C-le** syllables.

continuous sounds

in speech, those that can be pronounced and maintained for several seconds without distortion. Continuous sound consonants include **f**, **l**, **m**, **n**, **r**, **s**, **v**, **w**, **y** (as in yellow), and **z**.

controlled readers

are readers *controlled* by the deliberate selection of words with letters representing their most common or regular phonemes—those that are introduced in a sequenced, structured way.

cursive handwriting

rounded, joined letters with slanted strokes that usually do not require lifting the pen or pencil as words are written.

decoding

the techniques required to identify word parts and then whole words by segmenting words and syllables into grapheme – phoneme correspondences to name or read syllables and words.

diacritical notations

dictionary symbols used to indicate the pronunciation of graphemes, syllables, and words (breve, macron, schwa, etc.).

digraph

A *consonant digraph* is a combination of two adjacent consonants that express a single sound, such as **th** in **th**imble, **sh** in **sh**ipment, and **ph** in **ph**one; a *vowel digraph* (vowel pair or team) is a combination of two adjacent vowels that express a single long vowel sound as **ee** in m**ee**t, **eu** in **Eu**rope, and **oo** in m**oo**n.

diphthong

True *diphthongs* are speech sounds made by gliding one vowel phoneme into another in one syllable as **o** glided into **i** in **oi** (b**oi**l) and **o** and **u** in **ou** (cr**ou**ch). The produced sound occurs because of a change in the position of the tongue in the oral cavity. Another way to define a diphthong is to say that a diphthong is comprised of two consecutive vowels, each contributing to its sound. Some teachers refer to any vowel digraph as a diphthong. Others recognize only **au**, **aw**, **oi**, **oy**, **ou**, and **ow** as true diphthongs.

discrimination

auditory discrimination refers to the ability to auditorily distinguish (hear) similarities and differences between, among, and in words; *visual* discrimination refers to the ability to visually distinguish similarities and differences in letters and words that are graphically similar.

double-duty g and k

is a **g** or **k** that has two functions or *duties* in a word. For example, in the word **jungle**, the **g** is the final letter of the letter combination **ung**, and at the same time it is the first letter of the **C-le** syllable **gle**. Similarly, the **k** in **wrinkle** serves a *double-duty*.

dyslexia

As redefined by a Committee of Members of the International Orton Dyslexia Society (International Dyslexia Association) in 1994, *dyslexia* is a neurologically-based, often familial, disorder which interferes with the acquisition and processing of language. Varying in degrees of severity, it is manifested by difficulties in receptive and expressive language, including phonological processing, in reading, writing, spelling, handwriting, and sometimes in arithmetic. Dyslexia is not a result of lack of motivation, sensory impairment, inadequate instructional or environmental opportunities, or other limiting conditions, but may occur together with these conditions. Although dyslexia is life-long, individuals with dyslexia frequently respond successfully to timely and appropriate intervention.

encoding

In the Slingerland approach, *encoding* was often used synonymously with *blending* in B. Blending or Encoding on the auditory side of the daily lesson plan where phonetic words are spelled. The techniques for encoding require the segmentation of phonemes with their corresponding graphemes to spell words. (See blending and decoding.)

grapheme

a single letter, or more than one letter, that represents a single sound or phoneme.

Greek combining forms

are not the same as Latin and Anglo-Saxon roots and affixes. Connecting or *combining* Greek combining forms is somewhat similar to connecting smaller words to form compound words. Most Greek combining forms—Greek prefixes and roots—are usually found at the beginning of words: telegram, biography, hydrometer, psychology, monogram, to name just a few.

higher order thinking or analysis

thinking and analyzing beyond the level of merely finding facts, particularly in reading, by using application, analysis, synthesis, and evaluation skills.

homograph

one, two, or more words spelled alike but which have different meanings and pronunciations (the noun **rec**ord and the verb re**cord**).

homonyms

as used in *LessonPlanner* and this book, homonyms are really homophones (one of two or more words pronounced alike but with different meanings and spelled differently, such as **there, their, they're**. *Homonyms*, technically, are one of two or more words pronounced and spelled alike but that have different meanings (*pool* game and swimming *pool*).

homophone

one of two or more words pronounced alike but with different meanings and spelled differently (there, their, they're). Homophones are often referred to as homonyms.

inflection

the change of form that words undergo to mark case, gender, number, tense, person, mood, or voice.

irregular plural

a plural made by not adding **s** or **es**, the common or *regular* way to pluralize words (ox to oxen, foot to feet, and man to men).

key word

a word used to help trigger memory for the recall of the phoneme that is represented by a grapheme, for example, t - **turtle** - /t/ or /t/ as in **turtle**.

kinesthetic-motor

In this book, *kinesthetic-motor* refers to the memory for the sequence of movements necessary to trigger speech or form letters in writing.

LessonPlanner

a software product developed for teachers who use an alphabetic-phonics-based approach to teaching language arts or literacy skills to students with or without specific language disabilities (dyslexia). *LessonPlanner* was developed by the Lexia Institute, Los Altos, California.

letter combination

a group of letters which, when combined, make a sound that is different from the expected blend of their individual sounds. Common letter combinations include **ing**, **ang**, **ung**, **ong**, **eng**, **ink**, **ank**, **unk**, **onk**, **tion**, **sion**, **ture**, and others including **inc**, **unc**, and **onch**.

ligature

two letters together (tu, du, di) that make a sound which is different from the expected blend of their individual sounds; for example, /jo͞o/ in gra**du**ate rather than grad-**u**-ate.

literacy

succinctly, the ability to read and write

literacy-based

see the definitions for *meaning-emphasis* and *whole language*

macron

the straight line diacritical mark placed above a vowel to indicate that the vowel sound is long, i.e., pronounced the same as its name (**a**, **e**, **i**, **o**, **u**, etc.)

manuscript handwriting

letters as independent units that frequently require lifting of the pen or pencil when writing them and that are not connected in words. Manuscript handwriting is sometimes referred to as *printing.*

meaning-emphasis

In *meaning-emphasis* or *literacy-based* programs such as *whole language,* common words found in print are introduced with little or no regard to their letter-sound regularity. They include words that appear frequently in print. Students learning to read them are taught a variety of strategies or clues to decipher them from the content of pictures, word configurations, and the initial letters of words. In *meaning-emphasis* programs there is little attempt to control words so that the same letter represents the same sound in beginning readers. For instance, the words **some**, **do**, **don't**, **hot**, **spoon**, **spoil**, **ouch**, and **hope** might be presented in one reading lesson with the "**o**" in each word representing a different phoneme. The quality of the literature, not possible in controlled or phonics readers, is considered of greater importance.

memory

involves the reception, storage, and retrieval of sensory information. It is further delineated by the terms *short-term memory* that refers to limited memory that lasts only briefly and *long term memory* that refers to more lasting memory. Additionally, there is *visual memory* that refers to the reception, storage, and retrieval of visually presented information (graphemes, words, text) and *auditory memory* that refers to the reception, storage, and retrieval of auditorily presented information (phonemes, spoken words, spoken language).

monosyllable

one syllable, from the Greek *mono* meaning one.

morpheme

the smallest unit of meaning in words. A morpheme cannot be divided without altering or destroying its meaning. Morphemes that consist of complete words (**pin**, **proud**) are called free morphemes. Affixes (**re-**, **-ish**) and roots (**ject**, **dict**) are called bound morphemes.

morphology

the study of morphemes; their different forms, and the way they combine in word formation. For example, the word **unfriendly** is formed from **friend**, the adjective-forming suffix **-ly**, and the negative prefix **un-**.

multisensory

the use of auditory, kinesthetic-motor, and visual channels to reinforce learning.

non-phonetic

Non-phonetic words are often referred to as *sight* or *learned* words, or as *red flag* words by Slingerland teachers. They are words that do not conform to the expected grapheme - phoneme correspondences of English or by the rules and generalizations that usually govern spelling and decoding. Examples of such words are **laugh**, **yacht**, and **Wednesday**.

nonsense word

sometimes referred to as a *pseudoword*, is a word to which there is no real meaning attached, but which looks like a word because of its pattern or type; for example, closed syllable, v-e, r-controlled, etc. Nonsense words are useful when teaching elementary decoding skills because students will not recognize them and will be compelled to apply their decoding techniques.

open syllable

a syllable in which the vowel in the syllable is at the end (**o** as in n**o** and **o**/pen) or *open*, i.e., not closed with one or more consonants. An *open* syllable is usually long in an accented syllable (**o**'pen), but has a half long - half short or schwa sound in an unaccented syllable (c**a**/det', s**e**/dan', T**i**/bet', p**o**/lite', s**u**/perb').

perception

the ability to isolate and identify a specific stimulus among several stimuli. In the Slingerland approach, *perception* is an encoding auditory exercise where students are required to identify the vowel phonemes and graphemes in words.

phoneme

the smallest unit of speech that distinguishes one utterance from another. As examples: the words **pan** and **ban** differ only in their initial sounds /p/ and /b/, and **ban** and **bun** differ only in their vowels, /ă/ and /ŭ/. Therefore /p/, /b/, /ă/ and /ŭ/ are all phonemes of English. Depending on dialect, English has approximately 45 phonemes.

phonemics

the study of the distinctive sound units (phonemes) of a language and their relationship to one another.

phonemic awareness

the understanding that spoken words and syllables are made up of sequences of speech elements. This understanding is necessary for learning to read an alphabetic language, such as English, because the *elements* are represented by letters. Phonics will make no sense to a student lacking phonemic awareness.

phones

individual sounds, as they occur in speech.

phonetics

the systematic study of speech sounds or *phones*. There are three main areas: **articulatory phonetics** deals with the way speech sounds are produced; **acoustic phonetics** deals with the transmission of speech sounds; **auditory phonetics** deals with how speech sounds are perceived by the listener.

phonics

a reading and spelling approach to teaching literacy skills that focuses on pho-neme – grapheme correspondences. Sometimes *phonics* is confused with *phonetics*. Phonics can also be confused with *phonemic awareness*.

phonogram

Gillingham and Slingerland use *phonogram* to mean a vowel digraph (**ee** or **ay**) or a diphthong (a speech sound made by gliding from one vowel to another, such as **oi** in **oil**). Slingerland also includes **v-e** syllables as phonograms; these traditionally are not viewed as phonograms by Gillingham or others.

prefix

an affix added to the beginning of a base or root word that changes the word's meaning (**pre**scribe, **un**kind, **re**play).

r-controlled phonogram or syllable

a phonogram or syllable with an **r** at the end that alters the sound of the vowel that precedes the **r**; thus, the **r** *controls* the vowel sound so that it is neither purely long nor short, as in th**ir**d, **ear**th, and ch**ur**ch.

red flag words

non-phonetic, *sight* or *learned* words that do not conform to the expected grapheme – phoneme correspondences of English or by the rules and generalizations that usually govern spelling and decoding. Examples of such words are **said** and **yacht**. The term *red flag* is used by Slingerland teachers, especially.

root

sometimes referred to as a base or stem, is the smallest element of a word to which prefixes and suffixes can be affixed. The root can stand alone as a word (hash, fat) or not stand alone (ject, cis).

schwa

the reduced vowel sound in unaccented syllables, symbolized by /ə/; frequently spelled by **a** and **o** (c**a**det, p**o**lite), sometimes by **e** (r**e**gard), less frequently by **u**, **i**, and by vowel digraphs (s**u**perb, clar**i**ty, fam**ou**s).

scribal-o

is the vowel **o** in words like **month**, **brother**, **love**, **some**, and **wonder**, pronounced /ŭ/. For a detailed explanation for the **o** - /ŭ/ pronunciation, refer to the **scribal-o** story on page 56.

semantics

is the study of meaning; including literal, idiomatic, and colloquial meaning, as well as figurative and other non-literal language. It also includes the way words are organized to vary meaning.

sibilant

a speech sound such as /s/, /z/, /sh/, /zh/, /ch/.

silent-e

Although the **e** at the end of many English words is silent, **e** is a signal: It may signal a lengthening of the sound of the vowel or vowel digraph that precedes it (p**i**n to p**i**ne or br**ea**th to br**ea**the) or it may signal the softening of **c** and **g** (picni**c** versus noti**ce** and hu**g** versus hu**ge**). Since in English few words end with the letters **v** or **z**, silent-e may signal the necessity to *finish* words such as ha**ve** and free**ze**, and the **e** signals how to prevent the plural effect in words ending with a /z/ sound as in **please** and **tease** not to be confused with **pleas** and **teas**, respectively. Because of the many functions of silent-e, as well as to sounded or voiced **e**, this writer refers to **e** as the *ubiquitous* **e**. Silent-e should not be confused with what Slingerland refers to as **silent-e** syllables (ble, dle, stle, etc.), to what Orton-based instructors refer to as silent-e syllables (**v-e** as in safe, these, dime, home, and mule or flute), or to the Silent-**E** *Rule*.

soft c, soft g

The *soft* sound of **c** is /s/; the *soft* sound of **g** is /j/. The *hard* sounds for each, respectively, are /k/ and /g/.

S.O.S.

simultaneous oral spelling, a term coined by Gillingham to describe the techniques that are incorporated in teaching and learning to spell orally and write phonetic, ambiguous, and non-phonetic words using kinesthetic-auditory-visual associations to create linkages of sound with letter formations that impress and solidify recall of letter sequences in words.

specific language disability

see the synonymous definition for *dyslexia.*

stop sounds

sounds that can be pronounced (spoken, said, or enunciated) only for an instant because they are completely stopped in the oral cavity. The most difficult stop sound consonants include **b**, **c**, **d**, **g**, **h**, **j**, **k**, **p**, **q**, **t**, and **x**. Voiced stop sounds are /b/, /d/, and /g/; voiceless stop sounds are /p/, /t/, /k/.

strephosymbolia

literally means "twisted symbol" and was coined by Orton. The *twisting* of the symbols pertains to the tendency of people with dyslexia to reverse, invert, and transpose letters and syllables in words when reading or spelling.

syllable

a unit of spoken language consisting of an uninterrupted utterance and forming either a whole word (stomp) or a commonly recognized division of a word (cat/nip, re/ply, no/ tice/able).

syllabification, **syllabify**, **or syllable division:** the process of dividing or breaking words into separate syllables usually for decoding or encoding and spelling.

syllable types

In many Orton-based programs, identification of the six syllable types (closed, open, v-e, r-controlled, consonant-le, and diphthong or vowel digraph) is important. If students can identify syllable types they have more information about the pronunciation of the vowel units.

syntax

how words are put together to form phrases, clauses, and sentences, including English grammar.

trigraph

A *consonant trigraph* is a combination of three adjacent letters that represent a single sound, such as **dge** in bri**dge** and **tch** in ma**tch**.

voiced sounds

sounds in speech that require the vibration of the vocal chords for their production.

voiceless or unvoiced sounds

consonant sounds that are made without vibration of the vocal chords when produced.

vowels

letters of the alphabet whose phonemes open the throat or are voiced and unobstructed. In English the vowels, according to an old saying, are **a**, **e**, **i**, **o**, **u**, and sometimes **y** and **w**. The latter are referred to as semi-vowels. The **y** is a vowel when it acts as **i**'s twin: it is a consonant usually at the beginning of words and syllables and when pronounced /y/. **W** acts as a vowel when it does not have its consonant sound /w/, usually as **u**'s twin in phonograms such as **aw**, **ew**, and **ow**. Traditionally each of the common vowels has a short and long sound. *Short vowels* are typically found in monosyllabic words (had, bed, inch, lot, cut) or in accented closed syllables (**a**p/ple, **e**l/e/phant, **i**nch, **o**l/ives, **u**m/brel/la). *Long vowels* usually occur at the end of monosyllabic words (m**e**, h**i**, n**o**) or at the end of accented, open syllables (b**a**/by, m**e**/ter, t**i**/ger, p**o**/ny, t**u**/lip).

whole language

as used throughout this book, is a currently popular term for *literacy-based* or *meaning-emphasis* programs wherein common words found in print are introduced with little or no regard to their letter-sound regularity. They include words that appear frequently in print. Students learning to read them are taught a variety of strategies or clues to decipher them. In *whole language* the intention is for the learner to be actively, rather than passively, involved in the process of learning to read and write; that the skills of listening, reading, writing, and speaking be integrated, rather than taught separately; and that the literature used for reading and writing instruction reflect exemplary quality for a variety of expository and narrative forms.

word family words

In this book, word family words are words in which the vowel has an unexpected phoneme. For example, in the **ind** word family, it is expected that the vowel **i** followed by two consonants in a closed syllable would be pronounced /ĭ/ instead of /ī/.

yellow flag words

ambiguously spelled words such as **has** that could be spelled **haz** or **has**. Ambiguous words are phonetic but require making at least one spelling choice between or among its phonetic elements. The term *yellow flag* is used by Slingerland teachers, especially.

References

Adams, Marilyn J. (1990) *Beginning to Read: Thinking and Learning about Print.* Cambridge, Massachusetts: The MIT Press.

Anton, J., C. Murray, and J. Elkind. (1996) *User's Manual for LessonPlanner.* Los Altos, California: The Lexia Institute.

Akin, Florence. (1941) *Word Mastery—A Course in Phonics for the First Three Grades.* Cambridge, Massachusetts: Educators Publishing Service, Inc.

Barton, Susan. (1999) *Reading & Spelling System.* San Jose, California: Bright Solutions

Brady, Susan and L. Moats. (1997) *Informed Instruction for Reading Success: Foundations for Teacher Preparation* Baltimore, Maryland; ODS.

Bowen, Carolyn. (1980) *Angling for Words Study Book.* Novato, California: Academic Therapy Publications.

Bertin, Phyllis and P. Perlman, P. (1980) *Preventing Academic Failure.* Scarsdale, New York: Munroe Assoc.

California Department of Education. (1996a) California County Superintendents Educational Services Association, Curriculum and Instruction Steering Committee, Early Reading Instruction Subcommittee. *Guide to the California Reading Initiative.* Sacramento, California.

——— (1996b) California State Superintendent of Public Instruction, State Board of Education, and the California Commission on Teacher Credentialing Reading Program Advisory. *Teaching Reading, A Balanced, Comprehensive Approach to Teaching Reading in Prekindergarten Through Grade Three.* Sacramento, California.

Carnine, D., J. Silbert, and E. Kameenui. (1990) *Direct Instruction Reading.* New Jersey and Columbus, Ohio: Merrill, an Imprint of Prentice Hall, Englewood Cliffs.

Cox, Aylett R. (1992) *Foundations for Literacy: Structure and Techniques for Multisensory Teaching of Basic Written English Language Skills.* Cambridge, Massachusetts: Educators Publishing Service, Inc.

Enfield, Mary L. and V. Green. (1988) *Project Read Guides.* Bloomington, Minneapolis: Language Circle.

Gillingham, A., and B. Stillman. (1997) *Remedial Training for Students with Specific Disability in Reading, Spelling, and Penmanship.* Cambridge, Massachusetts: Educators Publishing Service, Inc.

Greene, Jane F. (1997a) *Language! A Curriculum for At Risk and ESL Students at Grades 4-12.* Longmont, Colorado: Sopris West.

———— (1997b) *Letters for Readers and Spellers—Phoneme Awareness Drills for Teachers and Speech-Language Pathologists.* Longmont, Colorado: Sopris West.

Healy, Jane M. (1990) *Endangered Minds: Why Our Children Don't Think.* New York, New York: Simon and Schuster.

Henry, Marcia. (1990) *Words.* Austin, Texas: Pro-Ed.

Herman, Renee. (1975) *Rationale: The Herman Method of Reversing Reading Failure.* Los Angeles: Romar Publications.

Hoover, Mary R., and M. Fabian. (1975) *Patterns for Reading.* Dubuque, Iowa: Kendall/Hunt Publishing Company.

Honig, Bill. (1996) *Teaching Our Children to Read: the Role of Skills in a Comprehensive Reading Program.* Thousand Oaks, California: Corwin Press.

Lindamood, C. H., and P. Lindamood. (1975) *The A.D.D. Program, Auditory Discrimination in Depth: Books 1 and 2.* Austin, Texas: PRO-ED.

McCulloch, Clara. (1990) *Selections for Teaching Reading Using the Slingerland Approach to Language Arts.* Cambridge, Massachusetts: Educators Publishing Service, Inc.

Moats, Louisa. (1995) *Spelling: Development, Disability, and Instruction.* Baltimore, Maryland: York Press.

Murray, Carol, and J. Munro. (1989) *30 Roots to Grow On—A Teacher's Guide for the Development of Vocabulary.* San Francisco, California: Murray Educational Services.

Orton Dyslexia Society. (1994) Definition of the committee members. In *Dyslexia: Newsletter of the New York Branch of the Orton Dyslexia Society*, ed. A. Bailin. New York, N.Y.

Orton, Samuel T. (1937) *Reading, Writing, and Speech Problems in Children.* New York: W. W. Norton.

Royal, Nancy L. (1987) *The Long Term Consequences of Specific Language Disabilities: the Secondary School Years.* Ann Arbor, Michigan: University Microfilms International.

Rudginsky, Laura T., and E. Haskell. (1985) *How to Teach Spelling.* Cambridge, Massachusetts: Educators Publishing Service, Inc.

Slingerland, Beth H., and M. Aho. (1985) *Learning to Use Manuscript Handwriting* and *Learning to Use Cursive Handwriting.* Cambridge, Massachusetts: Educators Publishing Service, Inc.

Smith, Margaret T., and Hogan, E. (1987) *MTA Reading and Spelling Program.* Cambridge, Massachusetts: Educators Publishing Service, Inc.

Slingerland, Beth H. (1971) *Book One—A Multi-Sensory Approach to Language Arts Instruction for Specific Language Disability Children: A Guide for Primary Teachers.* Cambridge, Massachusetts: Educators Publishing Service, Inc.

————— (1976) *Book Two—Basics in Scope and Sequence of a Multi-Sensory Approach to Language Arts Instruction for Specific Language Disability Children: A Guide for Primary Teachers.* Cambridge, Massachusetts: Educators Publishing Service, Inc.

————— (1977) *For Uniformity in Practices to be Followed by Staff Members of Summer School Sessions for the Introductory Courses.* Bellevue, Washington: The Slingerland Institute.

————— (1981) *Book Three—A Multi-Sensory Approach to Language Arts Instruction for Specific Language Disability Children: A Guide for Elementary Teachers.* Cambridge, Massachusetts: Educators Publishing Service, Inc.

Slingerland, Beth H., and C. Murray. (1987) *Teacher's Word Lists for Reference.* Cambridge, Massachusetts: Educators Publishing Service, Inc.

Spalding, R. B., and W. T. Spalding. (1980) *The Writing Road to Reading.* New York: Quill/William Morrow.

Texas Scottish Rite Hospital. (1989) *Dyslexia Training Program Video Tapes.* Dallas, Texas: Texas Scottish Rite Hospital.

Wilson, Barbara A. (1988) *Wilson Reading System.* Millbury, Massachusetts: Wilson Language Training.

Wolf, B. (1982) *Instructional Sequence for SLD Classrooms.* Renton, Washington: Renton School District.

Index

Auditory cards, 120
    phoneme-graphemes for first trimester, 136
    phoneme-graphemes for grade 4, 142
    phoneme-graphemes for grade 5, 143
    phoneme-graphemes for second trimester, 138
    phonemes spelled with consonants, 123
    phonemes with consonant digraphs, 123
    phonemes with dipthongs, 126
    phonemes with long vowels, 126
    phonemes with phonograms, 126
    phonemes with r-controlled phonograms, 129
    phonemes with r-controlled syllables, 129
    phonemes with short vowels, 125
    phonemes with trigraphs, 123
    phonemes-graphemes for grade 3, 139
    review of techniques, 133
    vowel perception and discrimination, 131
    yellow card exercises, 130
    yellow card exercises for c-le syllables, 130
    yellow card exercises for **ed** suffix, 130
    yellow card exercises for noun ending **us**, 131
    yellow card exercises for suffix **ous**, 131
    yellow card scope and sequence, 122
    yellow cards, 121
Auditory presentations, 119
Cursive instruction
    completing lower case, 36
    considerations for scope and sequence, 29
    first three or four lessons, 30
    review, 37
    second and third weeks, 32
    second month, 34
    third or fourth week, 33
Decoding, 77
    accenting two-syllable words, 99
    beginning **cvc** words, 78
    homonyms, 91
    letter combinations and phonograms, 85
    nonsense words, 80
    phonogram introduction sequence, 86
    pronunciation of 2-syllable words, 99
    Review, 112
    soft **c** and **g** words, 83
    suffix **ed**, 82
    syllabification Rule I, 99
    syllabification Rule II, 105
    syllabification Rule III, 104
    syllabification Rule IV, 107
    Three or more syllable words, 111
    two-syllable words, 97
    vowel-consonant-**e** words, 88
    word families, 91
    words with affixes, 109
Dictations, 189
Dyslexia, 12
Educators Publishing Service, 8

Encoding and spelling
    1-1-1 vowel rule, 185
    advanced suffixes and endings, 180
    ambiguous and phonetic words, 149
    closed two-syllable words with 1 consonant, 173
    closed two-syllable words with 2 consonants, 170
    common suffixes and prefixes, 177
    consonant-**y** rule, 186
    discriminating between /ă/ and /ĭ/, 148
    encoding techniques, 146
    ending /əs/ spelled ous or us, 181
    extended **1-1-1** vowel rule, 187
    homonym words, 165
    Latin and Greek roots, 182
    mixed blending, 163
    mixed multisyllable words with affixes, 178
    nonphonetic and phonetic words, 151
    non-phonetic words, 165
    nonsense words, 150
    one-syllable letter combination words, 154
    one-syllable phonogram words, 154
    phonetic words, 145
    review, 171
    scope and sequence, 144, 163
    sight words, 165
    silent-**e** rule, 184
    suffixes, 157
    suffixes added to base words, 164
    three or more syllables, 183
    two-syllable words with 1 open syllable, 174
    v-e words, 160
    word-family words, 165
    words, 176
Gillingham, Anna, 5
Grammar, 93
    integrating into dictations and compositions, 191
Grapheme, 18, 230
Graphemes
    LessonPlanner, 215
Handwriting
    historical perspective, 12
    importance, 11
    Slingerland program, 11
    Slingerland program, 14
Handwriting instruction
    cursive. *See* Cursive instruction
    preliminary considerations, 15
Handwriting instruction grade 1
    considerations for scope and sequence, 16
    first trimester, 20
    reviewing manuscript, 26
    second trimester, 22
    second trimester for non-SLD, 23
    third trimester for SLD, 23
Handwriting instruction grade 2
    continuing manuscript, 27
Handwriting instruction grade 3

cursive. *See* Cursive instruction
Independent writing, 190
Lesson plans
    content overview, 193
    Orton-Gillingham simultaneous multisensory, 201
    Slingerland simultaneous multisensory, 195
    whole language augmented with phonics, 206
LessonPlanner, 7
    graphemes with key words and phonemes, 215
    phonemes with keywords and graphemes, 219
Lexia Institute, 8
Multisensory techniques, 12
Orton, Samuel T., 5
Orton-based adaptations, 9
Orton-Gillingham-Stillman, 12
Phoneme, 18
Phonemes
    LessonPlanner, 219
Phonemic awareness, 119, 234
Phonogram, 24
Phrase and sentence writing, 188
Preparation for reading, 113
Reading from the book, 117
Scribal-o, 56
SLD, 5
Slingerland, Beth, 5
Specific Language Disability, 5
Spelling. *See* Encoding and spelling
Stillman, Bessie, 5
Strephosymbolia, 12
Syllabification. *See* Decoding
Visual cards
    Orton-Gillingham sequence, 40
    Orton-Gillingham, Slingerland comparison, 39
    rationale for levels, 44
    rationale for scope and sequence, 43
    rationales for introduction differences, 73
Visual cards beginning grade 1 or 2
    graphemes for second trimester, 47
Visual cards for continuing grade 2, 48
Visual cards for grade 3
    graphemes Level I, 52
    graphemes Level II, 55
    graphemes Level III, 56
    scope and sequence, 51
Visual cards for grades 5 and 6
    advanced oddities, 71
    graphemes advanced group I, 64
    graphemes advanced group II, 67
    scope and sequence, 63
Vocabulary, 93